The Value of Humanity in Kant's Moral Theory

The Value of Humanity in Kant's Moral Theory

Richard Dean

CLARENDON PRESS · OXFORD

OXFORD
UNIVERSITY PRESS

Great Clarendon Street, Oxford OX2 6DP

Oxford University Press is a department of the University of Oxford.
It furthers the University's objective of excellence in research, scholarship, and education by publishing worldwide in

Oxford New York

Auckland Cape Town Dar es Salaam Hong Kong Karachi
Kuala Lumpur Madrid Melbourne Mexico City Nairobi
New Delhi Shanghai Taipei Toronto

With offices in

Argentina Austria Brazil Chile Czech Republic France Greece
Guatemala Hungary Italy Japan Poland Portugal Singapore
South Korea Switzerland Thailand Turkey Ukraine Vietnam

Published in the United States
by Oxford University Press Inc., New York

First published 2006

British Library Cataloguing in Publication Data

Data available

Library of Congress Cataloging in Publication Data

Data available

Typeset by Laserwords Private Limited, Chennai, India
Printed in Great Britain
on acid-free paper by
Biddles Ltd., King's Lynn, Norfolk

ISBN 0–19–928572–1 978–0–19–928572–3

For Jim Leupp and Thomas E. Hill, Jr.,
two people who have provided me with vivid,
but very different, examples of how good will
can be combined with human nature

Contents

Acknowledgments

Although no chapter of this book has been published previously in exactly its current form, some important ideas and passages are borrowed from two of my previously published articles. I thank the following journals for permission to draw on these articles.

Parts of Chapters 2, 3, 4, and 5 are taken from 'What Should We Treat as an End in Itself?', *Pacific Philosophical Quarterly*, 77: 268–88.

Section 2 of Chapter 8 is a condensed version of 'Cummiskey's Kantian Consequentialism', *Utilitas*, 12: 25–40.

I owe thanks to many people for various kinds of help on this project. Most of all, I thank Tom Hill, who has been a great source of encouragement, ideas, and constructive criticism. Others who have read and provided useful comments on parts of this book include Geoffrey Sayre-McCord, Bernie Boxill, Jan Boxill, Jay Rosenberg, Doug Long, Jacob Ross, Arnulf Zweig, Michael Gill, Robert Johnson, Andrews Reath, David Cummiskey, Andrew Mills, Muhammad Ali Khalidi, Hans Muller, Joshua Andresen, and Cynthia Stark. In addition, the suggestions of two Oxford University Press referees were extremely helpful. Chapter 10 has benefited the most from others' comments, and besides those mentioned above, I thank Andy Siegel, Douglas Husak, Jeff Moriarty, Dave Weber, Hylarie Kochiras, Earl Spurgin, Samuel Bruton, John Callanan, Mary Macleod, and Eric Rubenstein for their assistance with that chapter. Others, who did not read parts of this book itself, nevertheless provided useful discussion or correspondence about some of the ideas in the book. I thank Dina Abou Salem, Stephen Engstrom, Allen Wood, and the members of the Beirut Philosophy Circle for helping in this way, and I especially thank Joshua Glasgow for taking the time to consider and disagree with my earlier article, 'What Should We Treat as an End in Itself?' I am almost certainly forgetting others who helped, and I apologize to them.

I thank the American University of Beirut for financial support in the form of a University Research Board long-term development grant, and I thank the Mellon Foundation for funding a summer research grant, administered via the Center for Behavioral Research at the American University of Beirut.

On a more personal note, I thank my colleagues in the philosophy department at the American University of Beirut for providing a remarkably productive and pleasant work environment. And I especially thank Dina Abou Salem for her support and understanding during the sometimes stressful process of completing this book.

R. D.

Abbreviations for Kant's Works

For the writings of Kant that I cite most frequently, I will use the following abbreviations, and will cite the works parenthetically in the text instead of in a footnote. Unless otherwise noted, page numbers will refer to the relevant volume of *Kant's gesammelte Schriften*, ed. Koenigliche Preussische Akademie der Wissenschaften (Berlin: Walter de Gruyter, 1908–13). This edition of Kant's work is commonly called the Akademie (or Academy) edition. When works of Kant other than those abbreviated below are cited, a reference will be given in a footnote.

Anth	*Anthropology from a Practical Point of View*, trans. Mary Gregor (The Hague: Martinus Nijhoff, 1974). Translated from *Anthropologie in pragmatischer Hinsicht abgefasst*, in volume vii of *Kant's gesammelte Schriften*, 117–333.
C1	*Critique of Pure Reason*, trans. Norman Kemp Smith (New York: St Martin's Press, 1965). Translated from *Kritik der reinen Vernunft*, first edition from volume iv of *Kant's gesammelte Schriften*, 1–252, second edition from volume iii of *Kant's gesammelte Schriften*, 1–594. References use standard A/B pagination for the two editions.
C2	*Critique of Practical Reason*, ed. Mary Gregor (Cambridge: Cambridge University Press, 1997). Translated from *Kritik der praktischen Vernunft*, in volume v of *Kant's gesammelte Schriften*, 1–164.
C3	*Critique of Judgment*, trans. Werner S. Pluhar (Indianapolis: Hackett Publishing Company, 1987). Translated from *Kritik der Urtheilskraft*, in volume v of *Kant's gesammelte Schriften*, 167–485.
G	*Groundwork for the Metaphysics of Morals*, ed. Thomas E. Hill, Jr., and Arnulf Zweig (Oxford: Oxford University Press, 2002). Translated from *Grundlegung zur Metaphysik der Sitten*, in volume iv of *Kant's gesammelte Schriften*, 387–463.
MM	*The Metaphysics of Morals*, trans. Mary Gregor (Cambridge: Cambridge University Press, 1996). Translated from *Die Metaphysik der Sitten*, in volume vi of *Kant's gesammelte Schriften*, 203–491.
R	*Religion within the Boundaries of Mere Reason*, ed. Allen Wood and George di Giovanni (Cambridge: Cambridge University Press, 1998). Translated from *Die Religion innerhalb der Grenzen der blossen Vernunft*, in volume vi of *Kant's gesammelte Schriften*, 1–202.

PART I
Good Will as an End in Itself

1

Introduction

One of the most pervasive ideas in contemporary moral discussions is that every person deserves basic moral consideration, because of the intrinsic value and dignity of humanity. And Immanuel Kant's ethical theory probably provides the most influential philosophical support for this idea. Despite the notorious difficulty of Kant's texts, many have found his ethical theory to capture some deeply compelling intuition about the inalienable worth of humanity.

So it is no surprise that of the different formulations that Kant offers of the Categorical Imperative, or fundamental principle of morality, the 'humanity formulation' seems to be the most intuitively appealing. This moral principle demands that every person must 'Act in such a way that you treat humanity, whether in your own person or in any other person, always at the same time as an end, never merely as a means' (G 429). Most contemporary readers will feel that this way of expressing the Categorical Imperative captures a plausible and important moral intuition, that there is something special about persons which makes them deserving of at least some basic moral consideration.

Specialists in Kant's ethics have also regarded the humanity formulation as important, of course, and have come to place increased emphasis on it in recent years. The intuitive appeal of the humanity formulation has long been recognized, as has its influence on moral issues in medical ethics and other areas of applied ethics. But recent commentators have also become more inclined to regard the humanity formulation as the central normative principle in Kant's ethics.[1] Partly this is because many have come to think that the universalizability formulation of the Categorical Imperative is deeply problematic, but it is also because of the humanity formulation's promise as an

[1] Thomas E. Hill, Jr., *Dignity and Practical Reason in Kant's Moral Theory* (Ithaca, NY: Cornell University Press, 1992), 38–57; David Cummiskey, *Kantian Consequentialism* (New York: Oxford University Press, 1996), 62; Allen Wood, *Kant's Ethical Thought* (Cambridge: Cambridge University Press, 1999), 111–55.

interpretative focal point and as a moral principle that may illuminate issues in applied ethics and moral theory.[2]

But despite its intuitive appeal and the scholarly attention it has received, it is far from clear precisely what the humanity formulation demands. Even the two most basic elements of the principle—what humanity is, and what is involved in treating it as an end in itself—require further explanation. Two main tasks of this book are to provide answers to these basic questions about the humanity formulation. And by answering these questions, I hope to accomplish a third task, of showing that the humanity formulation is a viable, in fact a powerful and useful, moral principle.

Explaining the moral obligations that are implied by the humanity formulation is a challenge. Kant himself provides examples of specific duties that supposedly follow from the humanity formulation,[3] but even in his own examples the exact connection between the general moral principle and the more specific duties is not always clear. And if Kant's own examples were pellucid, questions would still remain about how to apply the humanity formulation to situations that Kant does not discuss. The meaning of 'humanity' in the humanity formulation might be assumed to be an easier question, but this assumption would be incorrect. Kant's use of the seemingly straightforward term 'humanity' (in German, 'die Menschheit') is deceptively obscure. Closer examination reveals that it does not simply refer to 'human beings', as readers might naturally assume, but rather refers to some property possessed by rational human beings. And recent commentators on Kant's ethics have offered differing accounts of exactly what feature of rational beings is denoted by 'humanity'.

So, there are still important questions to be settled about the Categorical Imperative's demand that we treat humanity as an end in itself. In Part I of the book, I will argue for a non-standard reading of 'humanity' in the humanity formulation. I will argue that my reading renders the humanity formulation more consistent with the main ideas of Kant's ethics and with the particular passages in which Kant discusses humanity as an end in itself. In Part II of the book, I will employ the conclusions of Part I to examine several questions about the humanity formulation as a fundamental principle of morality. Some

[2] Regarding the problems with the formula of universalizability as a motive for increased emphasis on other formulations, see Hill, *Dignity and Practical Reason*, 121–2; Wood, *Kant's Ethical Thought*, pp. xii–xiv; Samuel Kerstein, *Kant's Search for the Supreme Principle of Morality* (Cambridge: Cambridge University Press, 2002), esp. 114–38, 168–91.

[3] In *Groundwork for the Metaphysics of Morals*, Kant only provides four such examples, but in *Metaphysics of Morals*, published twelve years later, he usually relies on the humanity formulation to ground the specific duties that he thinks result from applying the Categorical Imperative to human circumstances.

of these questions, about the justification of the principle and how Kant derives specific duties from it, are mainly of concern to scholars of Kant's ethics. But others deal more pragmatically with applying the humanity formulation to particular moral issues.

The point on which I break most sharply with previous commentators is the one which may at first glance appear to offer the least potential for disagreement, namely the meaning of 'humanity'. It may appear obvious that Kant is saying simply that all humans must be treated as ends in themselves, and so is just using 'humanity' as a general noun to identify all members of the human species. But contemporary commentators widely agree that this is not what Kant means by 'humanity'.[4] Kant speaks repeatedly of humanity as a property 'in' a person, and frequently uses 'humanity' interchangeably with 'rational nature'.[5] It also seems clear that Kant does not think that all members of the human species possess the characteristic that Kant calls 'humanity'. Humanity, in Kant's technical sense, is some sort of rational nature, and not all human beings have even a minimally rational nature (think of the severely brain damaged, for one example). Neither can Kant mean to limit the possession of 'humanity' or rational nature to only the human species, since Kant thinks that the requirements of morality apply equally to all rational beings, if there are rational beings other than humans. Kant even specifically states that it 'could well be' that there are rational beings on some other planet (Anth 332). For these reasons, it is generally accepted that Kant does not mean to say that precisely all and only human beings should be treated as ends in themselves, but rather that rational beings should be treated as ends in themselves, in virtue of some feature associated with rationality.

This idea of 'humanity' is not completely disconnected from the human species, since the 'rational nature' that Kant calls 'humanity' is the characteristic feature that distinguishes typical humans from all other beings that we know. Nevertheless, specialists in Kant's ethics regard Kantian humanity as some feature possessed by rational beings, and not just as the property of being a member of the human species.

This seems correct to me. But there is more disagreement than is generally recognized about exactly which characteristic of rational beings Kant means to pick out as the 'humanity' that must be treated as an end in itself. Christine Korsgaard identifies Kantian humanity as the power to set ends, Allen Wood identifies humanity as the power to set ends plus other powers associated with

[4] See Hill, *Dignity and Practical Reason*, 39; Wood, *Kant's Ethical Thought*, 119–20; Christine Korsgaard, *Creating the Kingdom of Ends* (Cambridge: Cambridge University Press, 1996), 110–11; Onora O'Neill, *Constructions of Reason* (Cambridge: Cambridge University Press, 1989), 137.

[5] Kant does this throughout *Groundwork* chapter 2, but esp. 429–39.

this end-setting (such as the power to organize those ends into a systematic whole), and Thomas E. Hill, Jr., identifies humanity as a wider range of rational abilities including the capacity to legislate and act on moral laws.[6] Several other authors equate humanity with the capacity for morality, often without specifying exactly what is involved in possessing this capacity for morality. Surprisingly little direct attention has been paid to the fundamental incompatibility of these different readings of 'humanity'. Perhaps the differences seem relatively unimportant, since all the proposed readings agree at least that the feature that Kant identifies as 'humanity', which must be treated as an end in itself, is some feature of rationality which is possessed by all competent, minimally rational adult humans.

But this is exactly what I think is mistaken. Humanity, in the sense of the humanity formulation, is indeed equivalent to some feature possessed by rational beings, but not by all minimally rational beings. Instead, 'humanity' is Kant's name for the more fully rational nature that is only possessed by a being who actually accepts moral principles as providing sufficient reasons for action. The humanity that should be treated as an end in itself is a properly ordered will, which gives priority to moral considerations over self-interest. To employ Kant's terminology, the end in itself is a good will.

Of course, many defenders of Kant's ethics will find the good will reading of the humanity formulation disturbing. And readers less sympathetic to Kant may think that if the good will reading is correct, it only confirms their darkest suspicions. The claim that beings with a commitment to morality are ends in themselves, and no other beings are, naturally gives rise to a number of reasonable worries. For one, the good will reading seems to render the humanity formulation repugnantly moralistic. Instead of grounding an egalitarian ideal of inalienable dignity for all, it appears to recommend passing judgement on others' moral character, and apportioning respect and rights in proportion to our judgements. An extremely moralistic principle of this sort would no doubt be ill suited to serve as the fundamental basis of an ethical system. In addition, the good will reading may seem to subvert much of the excellent scholarship on Kant's ethics that has been done in recent decades. By putting aside the too-prevalent view of Kant as a stuffy, overly demanding moralist with an unrealistic view of human psychology and the limits of human virtue, recent commentators have made a strong case for the philosophical justification and pragmatic application of Kantian moral principles, especially the demand

[6] Korsgaard, *Creating the Kingdom of Ends*, 17, 110, 346; Wood, *Kant's Ethical Thought*, 118–19; Hill, *Dignity and Practical Reason*, 40–1; Thomas E. Hill, Jr., 'Editor's Introduction' to Immanuel Kant, *Groundwork for the Metaphysics of Morals*, ed. Thomas E. Hill, Jr., and Arnulf Zweig (Oxford: Oxford University Press, 2002), 77.

that we treat humanity as an end in itself. It is natural to worry that the good will reading of the humanity formulation would undo much of this progress.

But the good will reading does not have the monstrous results that one might think. The good will reading does not make Kant's ethics implausible or morally repugnant. This is both because a good will, properly understood, is not such a rarity among humans, and because there are reasons to treat most humans with respect and concern, even if they do not fully earn this treatment by possessing a good will. Good wills are not rare, because a good will is not possessed only by a few moral saints, who always keep their commitment to morality firmly in the forefront of their thoughts, and never act wrongly. Instead, given the frailties of human nature that Kant freely acknowledges, in humans a good will generally takes the form of a commitment to moral principles that is compatible with significant degrees of self-deception, lack of attention to the moral dimensions of one's choices, and weakness of will. Once it is clear that a human good will is not a perfect will, it is quite plausible to suppose that good wills are not rare. And even when someone lacks a good will, this does not absolve us of our duties toward her (even if only a good will is an end in itself). Kant is quite aware of the human tendency to exalt oneself in comparison to others, and of the inherent obstacles to making reliable judgements of others' character. And he specifically acknowledges the importance of moral education, and encouraging others' moral development. For all these reasons, which are plausible to contemporary ears as well as firmly grounded in Kant's own stated views, we have good reason to avoid moralistic judgements and to try to treat all humans with respect and encouragement. Kant maintains that we cannot make reliable judgements about the moral state of others' wills, or even our own. We can only infer the state of someone's character from her actions, and Kant is quite explicit that these inferences are highly unreliable. One reason for this is that we have a strong tendency to regard our own motives and characters charitably, while being less charitable to others. So the good will reading is not accompanied by a moral requirement to assess who should or should not be treated as an end in herself. In addition, we have reason to treat even the villain with respect, since to fail to do so would have a corrupting influence on our own character and would also discourage her from coming to see the possibility of reforming herself. In Chapter 5 of this book, I develop further the claim that, given basic Kantian ideas, accepting the good will reading of the humanity formulation does not result in a morally repugnant view.

It seems that this worry, about the unpalatable implications of the good will reading, has been a major obstacle to accepting the idea that Kant equates a good will with the 'humanity' that must be treated as an end in itself. There must be some intuitive obstacle to the good will reading, because otherwise the abundant evidence in favour of it would have been acknowledged more readily. Reading 'humanity' as 'good will' renders the humanity formulation of the Categorical Imperative more consistent both with the other major ideas of Kant's moral philosophy and with the particular texts in which he discusses humanity as an end in itself.

One way in which the good will reading of 'humanity' fares better than minimal readings is in making Kant's basic claims about value in *Groundwork* consistent. Kant begins *Groundwork* with the claim that only a good will is good without qualification, and that only a good will has an incomparably high value, or dignity. Later in *Groundwork*, he says that only humanity is an end in itself, and only humanity has a dignity. A thorough analysis of these claims reveals that something that has an incomparably high value, and is valuable without qualification, must also be an end in itself. So good will must be the end in itself. The good will reading also explains why one should never choose to act immorally, because by choosing to act immorally, one is also choosing to sacrifice one's most valuable possession, a good will. Given the basic Kantian conception of value, which says that to be valuable is to be the object of rational choice, Kant's repeated claim that good will is an ideal to be pursued above all else also implies that a good will is what has highest value, and so is an end in itself. And besides fitting with Kant's claims about value, the good will reading of the humanity formulation does a better job than other readings of explaining why our duty to aid others in pursuing their ends does not include their immoral ends. The good will reading also allows stronger connections between the different formulations of the Categorical Imperative than any of the standard readings do. I explain these advantages of the good will reading in Chapter 3.

Besides making Kant's overall ethical theory more consistent, the good will reading is also supported by a narrower examination of the texts in which Kant specifically discusses the ideas of humanity and of treating something as an end in itself. Many of the particular passages that have been offered in support of other readings of 'humanity' are ambiguous, when examined in their context, and some even support the good will reading. One example of this is provided by the passages cited by Christine Korsgaard and others as evidence that Kant means to equate humanity with the power to set ends.[7] In *Metaphysics of Morals* 387, Kant says each person has a duty to raise himself 'more and more toward humanity, by which he alone is capable of setting himself ends', and in *Metaphysics of Morals* 392 Kant says that 'The capacity to set an end—any

[7] Korsgaard, *Creating the Kingdom of Ends*, 110.

end whatsoever—is what characterizes humanity'. But in each case, Kant goes on to clarify that the power to set ends is not a complete characterization of humanity, saying that the duty to cultivate one's humanity also includes the duty to accept moral principles as a sufficient reason for action. Of course, these are just examples, just two of the passages that have been offered in support of minimal readings. There are many other Kantian texts to be considered, and, not surprisingly, they are not entirely consistent. In Chapter 4, I examine the textual arguments for the various possible readings of 'humanity', and conclude that overall the textual evidence supports taking 'humanity' as 'good will'.

So, in the chapters of Part I of this book, I argue that both the large themes of Kant's ethics and the particular texts support the good will reading of the humanity formulation. And, contrary to first impressions, this does not render the humanity formulation or Kant's overall ethical theory repugnant or implausible. Then there is very good reason to suppose that it is good will that should be treated as an end in itself.

Part II of the book goes beyond arguing for a particular reading of 'humanity' in the humanity formulation. There are two main goals of the second half of the book. The first is to fit the humanity formulation (particularly the good will reading of the humanity formulation) into a fuller picture of Kant's overall moral theory. The second is to show that the humanity formulation, on the good will reading, is a viable moral principle, and provides substantial guidance on practical issues.

Toward the first and more scholarly end, I will provide a reconstruction of Kant's argument in *Groundwork* for accepting the humanity formulation as a basic moral principle, and then a strategy for moving from this general principle to particular duties, and examples of some of these particular duties.

But even if these exegetical aims are achieved, the reader may well be dissatisfied with the account I offer. The sceptical reader may feel that to exactly the extent that I succeed in making the case for the good will reading as an essential part of Kant's ethics, I also render Kant's ethics implausible, and irrelevant to contemporary discussions of pressing moral issues. After all, the inalienable worth and dignity of all humans is an appealing ideal, and so it is natural to resist basing a moral theory on an incompatible ideal which does not necessarily grant the highest sort of value to all humans. If the idea of a basic dignity and worth for all humans is based on a misreading of Kant's ethics, then many readers will be happy to regard this as so much the worse for Kant's ethics. While this attitude is understandable, I think the good will reading of the humanity formulation ultimately renders Kant's ethics more intuitively appealing and more useful in application, not less. Demonstrating this is the second of my two goals for Part II of this book. The good will reading makes Kant's ethics more pragmatically applicable because it leads to a treatment of Kant's 'kingdom of ends' as a constructivist device for moving from general moral principles to more particular guides to action. Furthermore, this use of the kingdom of ends reinforces the claim that the good will reading of the humanity formulation does not license the abuse of humans who lack good wills. It does this by providing an additional, non-ad hoc derivation of duties of acting respectfully toward all humans, even if some do not fully deserve this respect. I will also argue that treating good will as an end in itself is a more appealing fundamental moral principle than at least one widely accepted competing normative principle, namely the allegedly Kantian principle of respect for autonomy. This argument for favouring the humanity formulation over the principle of respect for autonomy will also suggest an intuitive reason for more generally favouring the good will reading of the humanity formulation over any principles based on the equal, literally inalienable worth of all persons.

So my overall aims in Part II of the book fall into two main categories. The first is to propose solutions to some interpretative problems, about the argument for the humanity formulation, and how this formulation of the Categorical Imperative grounds more particular duties. The second is to show that the good will reading of the humanity formulation is not only accurate as an interpretation of Kant, but is also a plausible and promising moral principle in its own right.

The first chapters of Part II, Chapters 6 and 7, focus mainly on issues of exegesis of Kant's moral theory. Chapter 6 offers a reconstruction of Kant's argument for the humanity formulation as a fundamental principle of morality, a version of the Categorical Imperative. Chapter 7 supplements this argument by providing a strategy for moving from the general principle of treating good will as an end in itself to particular duties that follow from this principle. Chapter 8 explains why (contrary to some powerful arguments offered by David Cummiskey) the duties that follow from humanity's incomparable value are not consequentialist duties to maximize the humanity that is so valuable. Chapter 8 also argues against an idea expressed even by some prominent non-consequentialist Kantians, that the Kantian duty of beneficence is literally a duty to make others' ends one's own, without fundamentally distinguishing between one's own ends and others'. Chapter 9 is less strictly interpretative, instead exploring a roughly Kantian strategy for arriving at conclusions about specific moral issues.[8] I argue for a connection between the good will reading

[8] More accurately, I re-examine a strategy already proposed by Thomas E. Hill, Jr., 'Kantian Constructivism in Ethics', in *Dignity and Practical Reason*, 226–50, 'A Kantian Perspective on Moral

of the humanity formulation and the use of the kingdom of ends formulation as a 'moral constructivist' device, and then employ this constructivist framework to examine the moral status of non-human animals. Then Chapter 10 explains that the principle of 'respect for autonomy', which is commonplace in applied ethics, is not just another way of stating the humanity formulation. In fact, the concept of autonomy employed in the widely accepted principle 'Respect autonomy' is quite different both from Kant's concept of autonomy and from his concept of humanity, and Kant's ethics provides only conditional support for the idea that we must 'respect autonomy' in the currently influential sense. Furthermore, I will argue that Kant's humanity formulation is at least in some ways better suited to serve as a basic moral principle than the currently influential principle of respect for autonomy.

Part II of the book, then, is concerned largely with some central issues, both scholarly and pragmatic, regarding the moral demand that we treat humanity as an end in itself, while Part I was concerned more specifically with establishing that 'humanity' refers to a good will. But there are strong connections between the two parts of the book. All of the chapters of Part II employ the idea that the end in itself is a good will, and Chapters 7 and 9 rely crucially on this idea. This is indirect evidence in favour of the good will reading, since it shows that taking 'humanity' as 'good will' can aid in resolving some lingering exegetical questions, and some pressing moral problems. The good will reading is fruitful, as well as textually justified. Another link between the two parts of the book is that several of the arguments and ideas essential to Part I are also directly applied to the issues of the second part. The most conspicuous example is the Kantian concept of value. The idea that rational choice is conceptually prior to value, rather than the reverse, plays a key role in Chapter 3 in establishing that Kant means 'humanity' to be read as 'good will', and then plays an essential role again in Chapter 6, allowing a reconstruction of Kant's argument for the humanity formulation, and in Chapter 8, showing that the humanity formulation does not lead to consequentialist duties. Another idea that is introduced in Part I and then goes on serve an important function in the second part is the idea that even if good will is what has highest value, the humanity formulation can still make moral demands about how to treat beings who lack good wills. This is important in Chapter 5 of Part I, as a defence against the charge that the good will reading allows mistreatment of humans who are not sufficiently concerned with morality, and again in Chapter 9, which explains that the humanity

Rules', in *Respect, Pluralism, and Justice* (Oxford: Oxford University Press, 2000), 33–55, 'A Kantian Perspective on Political Violence', in *Respect, Pluralism, and Justice*, 200–36, and 'Hypothetical Consent in Kantian Constructivism', in *Human Welfare and Moral Worth* (Oxford: Oxford University Press, 2002), 61–95.

formulation can demand appropriate treatment of non-human animals. So, even though the second part of the book has different aims from the first, it is nevertheless a further development of the main ideas of the first part.

A little more should be said about the theme of Kant's conception of value, and how it is central to this book. Chapter 6, the first chapter of Part II, offers an answer to one of the most basic questions about the imperative of treating humanity as an end in itself, namely why we should accept this principle as a guide to action. Kant's argument for the humanity formulation is quite cryptic, so significant reconstructive work needs to be done (G 428–9). Kant says that every rational agent must conceive of herself as an end in herself, and that she also must conceive of every other rational being in the same way. I attempt to develop a Kantian argument for both parts of this conjunction. I rely partly on the outstanding work already done by other commentators, but I think previous reconstructions of Kant's argument have erred by making the argument for the humanity formulation depend on claims about humanity's incomparable value. Since value, on the Kantian conception, is conceptually dependent on the choices that rational beings would make, the reconstruction of Kant's argument cannot rely on the claim that humanity has special value in order to arrive at the conclusion that one must treat humanity in certain special ways. This would get things backwards. The point of the argument is to establish some rational requirements regarding how to treat humanity, in order to justify the claim that humanity has an intrinsic and incomparably high value. The value claim is just a way of expressing the inviolable moral requirements, so it would be circular to justify the requirements by saying that humanity has a special value. This point has not been consistently captured in others' reconstructions, probably because Kant himself misleadingly presents the argument, in *Groundwork* 427–9, as if it may depend on prior claims about the 'absolute value' of humanity. But if there is no way to avoid this dependence on prior value claims, then the argument fails. Kant's concept of value is less clearly defined in *Groundwork* than in later works, but even in *Groundwork* Kant means value to be conceptually dependent on the choices that rational agents would make, and this is too central a concept to jettison.[9]

In Chapter 8, I argue that keeping in mind the conceptual priority of rational choice over value is especially pressing, given that losing track of this idea leads to misdescriptions of the duties that are generated by the humanity formulation. The less serious form of misdescription is to say that, according to the humanity formulation, each of us must regard all rationally chosen ends as having the same sort of value, regardless of whether the ends are one's own

[9] For the clearest statement of Kant's concept of value, see C2 57–64.

or someone else's. The intuitive problem with this position is not that there could never be more valuable or less valuable ends (since ends might have different value depending on the force of an agent's commitment to them) but rather that no moral room is left for placing a greater intrinsic value on one's own ends than on the ends of strangers.[10] This cannot be Kant's view, since he thinks we have only an 'imperfect duty' to help others attain their ends, meaning roughly a duty to adopt a principle of helping others at least sometimes (G 421–3, MM 449–50). The misdescription of Kant's ideas about the duty to promote others' ends stems from a failure to take account of Kant's concept of value. The humanity formulation does not say first that one must regard one's own ends as valuable, then that others' ends are equally valuable, resulting in a duty to regard others' ends in the same way as one's own. Rather, the humanity formulation argues that each of us must respect others' humanity, and can rationally demand equal respect for our own humanity. Part of respecting humanity is to give at least some weight to others' ends—the same weight we can rationally expect others to give our ends. At this point in the argument, it is still an open question how much weight we must give others' ends compared to our own, though it is settled that we must give the same sort of relative weight to others' ends as we can demand from them for our ends. Claims about value enter the picture only after the question is settled of how much weight each of us is required to give to others' ends. This picture is quite compatible with saying that each agent's own ends have fundamentally higher value for her than others' ends do for her.

One reason it is important to avoid this potential confusion is that the failure to employ Kant's concept of value, when conjoined with the claim that humanity has an incomparably high value and then pushed to its logical extension, results in consequentialism. In fact, this is the basic path that David Cummiskey follows in *Kantian Consequentialism*, to argue that although Kant himself was not a consequentialist, the central ideas of Kant's ethics in fact lead to consequentialist normative principles. Much of what Cummiskey says is correct, and his book at the least provides a stiff challenge that a non-consequentialist Kantian must meet. The challenge is to provide a reconstruction of the argument for the humanity formulation that does not have the humanity formulation underwriting consequentialist moral demands. The key to meeting this challenge is to keep firmly in mind that, for Kant, to call something valuable is only a way of capturing the idea that rational agents must treat it in certain ways. If the Kantian forgets this, then consequentialism

[10] Korsgaard seems to propose this account of the duty to promote others' ends. See Korsgaard, *Creating the Kingdom of Ends*, 127–8.

does indeed loom. If one says that each agent's humanity has an incomparably high value, and then asks how to treat all these incomparably valuable things, then the natural answer will be consequentialist. One must either maximize the number of beings who possess humanity or, as Cummiskey more plausibly maintains, maximize the necessary conditions for the development of humanity. The key to avoiding these consequentialist conclusions is to avoid allowing a non-Kantian notion of value to slip in prior to asking the question 'How should we act?' Instead, one must first find rational grounds for treating other rational beings (and their ends) in certain ways. Only after this has been accomplished can a thoroughgoing Kantian use talk of value as a sort of shorthand, to capture the choices that a rational agent would make regarding the objects in question. The threat of consequentialism, and the response based on Kant's concept of value, are a topic of Chapter 8.

Chapter 9 turns to a less scholarly and more urgently pragmatic question, about the moral consideration that non-human animals deserve. The idea that a good will is the criterion for distinguishing the beings that have the highest moral value may seem to be an extreme position, but it provides the grounds for a quite moderate position on the moral status of animals. One recurring idea in arguments for giving animals greater moral consideration is that it is arbitrary to single out some feature of rationality as a necessary condition for possessing the fullest sort of moral status. Tom Regan, Peter Singer, James Rachels, and Paul Taylor all employ some version of this 'arbitrariness' argument.[11] I agree that it is in fact arbitrary to claim that intelligence, linguistic ability, the ability to set ends, or even the capacity for morality provide a morally relevant criterion for distinguishing the beings that possess the fullest sort of moral status. The proponent of increased consideration for animals is justified in asking why any of these traits are necessarily connected with moral status. But the actual commitment to morality is not an arbitrary criterion. It is not arbitrary because anyone who argues in favour of changing our treatment of non-human animals is herself accepting that there is a special value to acting on moral principles. She may not acknowledge this explicitly, but she acknowledges it implicitly by attempting to rouse her opponent to accept the moral reasoning she offers as a sufficient reason for action. Her own arguments presuppose that there is at least prima facie reason to believe that acting on moral principles has a special and overriding value.

[11] James Rachels, *Created from Animals: The Moral Implications of Darwinism* (Oxford: Oxford University Press, 1990), 176–8; Tom Regan, *The Case for Animal Rights* (Berkeley and Los Angeles: University of California Press, 1983), 151–4; Peter Singer, *Animal Liberation* (New York: New York Review of Books, 1975), 1–7; Paul Taylor, 'The Ethics of Respect for Nature', *Environmental Ethics*, 3 (Fall 1981), 197–218.

But even if this is so, it does not mean that we may treat non-human animals in just any way we please. To show this, I elaborate on one of the points from Part I of this book, that even if a good will is what has highest value, there can still be moral restrictions on the way we treat beings who lack good will. This applies to humans who lack a commitment to morality, as I argue in Chapter 5, but also applies to non-human animals, which lack the cognitive capacities to possess a good will. The nature of these moral requirements, and their connection to the idea of a good will's special value, are best explained through an examination of Kant's idea of a kingdom of ends. One way to interpret the kingdom of ends formulation of the Categorical Imperative is that it provides a way to move from the general principle that humanity must be treated as an end in itself to more specific duties regarding how to act in the world, given the state of the world and given human nature.[12] In the hypothetical kingdom of ends, the members would all recognize one another as ends in themselves, and would give at least some weight to the ends of the other members. Taking into account these facts about the members of the kingdom of ends, plus the sorts of ends that we can predict they would have, will allow us to reach conclusions about some of the rules upon which the members of the kingdom of ends would agree. These specific rules, which are derived by using the kingdom of ends as an interpretative tool, are the rules that actually apply to us in the real world, even if some of us in the real world do not live up to the demands of these rules. The rules regarding treatment of non-human animals, I argue, would at the least include restrictions against inflicting needless pain on them. So Chapter 9 argues for some particular conclusions about duties toward non-human animals, but also provides a moral framework, based on the good will reading of the humanity formulation, for deliberating about other particular moral issues.

In Chapter 10, I examine the connections between the humanity formulation, the Kantian concept of autonomy, and the concepts of autonomy that are prevalent in contemporary discussions in bioethics. More specifically, I emphasize the important differences between each of these concepts. Relying on these differences, I conclude that the widely accepted contemporary principle that we must 'Respect autonomy' is related to Kant's humanity formulation only loosely. To respect autonomy, in the current sense, means roughly to allow beings to makes choices for themselves, especially important choices about the course of their lives. To find this duty in Kant's ethics, we must piece it together from various other duties, some perfect and some

[12] This 'constructivist' reading of the kingdom of ends formulation is suggested by Thomas E. Hill, Jr. See n. 8 above.

imperfect, which Kant derives from the various formulations of the Categorical Imperative. Far from being a basic Kantian principle, the current ideal of 'respecting autonomy' must be searched for in the penumbra of duties that Kant discusses more directly. I further conclude that the gap between the humanity formulation and the contemporary idea of respecting autonomy is evidence that the minimal readings of 'humanity' are mistaken, since if they were correct, then the humanity formulation would be saying something fairly close to 'respect autonomy'. Finally, I argue that some cases in bioethics, especially cases involving the duty of medical confidentiality, suggest that the good will reading of the humanity formulation is in at least some ways a more intuitively compelling moral principle than the principle of respect for autonomy.

I believe that Part I and Part II of the book are mutually reinforcing. The good will reading for which I argue in Part I is useful in Part II, allowing for progress toward answers to several difficult questions—questions about the argument for the humanity formulation, the duties it leads to, the fundamentally non-consequentialist nature of the humanity formulation, the moral status of non-human animals, and the connection between the humanity formulation and the contemporary principle of respect for autonomy. And the arguments of Part II show that the good will reading of the humanity formulation can play a central role both in Kant scholarship and in discussions of more general moral issues. Taken together, the two parts of the book go a long way toward explaining the humanity formulation's content, its implications, and the role it may play in further moral enquiries.

2

What Should we Treat as an End in Itself?

The humanity formulation demands that we treat humanity, in ourselves or others, always as an end in itself. But it is far from obvious what this means. The key ideas in the principle—humanity, and treating something as an end in itself—require further explanation. In the second half of this book, I will examine the specific requirements entailed as part of treating someone as an end in herself. Before turning to that, I will examine the other basic question about the humanity formulation, namely what the 'humanity' is that Kant thinks we must always treat as an end.

It may appear obvious that Kant means 'humanity' ('die Menschheit') to refer to human beings, so that the humanity formulation is telling us to treat all (and only) humans as ends in themselves. But this cannot be correct, as many commentators have pointed out.[1] Kant says that the 'humanity' or what he often calls 'rational nature' *in* a person is what has value as an end in itself, and this rational nature can be possessed by rational beings other than members of the human species, if there are any such beings. And, notoriously, Kant also seems committed to the position that not all members of the human species possess this feature. Whatever Kantian humanity is, it is lacked by the permanently unconscious, the seriously deranged, the severely brain damaged, and (perhaps most troubling) by very young children. I think the claim that not all humans qualify as ends in themselves is not quite as deeply problematic as some have taken it to be, for reasons I will discuss in Chapter 8, but the point for now is just that 'humanity' is not interchangeable with 'human beings', but rather refers to some property possessed by many humans and possibly by other rational beings.

[1] See for example Thomas E. Hill, Jr., *Dignity and Practical Reason in Kant's Moral Theory* (Ithaca, NY: Cornell University Press, 1992), 39; Allen Wood, *Kant's Ethical Thought* (Cambridge: Cambridge University Press, 1999), 119–20. I am not aware of any recent commentators who have held that 'humanity' in fact refers precisely to human beings.

This is the going view among Kant commentators, and it seems right to me. But I believe that standard views are mistaken about exactly which features constitute humanity, and who possesses humanity.

It has become common to think that 'humanity' refers to some minimal feature or features of rationality, necessarily possessed by any rational agent. I think this is mistaken, and that 'humanity' instead refers to a good will, the will of a being who is committed to moral principles. In this chapter, I will explain in more detail the Kantian concept of a good will, and I will present the alternative readings of 'humanity' proposed by other commentators. This will set the stage for the arguments of the first half of this book, in favour of the good will reading of 'humanity' and against others' minimal readings.

While my aims in this chapter are explanatory rather than argumentative, I hope that one point will become clear. Even among the more standard readings, which take humanity to be something possessed by all minimally rational beings, there is substantial divergence on exactly which (minimal) features of rationality constitute a being's humanity. The details of this disagreement have received surprisingly little scholarly attention. The most prominent recent commentaries on the topic have all maintained that humanity is a feature possessed by all rational beings, but have not explicitly addressed the differences in views regarding the exact nature of humanity.[2] Even if one rejects my reading of 'humanity' as 'good will', there remains a substantial question about what the humanity is that we must treat as an end in itself. But, of course, I hope to provide convincing evidence for taking humanity to be a good will.

1. What is a Good Will?

As a first step toward arguing that Kant says a good will (*gute Wille*) is what we must treat as an end in itself, I will state more precisely what a good will is.

There is an older view that identifies good will as a will that performs actions with moral worth, but this view has largely fallen by the wayside. Kant says an action has moral worth if (and only if) the action is in accord with duty and performed from the motive of duty (G 397–400). Since a good will is in some sense a will that is motivated by duty, it is perhaps natural to think that a good will is a will that chooses to perform actions with moral worth. H. J. Paton sometimes offers this as a definition of 'good will'. He

[2] See Hill, *Dignity and Practical Reason*, 38–57; Wood, *Kant's Ethical Thought*, 118–22; Christine Korsgaard, *Creating the Kingdom of Ends* (Cambridge: Cambridge University Press, 1996), 110–14.

says, 'A good will—under human conditions—is one which acts for the sake of duty'.[3] Lewis White Beck makes similar statements. In *A Commentary on Kant's Critique of Practical Reason*, he writes, 'An action having this motive (the motive of duty) is moral, and a being who acts from this motive has a good will'.[4] According to this view, a good will is exactly a will that performs dutiful actions because they are required by duty.

While this view is not wholly misguided, it is an oversimplification. None of us find ourselves always bound by duty in every situation. The 'moral worth' view of good will suggests that at those times when we choose an action that is morally permissible but not required, our good will fades. It is peculiar to think of a good will as something that comes and goes in this way. For these reasons, the strict identification of good will with moral worth is no longer widely accepted.

But there is something right about the view. Kant clearly means there to be a connection between good will and acting on moral principles. To have a will at all is to have the capacity to act for reasons, or on certain principles. The good will is distinguished by the principles on which it acts and 'is not good because of its effects or accomplishments ... it is good only by virtue of its willing' (G 394). The principle on which the good will acts is given by reason alone, and is in fact the Categorical Imperative (G 401–3). Since the Categorical Imperative is the fundamental moral principle, a good will is the will of an agent who acts on moral principles. This is the basic definition of a good will that Kant offers in *Groundwork*.[5]

But so far this sounds compatible with the idea that a good will is exactly a will that chooses to perform actions that have moral worth. *Metaphysics of Morals* and *Religion within the Limits of Reason Alone* provide the resources for a more detailed and satisfactory description of a good will.

Metaphysics of Morals offers the clearest description of different aspects of the will. The power that most obviously might be identified with the will is 'choice', or the power to choose, which Kant identifies as *Willkür* (MM 213). But there are other aspects of the will, the most important of which is *Wille*. Each rational agent's *Wille* provides her with practical laws to which her particular choices must conform in order to be fully rational.[6] The practical

[3] H. J. Paton, *The Categorical Imperative* (Philadelphia: University of Pennsylvania Press, 1947), 47. See also 55, for a virtually identical statement.

[4] Lewis White Beck, *A Commentary on Kant's Critique of Practical Reason* (Chicago: University of Chicago Press, 1960), 41.

[5] This very general account is not meant to be controversial, and accords with most commentators' views, e.g. Korsgaard, *Creating the Kingdom of Ends*.

[6] See e.g. MM 225–7.

laws that Kant emphasizes are the fundamental moral principles given by the different formulations of the Categorical Imperative.[7] A fully rational agent would limit her particular choices of actions to those that are morally permissible, or in other words would always allow her *Wille* to govern her *Willkür*. The will of an agent who is fully rational in this way is a good will.

But humans are imperfectly rational, so they can use *Willkür* to choose actions that are morally prohibited. We could imagine a 'holy will', which is not subject to inclinations that might lead it astray (G 414, 439). Since there is no possibility of a holy will choosing to act contrary to the principles legislated by reason, the moral law does not even appear to it as an imperative. It only makes sense to speak of obligations to act in certain ways if the obligated being could act otherwise. Humans obviously do not have holy wills. We could imagine a will that is short of a holy will, because it is subject to the temptations of inclination, yet still chooses always to act according to the principles of reason. Kant thinks (and intuition seems to fall on his side here) that humans do not have this sort of perfect, finite will either.

In *Religion within the Limits of Reason Alone*, Kant explains why humans are imperfectly rational and how they can nevertheless have good wills. Humans have a predisposition for respect for the moral law, which can motivate them to act on moral principles. But they also have inclinations, and a 'self-love' that motivates them to satisfy these inclinations.[8] So every human has an incentive of self-love and also an incentive unconditionally to respect and obey the moral law. Kant says the difference between a good and evil man 'must depend on subordination, i.e. which of the two incentives he makes the condition of the other' (R 36). In order for an agent's will to be good, she must have a commitment to act morally even when acting morally requires her to forgo the satisfaction of inclinations (she must make the moral law 'the supreme condition of the satisfaction' of her inclinations). If, on the other hand, someone took his inclinations 'as in themselves wholly adequate to the determination of the [*Willkür*], without troubling himself about the moral law (which after all, he does have in him), he would be morally evil' (R 36). Whether someone's will is good depends on whether he gives priority to morality or to satisfying his inclinations.

On this description, a good will is an enduring feature. This makes clear why it is not correct to say that a good will is precisely a will that performs actions that have moral worth. A good will is the will of an agent who is committed

[7] Presumably the Hypothetical Imperative is also legislated by *Wille*, and certainly an agent's choices must conform to the Hypothetical Imperative in order to count as fully rational.

[8] R 26, 36–7. Also, see C2 73–4.

to moral principles, and this commitment can be present even when one is not performing actions that display it. An agent only demonstrates that her will is good when she performs her duties because they are duties—that is, when performing actions that have moral worth. But her will can remain good when she merely chooses between different permissible ends, for her commitment to morality can remain.

But this commitment is fragile in human beings, because they have what Kant calls a 'natural propensity of the human being to evil'.[9] This propensity can take the form of giving priority to the principle of self-love, rather than moral law. 'Depravity' is complete subjugation of morality to the principle of self-love, ignoring the commands of the Categorical Imperative. 'Impurity' is recognizing and acting on the commands of morality sometimes, but only because doing so is consistent with the principle of self-love. But even though each human has the propensity to ignore moral demands or place greater emphasis on the demands of self-love, he also has freedom (R 35) and so 'is capable of' (R 45) resolving to act on moral principles at all costs. So it is within his power to have a good will.

This is so despite the existence of a third type of propensity to evil in man, a propensity that can lead even agents with good wills to act wrongly. This propensity is 'weakness of the human heart ... or in other words, the frailty of human nature' (R 29). Frailty can keep one from choosing particular right actions even though one truly wills to act on the moral law as one's supreme and overriding principle.[10]

> In other words, I incorporate the good (the law) into the maxim of my (*Willkür*), but this good, which is an irresistible incentive objectively or ideally (*in thesi*), is subjectively (*in hypothesi*), the weaker (in comparison to inclination) whenever the maxim is to be followed. (R 29)[11]

No human is fully free of this frailty, or at least its temptation, so man is only capable of 'an ever-continuing striving for the better', or 'gradual reformation'.[12] That is, a human agent can never regard herself as having won the struggle to be moral, with regard to her actions, and can only see herself as 'on a path of continual progress from bad to better'. But this frailty of human will is compatible with a commitment to act morally come what may, or 'that purity of the (moral) principle which he has adopted as the supreme maxim

[9] R 29, also e.g. R 29–39.

[10] See also MM 407–8, where Kant says weakness based on affect can coexist with a good will.

[11] The parentheses are Kant's, except for my substitution of the German *Willkür* for the translated 'will'.

[12] R 48. The remaining quotations in this paragraph are from the same page.

of his will'. To embark firmly on the path of continual moral improvement is to have the commitment to moral principles that marks a good will. So even human agents, frail and subject to temptation though they are, can have good wills.

It is now clear why a good will cannot be defined as a will that chooses actions with moral worth, and why even imperfectly rational humans can have good wills. A good will is not present only when an agent acts on the motive of duty. It endures when performing merely permissible actions and can even coexist with some intentional immoral actions.[13] One loses a good will not through weakness of will, but by giving priority to the principle of satisfying inclinations, because this principle 'by the goodness of which all the moral worth of the person must be assessed, is therefore still contrary to law, and the human being, despite all his good actions, is nevertheless evil' (R 31). Whether one's will is good is a matter of one's principles, not primarily of one's actions.[14]

Two points should be emphasized about my description of good will as the will of an agent who is committed to governing her *Willkür* with the moral principles dictated by *Wille.*

First, to dispel in advance a possible misunderstanding, my claim is that the humanity which we should treat as an end in itself is exactly a will that is good, not that the end in itself is just a commitment to morality. Placing a priority on moral principles is the feature that distinguishes a good will, but it is the whole will that is valuable, not just the commitment to morality. Not every will is good, but if the will is good, then it is valuable in all its aspects. And since, for Kant, the will is the most essential feature of a rational being, one might speak

[13] It is not obvious how Kant can account for the compatibility of good will and intentional immoral actions. It appears at first glance that by intentionally choosing to act immorally one must be taken to be renouncing one's unconditional commitment to morality. I briefly address this in Chapter 3.

[14] The description of good will as the will of a being who places a priority on morality over self-love accords for the most part with the accounts of other commentators who have written recently on the topic. Walter E. Schaller recognizes the importance of the *Religion* discussion of the goodness of human wills, and says that 'To have a good will is to have adopted the moral law as one's supreme maxim and to be unconditionally willing to do what is right, requiring no nonmoral motives or incentives for acting as duty requires. To have an evil will, on the other hand, is to be only conditionally willing to do what is right because one has subordinated the moral law to a maxim of self-love'. See Walter E. Schaller, 'The Relation of Moral Worth to the Good Will in Kant's Ethics', *Journal of Philosophical Research*, 17, (1992), 353. Similarly, Nelson Potter says that 'good will is a relatively permanent attribute of the agent's character, rather than a momentary aspect of an agent's action', and he analyses relevant *Religion* passages as saying that 'The good person gives priority to moral considerations, the evil person to personal desires'. See Nelson Potter, 'Kant and the Moral Worth of Actions', *Southern Journal of Philosophy*, 34, (1996), 228. Karl Ameriks also equates good will with 'the proper and complete individual character', rather than with a changing trait of particular actions. See Karl Ameriks, 'Kant on the Good Will', in Ottfried Höffe (ed.), *Grundlegung zur Metaphysik der Sitten: Ein kooperativer Kommentar*, (Frankfurt am Main: Vittorio Klostermann, 1989), 45–65.

(as I think Kant often does) of the being who possesses a good will as an end in herself.[15]

The second point is that, on Kant's account, a good will is not discernible through empirical observation. We can never have sufficient empirical grounds to reach definite conclusions about someone's character, because we can only observe her actions and not her principles.[16] Then, since a good will is a matter of one's principles and priorities, not one's actions, empirical observation can never tell us that someone has or lacks a good will. But Kant's point is not that we should then doubt whether there are any such things as commitment to principle, or as good or bad will. This is because Kant, of course, thinks that there are non-empirical justifications for accepting and employing these concepts.

In fact, the possibility of accepting moral principles as sufficient reason for action is one of the fundamental points on which Kant's ethics relies. In chapter 3 of *Groundwork*, Kant attempts to show that there is such a thing as a Categorical Imperative. To outline his strategy very roughly, he begins by claiming that we unavoidably find ourselves in situations of deliberating about what actions to perform, and that in order to make choices about what action to perform, we must take ourselves for practical purposes to be free to choose among different options. But we can only be free if it is possible to act on principles that we legislate to ourselves, principles that do not depend on our desires or inclinations. Only a Categorical Imperative, or moral principle, can meet this description. Since moral principles are a necessary condition of the possibility of an activity in which we unavoidably engage (the activity of deliberating about actions), we are justified in accepting the existence of moral principles. But then we must also regard it as possible to take moral principles as sufficient for action.[17] Only if this is possible can we act freely, because otherwise we would have no alternative to being 'determined' by our inclinations. So it follows from some of the most basic elements of Kant's ethics

[15] Of course, the very point at issue is whether humanity and a good will are equivalent, and I do not mean to beg that question here. My point is that Kant often speaks interchangeably of treating a person as an end in himself, and treating the humanity in a person as an end in itself. See e.g. G 428–9, 431, 435, 437–8. Whichever reading of humanity is correct, Kant means that humanity and the beings who possess humanity are ends in themselves. Allen Wood believes that Kant moves a little quickly on this point, and that humanity should be treated as an end in itself even when it is not instantiated in a person, but Wood does not deny that beings who do possess humanity should be treated as ends in themselves. See Wood, *Kant's Ethical Thought*, 144, and 'Kant on Duties Regarding Nonrational Nature', *Proceedings of the Aristotelian Society*, Supplementary Volume 72 (1998).

[16] See G 407, R 20, 30, 63, 68.

[17] Of course, I only mean that they are sufficient for action *given* the circumstances in which one finds oneself. Without a description of circumstances, it is not possible to see if or how a moral principle applies, and so no determinate action would result.

that we are justified in regarding it as possible to give priority to morality over inclination. Or, in other words, to have a good will.

Of course, the basic Kantian strategy alluded to above is controversial, and it is not my purpose to defend it here. The point is not that Kant's metaethics is clearly correct, but just that Kant's position entails a deep commitment to the possibility of possessing a good will. And this is so despite his claims that a good will is never directly observable.

This only establishes that lack of empirical observability does not provide reason to doubt that there could be good wills. It does not settle the question of how common good wills are, or whether any humans even possess a good will at all. That question will be addressed in Chapter 5.

So far, my aim has been simply to explain the Kantian idea of good will, which I believe is equivalent to the 'humanity' that Kant says we must treat as an end in itself. A good will is the will of a being who is committed to acting morally, who gives priority to moral principles rather than acting simply to satisfy her own desires, inclinations, impulses, or sentiments.

2. Others' Readings of 'Humanity'

In contrast to my proposal that humanity is equivalent to a good will (which a rational agent may fail to possess, if she fails to place sufficient priority on morality), other commentators have maintained that humanity is something that every minimally rational agent necessarily possesses. In fact, most other commentators have gone out of their way to emphasize that humanity must be a feature possessed by all functioning adult humans and any other rational beings that may exist. The spirit of these readings of 'humanity' is captured well in Allen Wood's statement, '"Humanity" clearly belongs to all mature members of our biological species'.[18] Indeed, it seems to be common practice in explications of the humanity formulation specifically to deny that humanity is equivalent to a good will.[19]

An examination of the reasons that have led commentators to eschew the good will reading of 'humanity' in favour of their minimal readings will wait until Chapter 4. My purpose here is just to clarify the different versions of the minimal reading. Despite other commentators' unanimity that humanity must be something that all minimally rational beings possess, the details of their definitions vary significantly. In fact, there has sometimes been a tendency for

[18] Wood, *Kant's Ethical Thought*, 119.

[19] Ibid. 120–1; Korsgaard, *Creating the Kingdom of Ends*, 123–4.

authors to slide between different definitions even within their own writings. This may be because the most urgent task has seemed to them to be the denial that humanity is good will, or it may be because the convenience of the Kantian labels 'rational nature' and 'rational beings' has obscured the need to clarify exactly what type or degree of rationality corresponds to humanity. Regardless of the reason, it seems that even among minimal readings of 'humanity', there is a need for more careful definition and consistency.

The minimal readings of 'humanity' fall into three categories, though the line between the second and third categories is not completely distinct.

The first category identifies humanity as just the power to set ends or make choices—in other words, as *Willkür*. This is a power that all rational beings possess, on Kant's picture of rational nature. To possess a will, for Kant, is the defining feature of rational agents, and *Willkür* and *Wille* are the two basic elements of the will, so every rational agent has the power to set ends for herself.

The second category of minimal reading also identifies humanity with some necessary features of rationality, but with a larger set of such features. Besides *Willkür*, other additional features that have been proposed include the power to legislate moral principles to oneself (*Wille*), the power to act on the Hypothetical Imperative, the ability to compare one's various contingent ends and organize them into a systemic whole, and the ability to employ theoretical reason to understand the world. The idea of the second type of minimal reading is that humanity is equivalent to a certain group of traits or abilities, which all minimally rational beings necessarily possess, and so all minimally rational beings must be treated as ends in themselves.

Supporters of both of these first two categories of minimal reading tend to take Kant's use of the term 'rational nature' ('vernünftige Natur') to be interchangeable with their own preferred reading.[20] In support of reading 'humanity' as 'the power to set ends', one might take it that by 'rational nature' Kant generally means the power to set ends, since it is this power that is most characteristic of rational agency. Or if one takes humanity to be equivalent to some larger group of traits, one might think that it is these traits taken together that constitute a minimum standard for rational nature.

A third sort of interpretation of 'humanity' identifies humanity as the capacity to act morally. This capacity for morality must be distinguished from possessing an actual commitment to act as morality demands (otherwise the 'capacity' reading of 'humanity' would be the same as the good will reading), but many commentators fail to specify exactly what they think constitutes a capacity for

[20] Not surprisingly, I think Kant often uses 'rational nature' to mean the more fully rational nature possessed by beings who are committed to acting on principles dictated by *Wille*.

morality. It seems that the best Kantian way to fill out the idea of the capacity for morality would begin with the ideas of *Willkür* and *Wille*. To accept moral principles as a determinant of one's actions requires the ability to choose among actions, or *Willkür*. And it requires access to moral principles, which on Kant's picture is provided by each agent's legislation of moral principles to herself through *Wille*. For a perfect or holy will, these ingredients might be sufficient to lead to moral actions, but for beings like humans who are also subject to inclination, there must also be some feeling that accompanies the choice to act on the moral law.

In *Groundwork*, Second *Critique*, and *Religion*, Kant explains the role that particular feelings play in making it possible for humans to act purely on moral principles. Reverence and the predisposition to personality are the feelings that are needed. Kant discusses reverence (*Achtung*) in *Groundwork* and Second *Critique*.[21] Reverence is a feeling that arises when we apprehend the reason-giving force of the moral law, and how our inclinations pale in importance compared to moral requirements. Kant distinguishes reverence from the typical sort of human feeling, in that it is 'not of empirical origin', instead being 'produced by an intellectual ground', namely the recognition of moral principles' unconditional power to command. Since this feeling is produced only by the recognition of the categorical force of morality, it is not the sort of pre-existing desire or inclination that robs an action of moral worth. One might think that the feeling of reverence would be enough to lead humans to act from the motive of duty, but in *Religion* Kant apparently says otherwise. He says we need an additional natural predisposition whose role is to serve as a 'subjective ground' for incorporating respect (*Achtung*) as a motivating force into our maxims' (R 27–8). This predisposition is what Kant calls the predisposition to personality, and he says it is a moral feeling. However, Kant has defined reverence as itself a subjective feeling (which is produced by an 'intellectual cause'[22]), so it is not clear why reverence can only have subjective influence by means of another, separate feeling.[23] What is clear is that for imperfect rational beings to have the capacity for moral action requires, according to Kant, the possession of not only *Wille* and *Willkür*, but also some moral feeling that disposes them to act in the ways that *Wille* demands.[24]

[21] See e.g. G 400, 401, 403, 436, 439, 440 and C2 73–85, 87–8. [22] C2 73.

[23] Kant even says, 'Respect (*Achtung*) for the moral law is therefore the sole and undoubted moral incentive'. C2 78.

[24] For more detailed discussions of moral feeling, see Andrews Reath, 'Kant's Theory of Moral Sensibility: Respect for the Moral Law and the Influence of Inclination', *Kant-Studien*, 80/3 (1989), 284–302, or Philip Stratton-Lake, *Kant, Duty, and Moral Worth* (London: Routledge, 2000), esp. 29–59.

If the capacity for morality consists in the possession of *Willkür, Wille*, and the predisposition to moral feelings such as reverence for moral law, then the capacity reading of 'humanity' can reasonably be seen as a variety of the second category of minimal reading. The second category of minimal reading takes humanity to be some set of traits possessed by all rational beings. *Willkür* and *Wille* are such traits, and on Kant's picture moral feelings are also possessed by all rational humans, at least. The only obstacle to saying that all rational beings must possess moral feelings is that a perfectly rational will, or holy will, presumably would not. Save for this exception, it appears that the best understanding of a capacity for morality would make the third kind of reading of humanity, the 'capacity for morality' reading, into roughly a species of the second category of reading of 'humanity'.

But there is a reason for treating the 'capacity' reading separately, at least a pragmatic reason. Many commentators have proposed reading 'humanity' as the 'capacity for morality' without specifying exactly what this capacity consists of. And even if the capacity for morality does depend on the possession of *Wille, Willkür*, plus moral feelings, there seems to be some intuitive appeal to the idea that a capacity or potential for morality has special value, and this intuitive appeal may be lost or blunted by reducing the capacity to its constituent characteristics. For this reason, and to allow the possibility that proponents of the capacity reading have in mind some other account of what the capacity consists of, it seems more charitable to treat the capacity reading separately from the more general second category of readings of 'humanity'.

Each of these three kinds of reading equates humanity with some features necessarily possessed by any minimally rational agent. This is unlike the good will reading, since agents could at least theoretically lack a commitment to act morally and so (if humanity is taken to be good will) lack the humanity we must treat as an end in itself.[25] I will refer to the non-good will readings as three versions of a 'minimal' reading of 'humanity', since they require less from an agent in order for her to count as possessing humanity.

Each of the three versions of the minimal reading receives support from some prominent commentators on Kant's ethics. Temporarily leaving aside any detailed examination of their arguments, I will here just give an idea of who has held which view.

Christine Korsgaard's considered view is that humanity is the power to set ends or make choices. She sometimes suggests a connection between humanity, as the power to set ends, and 'personality', or the setting of ends directed by

[25] If this seems implausible or morally repugnant, I ask the reader to wait until Chapters 5 and 9, which I hope will make the good will reading relatively easy to swallow.

moral principles, but she emphatically affirms that the mere power to set ends is what we must treat as an end in itself.

In chapter 1 of *Creating the Kingdom of Ends*,[26] Korsgaard says Kant identifies 'our humanity, our rational nature and capacity for choice' as the one thing that is an end in itself. She reiterates this in her chapter on the formula of humanity, saying, 'Kant takes the characteristic feature of humanity, or rational nature, to be the capacity for setting an end'.[27] Again, in her penultimate chapter, she defines 'humanity' as the capacity to propose an end to oneself, or 'the power of free rational choice'.[28] Korsgaard thinks that humanity is, to use the Kantian term, *Willkür*.

Korsgaard is firmly committed to her view of humanity as *Willkür*, yet she recognizes an apparent obstacle in Kant's statement that only a good will has unconditional value (G 393). She acknowledges that attributing unconditional value only to a good will may seem incompatible with the claim that it is the power to set ends which has value as an end in itself. She attempts to reconcile the two claims by saying that humanity (as *Willkür*) 'is completed and perfected only in the realization of "personality", which is the good will'.[29]

But this reconciliation is not viable. If the power of choice is an end in itself, then every minimally rational agent is necessarily an end in herself. If having a firm commitment never to act contrary to duty is a necessary condition for something being an end in itself, then it is at least theoretically possible that some minimally rational agents will not be ends in themselves. For all that has been said so far, it is possible that the best reading of 'humanity' is *Willkür*. But what is not possible is that two inconsistent readings of 'humanity'—as *Willkür* and as 'good will'—are simultaneously the best readings.[30]

More or less the same problem arises with Korsgaard's statement in chapter 1, that to identify the end in itself as *Willkür* 'is not different from saying it is a good will, for rational nature, in its perfect state, is a good will'.[31] The claim trades on an ambiguity in 'rational nature'. Fully rational nature in humans is of course equivalent to a good will, according to Kant—an agent always has sufficient reason to act morally, and a fully rational agent will always act on sufficient reasons. But at this point in her chapter, Korsgaard has just finished identifying rational nature as the 'capacity for rational choice'. If this is the rational nature she is talking about, then it does not make sense to speak of it being more or less perfect. It is something minimally rational agents have, and

[26] Korsgaard, *Creating the Kingdom of Ends*, 17. [27] Ibid. 110. [28] Ibid. 346.

[29] Ibid. 123–4.

[30] Unless, of course, we want to maintain that Kant himself is deeply inconsistent on this point, which is not the line Korsgaard is taking.

[31] Ibid. 17. See also ibid. 114, for a similar statement.

more completely rational agents have in just the same way. The ambiguity in her use of 'rational nature' does not support equating *Willkür* and good will. If anything, it suggests the possibility that it is misguided to read 'rational nature' as 'minimally rational nature'.[32]

But attributing this inconsistency to Korsgaard may be uncharitable. A rereading of Korsgaard's apparent attempt to equate *Willkür* and good will may make her position more plausible, though in the end still problematic. Perhaps she can be taken to mean that the power to set ends is what makes it possible to act on moral principles, since it is what makes it possible to act at all. So the power to set ends is what has special value, but it has this special value because it is in effect the capacity to act on the moral law. This would move Korsgaard's view from the first category of minimal reading, identifying humanity as *Willkür*, to the third category, identifying humanity as the capacity (but not the commitment) to act morally.

But it is very strange to say the power to set ends is what gives us the capacity to act morally. Besides the power to set ends, one must have the power to legislate moral laws to oneself (i.e. one must have *Wille*) and some incentive to follow the moral law. Kant does think humans have all these, and probably thinks that any finite rational being necessarily has these.[33] So Kant may well think that any being with *Willkür* must also have *Wille* and an incentive to obey *Wille*. But it is still not *Willkür* by itself that constitutes the capacity for acting morally.

So, in the absence of further explanation of how the 'capacity for morality' view of humanity is compatible with the 'power to set ends' view, it appears that Korsgaard's considered view is the latter.[34]

Allen Wood holds the second type of view of humanity, that humanity consists of *Willkür*, but also of other features possessed by all rational agents. He thinks that humanity 'encompasses all our rational capacities having no

[32] I believe that Kant usually uses it to denote something closer to the fully rational nature that includes possession of a good will.

[33] In *Religion*, Kant sometimes sounds as if it is just a contingent fact about human nature that we have both the incentive to obey the moral law and the incentive to satisfy our inclinations. But in fact it appears that Kant's moral theory implies that rational beings who are subject to inclinations must possess all the features that make it possible to act from moral motives. This is because we must take ourselves as free for practical purposes, and to take ourselves as free we must suppose it is possible to act on moral principles.

[34] David Cummiskey follows Korsgaard's lead in defining humanity as the power to set ends, in *Kantian Consequentialism* (New York: Oxford University Press, 1996). His only explicit definition occurs on p. 85, where he cites MM 392 and G 412 to say that the 'distinctive characteristic' of humanity is 'the capacity to set oneself an end'. He generally seems to be employing this definition throughout his book, and his frequent use of the phrase 'rational nature' is apparently meant to be equivalent.

specific reference to morality'.[35] Humanity includes a 'technical aspect' that allows us to find the best means to our contingent ends. It also includes a 'pragmatic aspect' that consists of the 'ability to compare our contingent ends and organize them into a systematic whole'.[36] And because humanity 'subjects my actions to rational guidance by an end', it also 'involves an active sense of my identity and an esteem for myself'. But *Willkür* is the central element of humanity, because 'The capacity to set ends through reason holds together the set of capacities constituting our humanity'.

In the paper 'Humanity as End in Itself', Wood includes a capacity for morality as part of humanity as well, but in *Kant's Ethical Thought*, he does not pursue this claim, and seems to have reconsidered it. In 'Humanity as End in Itself', Wood defines 'personality' as the 'rational capacity to respect the moral law and to act having duty or the moral law as a sole sufficient motive of the will',[37] and then says that 'Kant does not regard personality as distinct from humanity'.[38] But there is no attempt in *Kant's Ethical Thought* to include a capacity for morality as part of humanity, and in fact he excludes any moral aspects of rational nature from being constitutive of humanity. So Wood's considered view seems to be that humanity is a set of characteristics possessed by all rational agents, but that the capacity for acting on moral principles is not part of this set.[39]

In contrast, Thomas E. Hill, Jr.'s view of humanity falls in the third category, saying that humanity is (or includes) the capacity for morality. In 'Humanity as an End in Itself', Hill quite rightly says that Kant is equivocal in his use of the term 'humanity', but Hill settles on a basic definition of 'humanity' as 'only those powers necessarily associated with rationality'.[40] Specifically, he thinks the relevant powers associated with rationality are: to act for reasons in general; to follow principles of prudence (hypothetical imperatives); to set ends; to understand the world by using theoretical reason; and to legislate

[35] Wood, *Kant's Ethical Thought*, 118.

[36] Ibid. 119. Subsequent quotations in this paragraph are from the same page.

[37] Allen Wood, 'Humanity as End in Itself', *Proceedings of the Eighth International Kant Congress*, 1/1 (1995), 307.

[38] Wood may not be capturing Kant's use of 'personality' here. In the *Religion* passage Wood cites, Kant identifies personality as actual 'good character', not just the capacity for it. But Wood's real concern here does not seem to be with the term 'personality', but with identifying his concept of humanity with the capacity to act morally.

[39] In correspondence, Stephen Engstrom has also expressed what sounds like the second version of the minimal reading, but one which seems to include moral aspects. He says that he does not think Kant simply equates humanity with the capacity for morality, that 'the capacity for morality is not bare humanity, but rather humanity in a developed state ... namely a state in which it, as rational nature, can of itself be practical'.

[40] Hill, *Dignity and Practical Reason*, 40.

moral principles to oneself. Hill equates the self-legislation of moral principles with 'acceptance' of the principles.[41] Then he says, 'This implies that anyone who has humanity has a capacity and disposition to follow such principles'. So it seems most accurate to say that Hill means humanity to include *Wille* and the accompanying predispositions (e.g. the feeling of respect for the moral law) that make it possible for finite rational beings to act on moral principles. He repeats this in his editor's introduction to *Groundwork for the Metaphysics of Morals*, saying, 'Our humanity includes our capacity and disposition to follow the (allegedly) unconditional rational supreme principle of morality, but arguably it includes other aspects of rationality as well'.[42] So Hill takes 'humanity' in the humanity formulation to include several aspects of rational nature, including both the power to set ends and the capacity for morality.

John Rawls's most explicit statement about 'humanity' in the humanity formulation, in *Lectures on the History of Moral Philosophy*, resembles Hill's in that Rawls takes humanity to include both the capacity for morality—'moral personality, which makes it possible to have a good will and a good moral character'—and other, non-moral rational powers, or 'those capacities and skills to be developed by culture'.[43]

Several other authors identify humanity as the capacity to act morally or from moral motives, without explaining exactly what they mean. I believe the analysis offered earlier in this section, taking the capacity for morality as roughly the possession of *Willkür* and *Wille*, plus the capacity to feel reverence for the moral law and make this reverence a motive for action, is the best way to understand their position.

Barbara Herman does not argue extensively for any particular reading of the humanity formulation, but she seems to accept the idea of humanity as a capacity for morality. Near the end of *The Practice of Moral Judgment*, she says that rational nature is an end in itself 'Insofar as it is capable of morality'. She emphasizes that it also has dignity, or incomparable worth, then devotes a paragraph to explaining that a good will is not required in order for an agent to have dignity.[44] Instead, 'As rational agents, we each have the capacity to bring our will into conformity with the principle of good willing, so each has all the dignity there is to have'.[45] The capacity for acting morally is what she

[41] Ibid. 41.

[42] Immanuel Kant, *Groundwork for the Metaphysics of Morals*, ed. Thomas E. Hill, Jr., and Arnulf Zweig (Oxford: Oxford University Press, 2002), 77.

[43] John Rawls, *Lectures on the History of Moral Philosophy*, ed. Barbara Herman (Cambridge, Mass.: Harvard University Press, 2000).

[44] This is actually contrary to some of Kant's explicit statements. See G 435 and other texts that will be cited in Chapter 4. But, of course, the citing of a few passages is not in itself decisive.

[45] Herman, *The Practice of Moral Judgment* (Cambridge, Mass.: Harvard University Press, 1993), 238.

identifies as humanity. In the absence of further explanation, the best account of what the capacity for morality amounts to seems to be the account offered earlier in this section.

Similarly, Onora O'Neill settles on a 'capacity' reading of humanity without focusing heavily on the issue or precisely defining this capacity. She generally speaks of 'rational beings' as ends in themselves, which is indeterminate as a reading of 'humanity'. In one place she connects the idea of rational agency with 'willing', which sounds like a *Willkür* reading.[46] But she says that the reason rational beings are ends in themselves is that 'Rational beings presumably must be non-conditional values because they alone can will anything; hence they alone can have a good will'.[47] The best reading of this would seem to be that the capacity to act on the moral law is what should be treated as an end in itself, with the idea of this moral capacity left undefined.

Roger Sullivan more clearly holds the view that the capacity for morality is what should be treated as an end in itself. He says that 'the fundamental respect owed persons is not based on merit or achievement, not even on morally good character' but instead on 'the *capacity* to develop a morally good will'.[48] He suggests that rational agents are ends in themselves because they are 'able and obligated' to set ends, make choices, and 'to enact and act on genuinely universal laws of conduct for themselves and all others'.[49]

In some passages, H. J. Paton sounds as if he endorses reading 'humanity' as 'good will', but this is only because of a looseness in his use of the term 'good will'. He reminds the reader that only a good will is 'absolutely good, good in every respect, and the supreme condition of all good',[50] and notes that an end in itself must have absolute value. Then 'Since it has absolute value, we know already what it must be—namely, a good will'.[51] Later he reaffirms that the end in itself is 'a good or rational will itself'.[52] But in both cases, he quickly backs away from identifying humanity with an actual commitment to morality. In the first case, he says, 'This good or rational will Kant takes to be present in every rational agent, and so in every man, however much it might be overlaid with irrationality'. But since Kant does not think a good will is possessed by every rational agent, Paton is here using 'good will' loosely, to mean either the power to legislate moral laws to oneself, or the capacity to act on those laws as

[46] Onora O'Neill, *Constructions of Reason* (Cambridge: Cambridge University Press, 1989), 138.

[47] Ibid. 137.

[48] Roger Sullivan, *An Introduction to Kant's Ethics* (Cambridge: Cambridge University Press, 1994), 70.

[49] Roger Sullivan, *Immanuel Kant's Moral Theory* (Cambridge: Cambridge University Press, 1989), 197.

[50] Paton, *The Categorical Imperative*, 168.

[51] Ibid. 168–9. [52] Ibid. 177.

one's motive. And in the second case, after saying that a good or rational will is the end in itself, he says that 'even the human being capable of manifesting such a will, cannot be subordinated as a means'.[53] Paton is therefore not identifying humanity as a good will in the strict sense, as requiring a commitment to act as duty requires regardless of circumstances. Instead, he is holding a version of either the second view, identifying humanity as *Wille*, or the third view, identifying humanity as the capacity or capability of acting for duty's sake.

W. D. Ross similarly says that 'humanity' means 'good will', but actually holds something more like a 'capacity' view. He says, 'If there is something that has absolute value, there must be a duty to conserve this and to promote it to the best of one's ability. Now there is such a thing, viz. good will'.[54] But, as with Paton, this apparently unambiguous statement is misleading. Ross immediately adds that good will 'exists either actually or potentially in every man'. Again, on the next page, he says that what is to be valued in persons is their 'potentialities of virtue'. Like Paton, he has used 'good will' loosely, to signify the capacity for acting on the moral law.

This looseness in defining humanity seems representative of the relative lack of attention that Kant's notion of 'humanity' has received from Kant scholars in general, compared to some other, less central, ideas of Kant's ethics. I think there has been surprisingly little recognition of the differences between recent proposed readings of 'humanity', and few attempts to argue systematically for one reading over another. Sometimes there even appear to be internal inconsistencies within a given author's own most basic ideas about humanity. This is not to say that no good work has been done on the subject, of course—some of the good work has been mentioned in this chapter and more will be described in later chapters. But there does seem to be a need for deeper examination of the issue.

This is so even if my proposed reading of 'humanity' as 'good will' is wrong. Serious effort would be required to figure out exactly which minimal reading of humanity is correct. But I think compelling arguments can be offered in favour of the good will reading of 'humanity'. The next two chapters will take up that task.

53 Ibid.

54 W. D. Ross, *Kant's Ethical Theory* (London: Oxford University Press, 1954), 52.

3

The Good Will Reading Meshes With Major Ideas of Kant's Ethics

There are a number of good reasons for thinking that 'humanity', in the Kantian technical sense, refers to a good will rather than to features possessed by every minimally rational being. Perhaps the most compelling advantage of the good will reading over the minimal readings is that the good will reading does a better job of integrating Kant's claims about humanity with other central ideas of Kant's ethics.

In this chapter I will point out several ways in which the good will reading allows for more natural, more consistent, and richer connections with other elements of Kant's moral philosophy. One point on which the good will reading fares better than the minimal readings is that only on the good will reading are Kant's most basic claims about value in *Groundwork* consistent. The minimal readings force a deep inconsistency on Kant. The good will reading also does a better job of explaining why one should never choose to act immorally, of taking seriously Kant's description of humanity as a moral ideal, of explaining Kant's discussion of 'the highest good', of accounting for how to derive the duty to promote others' ends from the humanity formulation, and of providing a stronger connection between the different formulations of the Categorical Imperative.

My intention in this chapter is to focus mainly on these large themes of Kant's ethics, and to argue that accepting the good will reading of humanity is the best way to make the humanity formulation of the Categorical Imperative fit with these themes. Particular textual passages will of course play a role in these arguments, but my concern in this chapter is more to relate Kant's claims about humanity to other of his ideas, rather than to argue that any one particular passage defines humanity as good will. Looking closely at particular passages for evidence of the meaning of 'humanity' is also an important strategy, but a strategy which will wait until Chapter 4.

1. Attributions of Value in *Groundwork*

Several of Kant's central claims in *Groundwork* are about value. Indeed, chapter 1 of the book begins with a claim about the value of a good will, that only a good will is good without qualification (G 393). Then in chapter 2, the humanity formula demands that humanity be treated in certain ways because of its special value as an end in itself (G 428–9). And Kant also attributes a dignity, or incomparably high value, to both good will and humanity.

A careful examination of these value claims shows that unless Kant is being inconsistent in these basic claims about value, he must mean humanity and good will to be equivalent. Since my concern in this section is with examining Kant's claims about value, it is worth pointing out that the same German word, 'der Wert', is sometimes translated as 'worth' and sometimes as 'value'. This varies from translator to translator and also varies between different passages rendered by the same translator.[1] 'Wert' does not necessarily carry any greater moral connotation than the English 'value'.

There is certainly a prima facie case for thinking that Kant attributes the same kind of value to good will and to humanity. Kant says only a good will is 'good without qualification' ('ohne Einschränkung für gut') and also implies (by contrasting it with conditional goods) that it has an 'unconditional worth' ('unbedingten Wert') (G 393, 394). Then in his discussion of the end in itself, he says the end in itself must be an 'objective end' (G 427–8). What is unique about objective ends is that they have an 'absolute value' ('absoluten Wert'). In contrast, all relative ends, or ends based on inclination, have only a 'relative value' ('relativen Wert') or 'conditioned value' ('bedingten Wert') (G 427–8). Kant seems to use 'absolute value' as synonymous with 'unconditional worth', and to contrast this with 'relative value' or 'conditional worth'. And he appears to be attributing the former kinds of value to both humanity and to a good will.

Commentators have recognized and adopted the apparent interchangeability of these value terms. In discussing the good will, Korsgaard calls its value 'intrinsic', and unconditionally good,[2] and then her analysis of the humanity formulation depends on taking humanity to be unconditionally good.[3] Barbara Herman uses talk of unconditional goodness as if it is implied by or interchangeable with something being an end in itself.[4] And Paton feels free to

[1] This includes Arnulf Zweig, the translator of the edition of *Groundwork* which I quote below.

[2] Christine Korsgaard, *Creating the Kingdom of Ends* (Cambridge: Cambridge University Press, 1996), 118.

[3] Ibid. 121–3.

[4] Barbara Herman, *The Practice of Moral Judgment* (Cambridge, Mass.: Harvard University Press, 1993), 238.

use the ideas of absolute value, unconditional value, and value as an end in itself interchangeably.[5] Despite this, philosophers have, as far as I am aware, all baulked at the apparent implication of their usage, that humanity is the same as a good will because it has the same sort of (supposedly unique) value.[6]

The determination to resist this implication is put most pithily by Neil Cooper, in his one-page article 'The Formula of the End in Itself'.[7] Cooper first states that the humanity formulation is related to the universalizability formulation in that the universalizability formulation provides a standard that actions must meet, and when agents live up to that standard, they exhibit a good will. Since we know 'that the good will is the one thing which is unconditionally good', we must treat it as an end in itself. To treat it as a mere means is 'to treat it as if it were not unconditionally good', that is, 'as if it were not what it necessarily is'. So Cooper has assumed that unconditional goodness is equivalent to (or implied by) something being an end in itself, and he recognizes that this identifies a good will as the end in itself. But he says, 'One might try to remedy this deficiency in a Kantian spirit by making Kant's later distinction between *Wille* and *Willkür* and saying that every *Wille* is a legislating will and is thus a thing of value and good in the sense required'. Cooper does not explain why he takes the identification of good will with humanity to be a deficiency, or why this implication should be rejected.

My aim is to show that the equivalence of humanity and a good will is not an incidental or accidental consequence of some careless statements Kant makes about value, but rather the inescapable and welcome implication of Kant's most fundamental claims about value in *Groundwork*. In later sections I will argue that this equivalence is not a 'deficiency', but a deep, central point in Kant's ethics.

In the argument for the humanity formulation, Kant maintains that humanity is the only thing that is an end in itself (G 427–8). And in the opening paragraph of *Groundwork*, he states that a good will is the only thing good without qualification. I will first analyse what Kant means by calling something an end in itself, then what 'good without qualification' means. These analyses will lead to the conclusion that humanity must be the same thing as a good will.

[5] H. J. Paton, *The Categorical Imperative* (Philadelphia: University of Pennsylvania Press, 1947), 34, 168, 177.

[6] Although no commentator that I know of accepts the implication of the value claims, Samuel Kerstein admits there is 'an apparent tension that I am unsure how to resolve'. Samuel Kerstein, *Kant's Search for the Supreme Principle of Morality* (Cambridge: Cambridge University Press, 2002), 68.

[7] Neil Cooper, 'The Formula of the End in Itself', *Philosophy*, 63 (1988), 401–2.

Part of what Kant means by calling something an end in itself is that it has 'absolute value'.[8] He contrasts absolute value with the 'conditioned' or 'relative' worth possessed by 'subjective ends'. A subjective end has value only because some rational being has an inclination for it. For example, a chocolate bar has value for me only if I desire chocolate. The chocolate bar's value is relative because it only has value to someone with the right inclination. Its value is conditioned because an agent's inclination for it is a necessary condition of its having value for that agent. In contrast, an end in itself has absolute value, meaning a value for every rational agent, regardless of her inclinations. So Kant calls an end in itself an 'objective end', as opposed to a subjective end.

But Kant may mean to include more in the concept of an end in itself. He clearly attributes to humanity a value that is not only independent of inclinations, but also incomparably higher than the satisfaction of any amount of inclinations. What is not as clear is whether this is an entailment of the claim that humanity is an end in itself, or a conceptually distinct addition to his description of humanity's value. Kant says that humanity has a dignity, which means it 'is exalted above all price and so admits of no equivalent' (G 434). Besides having a value independent of inclinations, humanity also has a value so incomparably high that it is never worth sacrificing it in order to satisfy any amount of inclinations. This is why humanity can serve as 'the supreme limiting condition on all subjective ends' (G 431).

There is reason to think Kant took this idea of dignity to be included in the concept of something being an end in itself. When he introduces the term 'dignity', he uses it interchangeably with 'inner worth', and contrasts it with 'relative worth' (G 435). The distinction between relative value and intrinsic value here is the same distinction he made earlier, in his discussion of the humanity formulation, between relative and absolute value. This suggests that he means the idea of absolute value to include dignity, in addition to value that is independent of inclination. And he then argues as if the claim that something is an end in itself directly implies that it also has a dignity (G 435, MM 434–5).

But for the purpose of showing that humanity and a good will must be equivalent, it does not really matter whether having a dignity is part of the concept of being an end in itself. It is enough to have established that '*x* is an end in itself' either means '*x* has value independent of inclinations' or '*x* has value independent of inclinations and *x* has a dignity'. If the latter analysis is correct, then something that has value independent of inclination and has a dignity obviously must be an end in itself. Almost as obviously, if having inclination-independent value is by itself a sufficient condition for something

[8] All references in this paragraph are to G 427–8.

to be an end in itself, then something that satisfies this condition and also happens to have dignity must be an end in itself. So whichever analysis is correct, it must be true that:

(P1) If x has value independent of inclinations and x has a dignity, then x must be an end in itself.

This conditional, along with some additional premisses, will show that humanity must be equivalent to a good will.

An analysis of the meaning of 'good without qualification' will yield the most important of these additional premisses.

Kant begins *Groundwork* with the claim that only a good will is good without qualification. At least part of what it means to be good without qualification is to be valuable in all possible circumstances.[9] This is shown by the strategy Kant employs in arguing that only a good will is good without qualification (G 393–4). His argument is an argument by elimination, and when he tries to show that other candidates are not actually good without qualification, he does it by showing that in some circumstances they are not valuable. Talents such as wit, qualities of temperament such as courage or resolution, gifts of fortune such as power and wealth, and even qualities commonly thought of as virtues, like moderation and reflectiveness, can lack value sometimes, namely when possessed by someone without a good will. Since Kant thinks that lacking value in some possible circumstances is evidence that none of these things is good without qualification, we can conclude that at least part of what Kant means by calling something good without qualification is that it is valuable in all possible circumstances.

Kant also may mean to include having a dignity in the concept of being good without qualification. He does repeatedly state that a good will has a dignity. He says that a good will is the 'highest' and 'pre-eminent' good (G 401), that it is 'to be treasured as incomparably higher than anything it could ever bring about merely in order to satisfy some inclination' (G 394), and that morality has a dignity (G 435). He offers these statements casually, as if they follow naturally from the claim that a good will is good without qualification. But since he never explicitly says that dignity is included in the concept of being good without qualification, they may be conceptually distinct claims.

[9] Saying 'valuable in all circumstances' instead of 'good in all circumstances' may seem like an illegitimate slide from moral value to value in general, but it is not. Kant does not try to show specifically that a good will is morally good in all circumstances, but rather that it has value in all circumstances. If this is not clear from Kant's argument itself, he makes it clear immediately afterward by putting the discussion in terms of the good will's value, or *Wert*.

This question need not be settled in order to establish that humanity is equivalent to a good will. It is enough to have shown that '*x* is good without qualification' means either '*x* is valuable in all possible circumstances', or it means '*x* is valuable in all possible circumstances, and *x* has a dignity'. Whichever it means, it is true (for reasons analogous to those discussed above when conditional P1 was offered) that:

(P2) If *x* is valuable in all possible circumstances and *x* has a dignity, then *x* must be good without qualification.

This conditional will serve as a premiss in the argument that humanity must be equivalent to a good will.

An additional step is needed in order to establish this equivalence. It is clear that Kant means to say that humanity has a dignity (although it is not as clear whether this is part of the concept of an end in itself). But in order for conditional P2 to be useful, it must also be shown that humanity has a value in all possible circumstances. Analogously, it is clear that Kant thinks a good will has a dignity, but for conditional P1 to be useful it must also be shown that a good will has value independent of inclinations. And, in fact, it can be shown that humanity has a value in every possible circumstance, and that a good will has a value that is independent of inclination. This is because something has value in every possible circumstance if and only if its value is independent of inclinations.

Something that has value independent of inclinations will necessarily have a value in every possible circumstance. Suppose something has a value that is not conditional on an agent's inclinations. Her inclinations do not provide her with the reason to choose the thing, so it must be her rationality itself that provides her with such a reason. Every agent's rational nature, if we exclude the influence of her inclinations, will tell her the same thing, so every rational agent will have reason to choose (to preserve, cultivate, respect) something that has value independent of inclinations. This is what Kant means when he says an end in itself, which has value independent of inclinations, is 'necessarily an end for everyone' and a 'supreme practical ground' (G 428–9). Reason tells every rational being that an end in itself is valuable, so an end in itself provides a 'universal principle' that is 'valid and necessary for all rational beings' (G 428). Inclinations vary from agent to agent and moment to moment, so a value that depends on inclination may be transient. But a value determined only by necessary features of rationality will not vary. Something with a value that is independent of inclination will have this value in every possible circumstance.

And something that has value in every possible circumstance must have a value that is independent of inclination. Whether any agent has a particular inclination is a contingent matter. So if something's value depends on inclination, then it would not have value in every possible circumstance. There would be a possible circumstance in which no agent had the inclinations that made it valuable. If something has value in every possible circumstance, that value must not depend on inclination. So something has a value independent of inclination if and only if it has a value in all possible circumstances.

The equivalence of humanity and a good will can now be established.

Humanity has value independent of inclinations, Kant says. This means it must also have a value in every possible circumstance. Kant also says humanity has a dignity. If humanity has value in every possible circumstance and has a dignity, then according to conditional P2, humanity must be good without qualification. But only a good will is good without qualification, so humanity must be a good will.

And a good will must also be equivalent to humanity. Since a good will has value in all possible circumstances, it must also have a value that is independent of inclination. And Kant attributes a dignity to a good will. These facts, along with conditional P1, tell us that a good will is an end in itself. Since only humanity is an end in itself, a good will must be humanity. And if a good will is humanity, and humanity a good will, then they are equivalent.

This equivalence is also suggested by Kant's claims that good will has its value 'in itself' or 'considered in itself' (G 394). He explains that this means its value does not lie in 'its adequacy to any proposed end'. He reiterates later in *Groundwork* that the good will has its value 'without any limiting condition (the attaining of this or that end), [so] we must abstract completely from every end that has to be brought about (for such an end would make any will only relatively good)'. That is, the good will's value does not derive from its satisfying some inclination-based end. It is not just a subjective end, valuable as a means to satisfaction of inclination. Instead, it is an objective end, or end in itself. So it must be the same thing as humanity, which is the only end in itself.

Again, a good will must be equivalent to humanity unless Kant is just being inconsistent about two of the central claims of *Groundwork*, that only a good will has unconditional value and only humanity is an end in itself.

Kant's discussion of dignity provides additional evidence that he is not just guilty of inconsistency, and really means to equate humanity and a good will. He says only one thing has dignity (G 435). Since he has earlier attributed dignity to both humanity and a good will, he must mean them to be identical. In fact, he says as much: 'Now morality is the only condition under which a rational being can be an end in itself ... Therefore morality, and humanity so far as it is capable of morality, is the only thing that has dignity'.[10] By morality here he means 'the mental attitude' or the 'intentions—that is ... the maxims of the will' that lead to actions such as 'fidelity to promises and benevolence out of basic principles (not out of instinct)' (G 435). In other words, he means the commitment to moral principles that is only possessed by someone with a good will.

One last point about dignity also supports reading 'humanity' as 'good will'. Above I deferred discussion of the issues of whether the concepts of the end in itself or of goodness without qualification included the idea of dignity. It does not seem that either concept directly implies an incomparably high worth, yet Kant talks as if humanity (or a good will) does obviously have this dignity. His attitude can be explained if we admit the equivalence of humanity and good will.

The idea of an end in itself is of something that has value for every agent regardless of her inclinations. But this does not seem to imply incomparable value. One can imagine that something could be worthy of at least some consideration at all times, by all agents, and yet that its value could in some cases be overridden for the sake of inclination. The idea of inclination-independent value does not by itself imply a value greater than the value of any amount of inclination satisfaction.[11] Similarly, the idea of being good without qualification only implies having some value in every possible condition or circumstance, but does not seem to imply that this value will always be so high that something good without qualification should never be acted against.

But in the case of the good will, it is possible to surmise Kant's reason for thinking it also has a dignity. The justification for this attribution of dignity lies not in the idea that a good will is good without qualification, but in the idea that it is itself the condition for the goodness of all other things. Kant makes this latter claim in the same passages as the former, in the opening paragraphs of *Groundwork*, and both claims are meant to be based on 'common rational knowledge of morality'.[12] If possessing a good will is the necessary condition for the value of all one's other ends, then of course it would not make sense

[10] G 435. In conversation, both Robert Johnson and Stephen Engstrom have suggested that this passage might also be taken to support the capacity reading. I think it is much better support for the good will reading, both because of the textual context mentioned immediately below, and for other reasons I will discuss in Chapter 4, section 2.

[11] This is consistent with distinctions that Wood draws between different conceptions of value. Allen Wood, *Kant's Ethical Thought* (Cambridge: Cambridge University Press, 1999), 114–18.

[12] G 393 (the phrase appears in the title of Kant's first chapter).

to give up one's good will (e.g. by choosing to act immorally)[13] in order to achieve other ends that would lack value once achieved.

The idea that a good will has dignity is not strictly based on the idea that it is good in all circumstances. And the claim on which it actually is based, that a good will is the necessary condition of the goodness of other ends, may be more controversial than Kant believes. But at least Kant does appear to have some basis for saying that a good will has incomparable worth, if we grant him his supposedly common-sense idea that a good will is the condition of the value of all of an agent's other ends.

If humanity is equivalent to a good will, then Kant has exactly the same justification for saying that humanity has this incomparable worth.[14] If humanity is a good will, then humanity is the necessary condition of the goodness of all one's other ends, so it never makes sense to give up one's humanity. Humanity has more value than the satisfaction of any amount of inclination, because if one lacks humanity, then satisfying one's inclinations is valueless.

If humanity is something other than a good will, if it is some minimal feature of rationality that is necessarily possessed by any rational being, then Kant still owes an explanation of why humanity has a dignity. In the absence of such an explanation, his claim that humanity has a dignity seems to count in favour of equating humanity with good will.

The relations between *Groundwork*'s central claims about value support reading 'humanity' as 'good will'. Kant claims that a good will has an incomparable value in every imaginable circumstance, and humanity has a value that is incomparable and independent of inclination. And, given the Kantian framework in which they are embedded, these claims amount to the same thing.

2. Why we Should Resolve to Act Morally

On either the good will reading or the minimal reading (in any of its variations), the humanity formulation provides one sort of reason not to act immorally. But the good will reading can go on to offer an additional reason that the minimal readings do not.

[13] The idea of giving up or sacrificing one's good will may call to mind images of suicide or of inducing brain damage, but surely the more common way to lose one's good will is just by abandoning one's commitment to morality.

[14] Here I am overlooking the difficulty of moving from 'my good will has incomparable value for me' to 'everyone's good will has incomparable value for me'. I will take this up in Chapter 6, on the argument for the humanity formulation.

Uncontroversially, the humanity formulation attributes a special value to humanity (however one reads 'humanity'). This value provides a reason to act in certain ways—not to destroy humanity, not to use humanity as a mere means to something of lesser value, but instead to respect beings who possess humanity and to perfect oneself. When an agent acts immorally by failing to treat humanity as incomparably valuable, she ignores what the humanity formulation says we have reason to do. The defenders of any reading of 'humanity' would agree that in this sense the humanity formulation provides a reason never to act immorally. But only the proponent of the good will reading can add that an agent who chooses to act immorally is sacrificing her own most valuable possession. If the good will reading is correct, then the humanity formulation tells us that what has the absolute and highest value is a good will. This provides a clear reason to refrain from immoral action. By choosing to act immorally, one would be compromising one's good will and so putting into jeopardy one's possession of the most precious thing imaginable.

This might seem inconsistent with the idea that one can retain a good will even when one acts immorally,[15] and there is in fact a tension between the two claims. But it is a tension that arises from a fundamental feature of Kant's ethics, and not a contradiction. Kant's approach to ethics primarily emphasizes the first-person deliberative question 'What should I do?' rather than the third-person evaluation of others' actions. From this deliberative perspective, one always has an overriding reason never to choose to act immorally. When one chooses to act immorally, one must take oneself not only to be choosing a particular prohibited action, but also to be choosing to abandon the unconditional commitment to morality.[16] One must take oneself to be sacrificing one's good will. Since this involves giving up the thing of highest value, one can never be rationally justified in so choosing. But this is compatible with believing about someone else, or even about one's own past behaviour, that a certain degree of wrong action is compatible with retaining a good will. When explaining or evaluating wrong action, it makes sense to attribute some of it to weakness of the will, but when choosing what to do, one must take oneself to be strong enough to choose whatever one will. So when deciding what to do, the idea that a good will has an incomparable value provides one with an overriding reason never to choose to act immorally.[17]

15 This claim was made in Chapter 2 of this book.

16 Kant says, 'a disposition to surrender at times to vice, in order to break away from it gradually, would itself be impure and even vicious, and so could bring about no virtue (which is based on a single principle)'. MM 477.

17 See especially R 77.

This point can be put in the terms Kant uses in *Religion*. It is true that frailty, or weakness of will, is compatible with a supreme maxim of obedience to duty, because 'the frailty of human nature' consists of 'not being strong enough to comply with its adopted principles' (R 37). But one cannot plan to act from frailty. If one is deliberating about what to do and decides to act contrary to the moral law, one must take oneself to be elevating the principle of self-love to a higher status than the principle of acting for duty's sake. This is equivalent to abandoning the unconditional commitment to morality that constitutes a good will. One has good reason never to do this, if the good will is what has absolute and incomparable value. To do so would be to lose one's most valuable possession.

The minimal reading does not provide this sort of reason never to act immorally. According to any of the three versions of the minimal reading, what has highest value is something that all minimally rational agents possess and cannot lose. So an agent who chooses to act immorally need not take herself to be giving up something of incomparable value.

This is obvious on the first version of the minimal reading, which takes humanity to be *Willkür*, or the power to choose. Acting immorally does not typically cause the agent to lose the power to make choices in general.

And the second version of the minimal reading fares no better. This reading identifies humanity as the possession of traits such as *Willkür*, *Wille*, and theoretical reason. An agent's *Wille* legislates moral laws to her, and it might seem that enough immoral action could jeopardize her *Wille*, or silence the voice of conscience. But Kant insists that this is not so. Every minimally rational agent retains *Wille*, despite any of his actions. 'The law ... imposes itself on him irresistibly, because of his moral disposition', even if he chooses to ignore it (R 36). *Wille* remains as a 'germ of goodness' even in a villain (R 45). One does not lose *Wille* by choosing to act immorally, and neither does one lose any other traits that are necessary components of rationality.

The third version of the minimal reading identifies humanity as the capacity for moral action, and this capacity is best understood as *Wille* plus the predisposition to have feelings (of reverence) that can motivate one to follow *Wille's* commands. But an agent does not lose this capacity when she chooses to act immorally. As shown above, Kant thinks an agent never loses *Wille*, and neither does she lose the predisposition to act morally. Kant says the three predispositions of human nature, including the predisposition to personality (where personality is acting on the moral law as an unconditional incentive), 'belong to the possibility of human nature' so that humans 'cannot eradicate' them (R 28). An agent choosing to act immorally could be fully aware that she still possesses the capacity to act morally, so she need not take herself to be losing her most valuable possession.

It is not surprising, of course, that any minimal reading of 'humanity' must see humanity as something that cannot be lost. That is what distinguishes the minimal readings from the good will reading. The minimal readings make humanity something that every rational agent necessarily possesses. So the good will reading offers a reason for refraining from immoral actions that the minimal reading does not.

3. Value, and Humanity as an Ideal

The claim that humanity has an incomparably high value and so should never be sacrificed by acting immorally is consistent with the overall spirit of *Groundwork*, since claims about value lie at the core of that work.

But this reason for behaving morally may ring oddly to Kantian ears. It seems to presuppose that value is conceptually prior to the imperatives of reason, and this will sound un-Kantian to those familiar with Kant's overall account of value. A fundamental point about value, on Kant's picture, is that value is conceptually dependent on rational choice, rather than the reverse.

Although Kant is not as explicit about this in *Groundwork* as in later works, the idea does seem to be present even there, albeit in nascent form. In the passages immediately leading to the humanity formulation, it may sound as if Kant is first claiming that humanity has an absolute value, and that this value is the conceptual ground of the imperative to treat humanity in a special way (G 428–9). But he makes clear elsewhere in *Groundwork* that the connection between value and rational principles must run in the other direction. He says that it is 'law-making', the activity of rational willing, 'which determines all worth' (G 436). And he says that the reason we view some things as valuable is that 'every practical law presents a possible action as good' (G 414). It is the commands of practical reason that determine value.

But this position is not as thoroughly developed in *Groundwork* as it is later, in the Second *Critique*. There, Kant identifies the valuable as that which is an 'object of practical reason' (C2 57). First, Kant emphasizes in Second *Critique* 58–61 that the merely agreeable is not always good, nor is the disagreeable always bad. Sometimes a disagreeable thing (a painful medical procedure, to use Kant's example) can be seen to be good because of the overall positive 'influence this contingency has on our whole existence and our satisfaction with it'.[18] So a rational being's 'reason certainly has a commission from the side of his sensibility which it cannot refuse, to attend to its interest and to form practical maxims with a view to happiness'. Only if a rational being wills an end as contributing to his happiness does it have value. But this is only a necessary condition for value, not a sufficient condition. A rational being does not 'use reason merely as a tool for the satisfaction of his needs as a sensible being'. He also has a 'higher purpose', of accepting a principle that is a 'practical law *a priori*'—a Categorical Imperative—and making it 'the determining ground of the will without regard to possible objects of the faculty of desire' (C2 62). Only choices that conform to moral law confer value, so it is 'the moral law that first determines and makes possible the concept of the good' (C2 64). Value is not determined by one's desires or feelings, nor is it a property that is passively perceived. Instead value is conferred by the choices of a being who acts upon rational principles of both prudence and morality.

This Kantian concept of value generates a worry, that one is getting things backwards by saying (as I did, in section 2) that a good will's incomparable value provides a reason never to choose to compromise one's good will by acting immorally. The question of what choices an agent is rationally required to make must be settled before value is attributed to an object. I think there is a basis for this worry. Strictly speaking, rational choice is conceptually prior to value. But this does not stop Kant from putting large segments of his ethical writings in terms of value, nor should it mean that those commenting on Kant's work must eschew value talk. Kant presumably puts many of his points in terms of value because it is a familiar language in moral philosophy, and makes for a clearer presentation of some of his difficult ideas. Similarly, I see no reason to avoid discussing Kantian answers to the traditional question, 'Why be moral?' nor to be squeamish about employing value terms in that discussion.

Of course, it is important for any commentary not to distort the authors' actual ideas, but I think that my discussion did not. Rather it put Kant's ideas into terminology suited to the question of why one should choose to be moral. This is consistent with recognizing that to attribute incomparably high value to humanity is fundamentally to claim that rational agents would always seek to attain or preserve their humanity. If humanity has an incomparably high value, then Kant must think that every rational being is rationally required to strive toward humanity as an ideal. If Kant does claim this, then it may be illuminating to put the point in terms of value.

[18] This quotation and the next two are from C2 61.

So, in order to see if Kant means to attribute the highest sort of value to humanity, it is important to ask the conceptually prior question of whether Kant says that we should adopt humanity as an ideal toward which to strive above all else. If so, then humanity apparently has the highest sort of value, and taking humanity as good will does provide a reason to choose to act morally and make one's will a good will.

Kant does declare humanity to be an ideal toward which we should strive. In the First *Critique*, he proposes that, corresponding to the Idea of humanity ('die Menschheit', the same word as he uses in the humanity formulation), we have an 'ideal' or 'archetype' of 'a man [*Mensch*] existing in thought only'. Kant continues that 'We have no other standard for our actions than this divine man within us, with which we compare and judge ourselves, and so reform ourselves'.[19] In *Religion*, Kant again takes humanity as an ideal, by speaking of 'the dignity of humanity which the human being must respect in his own person and personal vocation, and which he strives to achieve' (R 183). This is consistent with a proposal Kant makes, that Jesus can serve as an ideal of moral perfection. Kant says, 'Now it is our duty to elevate ourselves to this ideal of moral perfection, i.e. to the prototype of moral perfection in its entire purity' (R 61). But accessibility to this prototype is not in fact dependent on Christian faith, for 'the required prototype always resides in reason' and 'each and every human being should furnish in his own self an example of this idea' (R 63). In *Metaphysics of Morals*, Kant also states that we have a duty to the 'cultivation of morality' or of 'moral perfection' (MM 392, 446). By this he means that one is obligated both to strive toward 'fulfilling all one's duties' (MM 446) and to 'strive with all one's might that the thought of duty for its own sake is the sufficient incentive of every action conforming to duty' (MM 393). He says that this duty to increase one's moral perfection is a duty 'regarding the end of humanity in our own person' (MM 447), and that the duty is to increase the perfection belonging 'to man as such (properly speaking, to humanity)' (MM 387).

So, Kant thinks that we must seek to reach a moral ideal of acting rightly and giving priority to moral law, and he calls this ideal 'humanity'. Then if we must always strive toward an ideal of humanity, regardless of circumstances or opposing inclinations, the most accurate way to describe the value of humanity is to say that it is absolute and incomparably high. So the claim of the previous section is accurate, though only a shorthand for saying that we must always choose to try to attain the ideal provided by humanity.

[19] C1, A569, B597. Any doubt that this ideal includes moral perfection is removed by noting that that Idea of humanity is also an Idea of 'Virtue, and therewith human wisdom in its complete purity'.

Kant's portrayal of humanity as a moral ideal also provides independent evidence for the good will reading of 'humanity'. It is obvious that the minimal readings of 'humanity' do not fit well with the claim that humanity is a moral ideal. If humanity is something that all rational beings necessarily possess, then it does not make sense to speak of striving toward humanity. Everyone already has it.

And, in fact, another way to describe the ideal of humanity is as an ideal of good will. We must strive to make moral law a sufficient motive for our choices, and must try to act in the ways that morality demands. These are precisely the distinguishing features of a good will. The fact that Kant uses the name 'humanity' for this ideal standard shows that he means 'humanity' to be a name for a morally good will. Both a good will and humanity provide the archetype toward which imperfect humans must strive, both good will and humanity possess an incomparably high value, and they are in fact the same thing.

This conclusion is not undermined by Kant's further statements, that our duty to pursue this moral ideal is only an imperfect duty. Kant says that a being's duty to strive for moral perfection is 'only a wide and imperfect duty to himself' (MM 446). This means that the agent is only bound by duty to adopt a certain maxim for action, without specific actions being demanded. In the case of the duty to seek moral perfection, this means that one must adopt a maxim of seeking to make the Categorical Imperative a sufficient motive for one's will, but that the particular acts that embody this maxim are unspecified. This may appear to defeat the claim that humanity has incomparably high value in all circumstances, since if it did have this value, it seems that one would be required to strive toward this ideal always.

But, in fact, a closer look at the text shows that one *is* required to strive toward the moral ideal of humanity at all times. Kant says the duty to pursue this ideal 'is a narrow and perfect one in terms of its quality', and 'with regard to its object'.[20] It is only the imperfections or 'frailty' of human beings that make it a wide duty for us. We must always strive for moral perfection, but given our natures, it is not clear to us at every given moment how best to do this.[21]

One reason that the duty to pursue moral perfection is only a wide duty is that 'The depths of the human heart are unfathomable'.[22] We cannot discern

20 All quotations in this paragraph are from MM 446.

21 For a more detailed discussion of the senses in which this duty is wide and in which it is narrow, see Mary Gregor, *Laws of Freedom* (Oxford: Basil Blackwell, 1963), 172–6.

22 MM 447. Kant also makes very similar statements in MM 392 and R 48.

the principles we act on, so we can never rest easy in the knowledge that we are making the Categorical Imperative the ground of our action. It will never be clear to us how closely we have approximated the ideal of a good will. So in any given case, it is not clear what sort of exertion counts as living up to the standard of a good will. If it is not clear what counts as living up to this ideal, then it is not clear what I must do in order to act on the maxim of striving toward the ideal. In addition, we are prone to vices that tend to attach to our very efforts to be virtuous (MM 447). While Kant is not specific about what vices these are, it is plausible to think that among them are the moralistic zeal of the 'fantastically virtuous' person who 'allows nothing to be morally indifferent and strews all his paths with duties, as with man-traps' (MM 409) and the 'moral arrogance' that comes from comparing oneself with other people instead of with the demands of the moral law. The wideness of a duty is a 'permission to limit one maxim of duty by another', and the duty of seeking moral perfection must be balanced against the duty to avoid vices of self-absorption, delusion, and arrogance. Because of these limits or weaknesses of our nature, it is not clear to us exactly what actions or efforts of will should count as acting on the maxim of striving toward the ideal of moral perfection.[23]

Nevertheless, we must make it our principle always to 'strive for this perfection' as best we can, given our limits. Only by this continual effort can we make 'continual progress'. For humans, the commitment to morality over inclination can only be a 'good (though narrow) path of constant progress',[24] not a completed project of attaining a good will. But this striving itself is the form a human good will takes. To someone who could see the 'intelligible ground of the heart (the ground of all the maxims of the power of choice)', this 'endless progress' counts as 'the same as actually being a good human being'. To adopt the principle of striving for a good will is what counts for us as having a good will, given the limits of human nature and knowledge.

[23] Kant's recognition of the vices that can result from an excessive concern with one's own virtue should help dispel some potential qualms about the idea that a good will is a person's most valuable possession. One should never sacrifice one's good will, but this does not mean one should be absorbed in one's own character at the expense of others, nor that one should pursue a 'clean hands' policy of refusing to get involved in complex moral situations or letting others perform the morally questionable acts from which one benefits. Instead, the way to live up to the ideal of moral humanity is to strive to do what seems morally best, all things considered. For a discussion of the general issue (rather than a close examination of Kant's texts), see Thomas E. Hill, Jr., 'Moral Purity and the Lesser Evil', in *Autonomy and Self-Respect* (Cambridge: Cambridge University Press, 1991).

[24] R 48. The additional quotations in this paragraph are from the same passage in *Religion*.

4. Why we Should Only Promote Others' *Permissible* Ends

Another way in which the good will reading seems preferable to the minimal reading is that it better accounts for how the duty to promote others' ends is derived from the humanity formulation. More specifically, only the good will reading can justify excluding others' immoral ends from this duty.

Kant uses the duty to further others' ends as an example of how imperfect duties to others follow from the humanity formulation (G 430). But his description is sketchy at best.

Recent commentators have tried to make the argument more intuitively plausible, and their general strategy seems promising. The humanity formulation tells us to treat humanity with respect, because of its incomparable value. Taking humanity as the power to set ends, Korsgaard and Wood say that respecting someone's power to set ends requires treating her ends as valuable.[25] And to treat ends as valuable is to recognize that these ends provide some reason for you to act. So the duty to treat end-setters as valuable implies taking steps, at least sometimes, to assist them in furthering their ends. This much sounds right.

But presumably these commentators would wish to follow Kant in excluding immoral ends from the duty to promote others' ends. Kant says we have no duty to 'give a lazy fellow soft cushions' or 'see to it that a drunkard is never short of wine' (MM 480–1). And this intuitively seems correct.

The problem is that the minimal readings of the humanity formulation provide no principled reason for excluding such ends.

If the first version of the minimal reading is right in saying that *Willkür*, the bare power to set ends, has an absolute and incomparable value, then this power is what we should respect. And, according to the argument above, showing respect for an agent's power to set ends requires us to treat her ends as valuable. The minimal reading leaves no room for adding that sometimes the power to set ends lacks value, and thus fails to deserve respect. So any time an agent exercises this power and sets an end, we should show respect for her end-setting power by treating her ends as valuable. The first version of the minimal reading provides no rationale for excluding immoral ends from this duty.

And it does not help to suppose, as the second version of the minimal reading does, that humanity must include *Wille* as well as *Willkür*. An agent

[25] See especially Korsgaard, *Creating the Kingdom of Ends*, 127–8; Wood, *Kant's Ethical Thought*, 149–50.

always possesses *Wille*, even if she ignores its directives and sets impermissible ends. Even when she did this, we would need to treat her 'humanity'—her possession of *Wille* along with the power to set ends—with respect, and so would be led to regard even her impermissible ends as valuable. It does help, in a limited way, to suppose that besides *Wille* and *Willkür*, humanity might also include the power to form a consistent concept of happiness, understood as a package of one's contingent ends. This helps because in some cases the lazy person's pillows or the drunkard's wine (or the crack addict's pipe, the robber's gun, etc.) may only aid her in gaining particular ends that overall undermine her other ends. But this does not show that one never has a duty to assist an agent in attaining her immoral ends, because it does not provide a reason to refuse assistance to the person whose happiness (as a roughly coherent package of contingent ends) is consistent with, or even formed primarily by, her vices. If someone's most fundamental aim is to lie on the couch all day watching television and drinking beer, then the second version of the minimal reading provides no rationale for denying that we have a duty to bring her the remote control or the bottle opener. The second version of the minimal reading cannot provide a general rationale for failing to treat immoral ends as valuable.

Nor can the third version of the minimal reading, which takes humanity to be the capacity for morality. The most plausible way to describe the capacity for morality is as the possession of *Willkür*, *Wille*, and the feelings that allow one to act on *Wille*. But if this is what humanity is, then to respect an agent's humanity seems to require treating all her ends as valuable. The essential distinction between the good will reading and the capacity reading is that the capacity reading takes the mere capacity for morality to be the end in itself, which must be treated in special ways regardless of whether that capacity is realized. The agent who subordinates the commands of *Wille* to the satisfaction of inclination is still an end in herself, and duties that follow from the humanity formula would demand that she receive the same treatment as someone who actually acts on *Wille's* commands. An agent deserves the same treatment when she sets immoral ends as when she regulates her end-setting with *Wille*, because she still has the capacity for morality. So if her morally permissible ends must be treated as valuable, then, according to the capacity reading of the humanity formula, so must her immoral ends.

Unlike the minimal readings, the good will reading can provide a rationale for excluding immoral ends from the duty to promote others' ends. On the good will reading, the power to set ends is not what the humanity formulation demands that we respect, nor is the proper object of respect the mere possession of *Wille* and *Willkür*, nor these plus the predisposition to have moral feelings of reverence for the law. The proper object of respect is the will of an agent who conforms her *Willkür* to the demands of *Wille*, and so is committed to setting only permissible ends. This sort of will is fully rational, within human limits, and it is only an agent's rational end-setting that confers value. If an agent's end-setting is not regulated by moral principles, then her willing is defective and does not confer value.

What matters is not whether her end happens to be permissible in a particular case, but whether the end is set by a will that is rational. This means that if an agent lacks a commitment to regulate her choices with moral principles, her ends have no value. A commitment to morality is the necessary condition of the value of an agent's ends.

This should not be surprising, as an interpretation of Kant. It is just another way of saying that a good will is the necessary condition of the goodness of all other things, the 'highest good and the condition of all the rest' (G 396). It also accords with the idea that a good will is 'the indispensable condition of our very worthiness to be happy', when happiness is understood as the satisfaction of one's ends (G 393). Kant is consistent in maintaining, in both earlier and later writings, that virtue is the necessary condition of one's worthiness to be happy.[26]

This is not to say that only morally obligatory ends, or ends demanded directly by duty, have value. The proper object of respect is the will, including the power to set ends, of an agent who is committed to morality. If an agent has a good will, then all her permissible ends have value and provide some reason for others to act.

But it is also important to notice that only her permissible ends, not necessarily all of her ends, have value. An agent's good will is a necessary but not sufficient condition of the value of her ends, because immoral ends lack value even if possessed by an agent with a good will. When an agent possesses a good will but sets an end that she knows is morally prohibited, her willing is defective. The defect in this case is not that she lacks a good will, but that the particular end she wills is inconsistent with the general principle of acting on moral principles, which she also wills. The defect in the will is inconsistency. There are two ways in which an agent's will can be defective, and so fail to confer value on the ends willed. The agent may lack a commitment to always act morally, or may have this commitment but choose to act contrary to it.[27]

[26] Kant, C1 A 813, B 841, MM 482, C2 110, 130, 142–8, C3 450, Anth 326, 'On the Common Saying: ' "This May be True in Theory, but it does Not Apply in Practice" ', 278.

[27] Presumably, choosing in ways that are inconsistent with the Hypothetical Imperative can also fail to confer value on one's ends. Suppose I place value on certain ends, and lesser value on some ends that

The good will reading of 'humanity' can account in detail, and in a way endorsed by Kant, for the restrictions on the duty to further others' ends, while the minimal readings of the humanity formulation cannot.

If anyone doubts that Kant really means to affirm that a good will is a necessary condition of a being's worthiness to be happy (i.e. to achieve her contingent ends), Kant's extensive discussion of the 'highest good' should put these doubts to rest. In fact, an examination of some of Kant's statements about the highest good serves in several ways to reaffirm the idea that it must be good will that has a dignity, or the highest possible value. Since Kant clearly attributes dignity to humanity, this again suggests that humanity must be equivalent to a good will.

Throughout several texts, Kant consistently describes the highest good as a state in which happiness is proportioned to virtue, that is, in which every being's contingent ends are satisfied to an extent that is proportional to her virtue.[28]

Already, the definition of the highest good shows that Kant really means to say that beings only deserve happiness (satisfaction of their ends) to the extent that they are virtuous. He is quite emphatic that 'happiness is something that, though always pleasant to the possessor of it, is not of itself absolutely and in all respects good but always presupposes morally lawful conduct as its condition' (C2 111). And earlier he has said that when a vicious person suffers, 'everyone would approve of it and take it as good in itself' (C2 61). Kant even uses 'virtue' and 'worthiness to be happy' as interchangeable terms (C2 110, C1 A810, B838). The idea that the best state of affairs proportions happiness to virtue reinforces the point that the humanity formulation ought not to demand that we aid others in achieving their immoral ends. The fact that the minimal readings do demand this tells against them.

A closer look at Kant's discussion of the highest good provides further support for the good will reading. In the Second *Critique's* 'Dialectic of Pure Practical Reason', Kant feels that he must begin his discussion of the highest

are clearly inconsistent with these. The Hypothetical Imperative demands that I drop some of these ends, because I cannot will the means to all of them. If I do not drop some of the ends, then some of them (one wishes to say the ones I value less) lack value and others have no duty to aid me in achieving them. This is the only justification I can see for Kant's restriction on the duty to promote others' ends, that 'it is open to me to refuse them many things that they think will make them happy but that I do not' (MM 388).

[28] C1, A808–15, B836–43, R 5, 'What is Orientation in Thinking?' 139, C2, 108–20, C3, 450. For more thorough discussions, see Stephen Engstrom, 'The Concept of the Highest Good in Kant's Moral Theory', *Philosophy and Phenomenological Research*, 52/4 (Dec. 1992), 747–80 and Andrews Reath, 'Two Conceptions of the Highest Good in Kant', *Journal of the History of Philosophy*, 26/4 (Oct. 1989), 593–619.

good by dispelling a possible confusion which can 'occasion needless disputes' (C2 110). The worry, which is left mostly implicit in his discussion, is that he has in fact already described something else as the highest good. He has described good will as having a dignity, or incomparably high value. He has even said exactly that it is the 'highest good' (G 396). So how can he now claim that something else, namely happiness in proportion to virtue, is the highest good? Kant eliminates the grounds for this worry by pointing out an ambiguity in the concept of the 'highest'. In one sense, he says, virtue or good will is the highest good, because it is the 'supreme' good, and its presence is the 'supreme condition of whatever can even seem to us desirable'. Nothing else has value unless it is accompanied by virtue, or a good will. But in another sense, virtue is not yet the highest good, because it is not a complete good. This is because, as finite beings with desires, we cannot be completely satisfied with a state in which our desires are not satisfied. 'To need happiness, to be also worthy of it, and yet not to participate in it cannot be consistent with the perfect volition of a rational being' (C2 110). But the happiness that is part of the highest good cannot lead one to act contrary to virtue, since the happiness that is part of the highest good only has value if accompanied by virtue. Seeking the highest good, of happiness in proportion to virtue, cannot lead one to give up one's good will. Kant is not being inconsistent with his earlier claims that a good will has the highest value, since in the strongest sense, it does have the highest value. And the more 'complete' value of happiness proportioned to virtue does not in any way conflict with it as an aim.

But Kant's explanation only reconciles the claims that *good will* (virtue) has incomparably high value and that it nevertheless only forms part (the 'supreme' part) of the highest good. What about Kant's claims throughout *Groundwork* that it is *humanity* that has a dignity, or incomparably high value? These are left unexplained, if humanity is something less than a good will. If humanity is *Willkür*, then Kant provides no hint of how the claim that *Willkür* has incomparable value would be consistent with the concept of the highest good as happiness in proportion to virtue. If humanity includes *Wille*, or includes the (unrealized) capacity for morality, then still there is no obvious way to reconcile the claims that humanity has the highest value and that the highest good consists of happiness in proportion to virtue. The highest good does not make the mere capacity for morality into the criterion for worthiness to be happy. If the mere capacity for morality makes one worthy of happiness, it would not make sense to speak of a 'proportionality' between happiness and virtue, since all rational beings equally possess the capacity for morality. The 'supreme good' that forms part of the 'highest' good is actual virtue, not merely the potential for virtue. So, if humanity is something other than virtue, Kant appears stuck with a deep inconsistency, the seemingly incompatible claims that humanity has the highest value and that happiness proportioned to virtue is the highest good.

This provides yet another reason in favour of reading 'humanity' as good will. Only on this reading is the humanity formulation of the Categorical Imperative consistent with Kant's position on the highest good.[29]

5. The Connection between the Different Formulations of the Categorical Imperative

Another advantage of the good will reading over the minimal readings is that it provides stronger connections between the humanity formulation and the other formulations of the Categorical Imperative.

On the good will reading of humanity, strong thematic and conceptual links can be found between the humanity formulation and the universalizability, autonomy, and kingdom of ends formulations.[30] None of the minimal readings provides equally strong connections to all of the other formulations. The second version of the minimal reading, which takes humanity to be the possession of *Wille*, *Willkür*, and possibly other features of rationality such as the capacity to organize one's ends into a consistent whole, can link the humanity formulation to the universalizability formulation and the autonomy formulation, but not to the kingdom of ends formulation. The third version of the minimal reading, which takes humanity to be the capacity for morality, can make roughly the same connections as the second version, but also fails to link the humanity

[29] And it is not as if Kant's idea of the highest good is a casual addition that is easily jettisoned. As Jerome Schneewind explains in his remarkably educational book, *The Invention of Autonomy*, one large historical influence on Kant's practical philosophy was the antivoluntarist idea that we must share with God the same sort of access to the principles of morality. Morality is not simply a matter of God's fiat, but rather is comprehensible to us through our power of reason. Since we can see the same principles of morality as God, we can infer that our moral goodness will also seem good to God, and will be rewarded. The point of Kant's use of the idea of the highest good is that we have licence to believe in God because only a being such as God could ensure that happiness will eventually be apportioned according to virtue, so only God could allow the highest good to be achieved. Schneewind says, '[Kant's] account of God's indispensability to morality is also common among the opponents of voluntarism. From Hooker through Leibniz and Wolff, they assign God the task of assuring us that we live in a morally ordered universe'. Jerome Schneewind, *The Invention of Autonomy* (Cambridge: Cambridge University Press, 1998), 511.

[30] I will focus only on these formulations, leaving aside the surprisingly contentious issue of how many formulations of the Categorical Imperative there actually are. I take it as fairly clear that the 'law of nature' formulation, if it is distinct from the universalizability formulation, will have the same sort of connections with the other formulations as the universalizability formulation does.

formulation to the kingdom of ends formulation. The first version of the minimal reading fares worst of all. If one takes humanity to be merely the power to set ends, then the humanity reading seems thematically disjoint from all the other formulations of the Categorical Imperative.

Any of the readings of 'humanity', except for the *Willkür* reading, can draw a connection between the universalizability formulation and the humanity formulation. The universalizability formulation of the Categorical Imperative provides a formal requirement that an agent's maxim of action must meet in order to be morally permissible, namely that it should be possible to will the maxim as universal law. As a version of the Categorical Imperative, the universalizability formulation demands that the agent act only on maxims that meet this requirement. On the good will reading of humanity, the humanity formulation then tells us that complying with this moral requirement (or, more precisely, having a commitment to always comply) confers on an agent an incomparable value that must never be ignored, 'for it is precisely the fitness of his maxims to make universal law that marks him out as an end in himself' (G 438). So the good will reading ties the humanity formulation to the universalizability formulation, in a way supported by Kant's texts.

But there is also a natural connection between the two formulations if humanity is taken to be the mere capacity to act on moral principles (the third version of the minimal reading). The connection, according to the capacity reading, is that the universalizability formulation provides a moral principle that we must obey, then the humanity formulation says that the capacity to recognize and act on this principle has special value. Similarly, the second version of the minimal reading, by including *Wille* as part of the set of features that constitute humanity, can be used to posit a connection between the universalizability and humanity formulations. *Wille* is the aspect of will that presents every rational being with moral principles, so one could say that the universalizability formulation is a fundamental principle of morality, and that humanity is valuable because humanity includes the *Wille* that presents an agent with the moral principle. So both the second and third version of the minimal reading provide the material to render fairly strong, natural connections between the universalizability and humanity formulations.

But the first version of the minimal reading, which takes humanity to be the power to set ends, does not fare as well. The universal law formulation gives a formal requirement that a permissible maxim must meet, but then the humanity formulation would not make meeting this requirement a necessary condition for having the highest sort of value. The humanity formulation would not even make the capacity to act on moral requirements the feature that distinguishes an end in itself, nor would it say the end in itself is distinguished by its ability to legislate moral requirements to itself. Instead the humanity formulation would shift its emphasis to merely setting ends, rather than regulating one's end-setting with moral requirements. While the second and third versions of the minimal reading, like the good will reading, allow a connection between the humanity and universalizability formulations, the first does not.

The same is true of the search for a connection between the humanity formulation and the autonomy formulation of the Categorical Imperative. The good will reading does lead naturally from the humanity formulation to the autonomy formulation, and the second and third versions of the minimal reading also draw a strong connection between the formulations. But if humanity is just the power to set ends, there is no apparent link.

The formula of autonomy is, oddly, not presented as a directly action-guiding imperative. In the initial presentation of the autonomy formulation, Kant says that from the ideas of the universalizability and humanity formulations, 'there follows our third practical principle of the will: the supreme condition of the will's harmony with practical reason is the Idea of the will of every rational being as a will that legislates universal law' (G 431). This idea is not really quite an imperative. It does become reasonably clear that as an imperative, the idea of the autonomy formulation would demand more or less that one must act only on maxims that are consistent with the universal laws legislated by every rational will. This still does not seem to provide enough content to clearly guide an agent's choices, without supplementation from the other formulations.

Instead of providing another imperative to regulate choices, Kant seems more concerned here with introducing the idea that every rational being legislates universal moral principles to herself, that the source of the Categorical Imperative is the agent's own rational will. He goes on to rely on this idea in two important ways. In chapter 3 of *Groundwork*, autonomy plays a key role, since Kant argues that every agent must take herself to be autonomous, and that she therefore must accept the moral principles that are autonomously prescribed by her own *Wille*. But even before the arguments of chapter 3, Kant employs the notion of autonomy to show why 'the previous efforts that have been made to discover the principle of morality ... have one and all had to fail' (G 432). They were bound to fail because they followed a flawed strategy to try to explain why everyone is inescapably obligated by the laws of morality. They tried to make this necessarily obligating force depend on an appeal to some other interest, some contingent desire or aim. But no contingent interest could create inescapable obligation, because the agent could always escape the obligation by abandoning her interest. The only way to account for necessary and inescapable obligation is through the idea of autonomy, that an agent is 'subject only to laws which they themselves have given but which are nevertheless universal' (G 432). If an agent unavoidably tells herself to act on certain principles, then she is unavoidably subject to those laws, or so Kant thinks.

This role of the idea of autonomy suggests the link that can be made between the humanity formulation and the autonomy formulation, if humanity is taken to be just the capacity to act on moral principles. If humanity is the capacity for morality, then the humanity formulation raises an obvious question for the ingenuous reader, the question 'Why is the capacity for morality so special?' Kant's discussion of autonomy can be seen as providing an answer to that question. The capacity for morality is valuable because this capacity includes the power to be the most powerful kind of ruler imaginable. One gives oneself commands that are valid for oneself and for all other rational agents, commands that inescapably demand obedience at all costs. So there is in fact a natural tie between the humanity formulation and the autonomy formulation, on the third minimal reading of 'humanity'.

The second reading, which takes humanity to be some set of features of rationality, can make a similar connection between the autonomy and humanity formulations. Kant's idea of autonomy as the power to give oneself universally binding imperatives could explain why the possession of *Wille* makes a rational being so valuable. It is *Wille* that legislates these principles, so a being who possesses a set of traits that includes *Wille* can be seen intuitively as being special. So if humanity includes *Wille*, we can see why Kant would attribute such a high value to humanity. This line of thought may draw support from Kant's statement that 'the lawgiving itself, which determines all worth, must for that reason have a dignity—that is, an unconditioned and incomparable worth'.[31] The humanity formulation raises a question that the autonomy formulation helps answer.

But on the good will reading of 'humanity', the humanity formulation also raises a question that the autonomy formulation answers. The question is 'Why does being committed to obeying moral principles make someone so valuable, instead of making her a slave?' Might not the person who cares about doing the right thing just lack independence? The autonomy formulation responds to this potential worry by pointing out that the person with good will is not a slave to any external tyrant or law. Instead, she is doing what her own power of reason tells her is best. Furthermore, her

[31] G 436. I say the quotation only 'may' support the idea because I believe the 'law-giving' described in the quotation is not the *Wille*'s legislation of moral principles, but is the willing of particular maxims that pass the tests provided by moral principles. I will address this point further in section 1 of the next chapter.

power as legislator of moral principles is so great that her principles outweigh all contrary considerations, and are the same principles that will bind every rational being. In his summary of the arguments of *Groundwork* chapter 2, Kant himself expresses the connection between good will and the autonomy formulations in just this way. Kant says,

> although the concept of duty includes the idea of a person's subjection to the law, we nevertheless attribute a certain sublimity and dignity to the person who fulfills all his duties. For although there is nothing sublime about him just in so far as he is subject to the law, there is sublimity to him in his being at the same time its author and being subordinated only for this reason to this very same law. (G 439–40)

Similarly, in *Groundwork* 434, Kant speaks of 'the dignity of a rational being who obeys no other law than that which he himself also enacts'. So, the good will reading of humanity strongly links the humanity formulation to the autonomy formulation, in that the humanity formulation raises a question that the autonomy formulation answers.

The first minimal reading of 'humanity', which takes humanity as the power to set ends, does not provide any such apparent link. Kant's idea of autonomy has to do with legislating moral laws, not just setting contingent ends. A defender of the 'power to set ends' reading of 'humanity' might point out that *Willkür* is part of what makes moral action possible, because it is what makes any action possible. But this is not a strong link to the autonomy formulation, because the emphasis in Kant's discussion of autonomy is on the legislative activity of *Wille*. The question 'Why is end-setting valuable?' is not answered by Kant's statements that the legislation to oneself of unconditionally binding principles is what makes humanity so valuable. In the attempt to connect the humanity formulation and the autonomy formulation, only the 'power to set ends' reading is not up to the task.

But none of the minimal readings provides the material for strong, natural connections between the humanity formulation and the kingdom of ends formulation. Only the good will reading provides such a link.

The kingdom of ends formulation of the Categorical Imperative demands that one act only on maxims that 'harmonize with a possible kingdom of ends' (G 436). As the name suggests, the kingdom of ends is a kingdom or union of beings who are ends in themselves, a 'systematic union of different rational beings under common laws' (G 433). Kant's goal in exploring this 'fruitful concept' seems to be to help us see what specifically would be involved in regulating our behaviour with the moral principle of treating others as ends, as opposed to acting mainly to satisfy our own contingent ends. This captures the idea of Kant's statements that in the hypothetical kingdom of ends, 'since these [moral] laws are directed precisely to the relation of such beings to one another as ends and means', we can 'conceive a whole of all ends systematically united (a whole composed of rational beings as ends in themselves and also of the personal ends which each may set)' (G 433). The point of positing the concept of the kingdom of ends is to help sort out our specific duties toward each other as ends in ourselves, and the connection of these duties to our own and others' contingent ends.[32]

The members of the hypothetical kingdom of ends are of course ends in themselves, but this is only because they are, by hypothesis, committed to acting on moral principles. Kant says it is a being's 'morally good disposition, or virtue' that 'renders him fit to be a member in a possible kingdom of ends' (G 435). Later, Kant reiterates, 'A kingdom of ends would actually come into existence through maxims whose rule the categorical imperative prescribes as a rule for rational beings, if these maxims were universally followed' (G 438). Similarly, in chapter 3 of *Groundwork*, Kant speaks of a 'universal kingdom of ends in themselves', and says that 'we can belong as members only if we are scrupulous to conduct ourselves in accordance with maxims of freedom, as if they were laws of nature' (G 462–3). And Kant must say this. The point of the kingdom of ends is to provide an ideal, illustrative model of the behaviour that would be involved in treating one another as ends. So Kant must suppose that the members of the kingdom of ends all obey the Categorical Imperative of treating one another as ends in themselves. Then, once reflection on the hypothetical kingdom of ends makes clear what behaviour is demanded as part of treating others as ends in themselves, one is morally obligated to conform to this kind of behaviour, even in the real world, where one 'cannot count on everybody else therefore being faithful to the same [moral] maxim' (G 438). Kant does suppose, and must suppose in order to achieve his philosophical purposes, that a commitment to acting on moral principles is the defining feature of members of the kingdom of ends.

Then the link between the humanity formulation and the kingdom of ends is obvious, if humanity is a good will. The humanity formulation says that a good will, the will of a being who is committed to morality, is the end in itself. Then the kingdom of ends formulation uses the idea of a union of beings who are committed to morality, to help identify the actions that are necessarily involved in treating others as ends in themselves. The idea of what qualifies a being as an end in herself, and a member of the kingdom of ends,

[32] Controversially, this may be part of what Kant means by saying that the kingdom of ends formulation helps to bring the universalizability formulation 'closer to intuition'. G 437. In Chapter 9, I pursue further issues having to do with the kingdom of ends formulation, its role, and its connection to the humanity formulation.

is perfectly consistent between the humanity formulation and the kingdom of ends formulation.

In contrast, all of the minimal readings lead to a glaring inconsistency between what counts as an end in itself in the humanity formulation and in the kingdom of ends formulation.

Kant does, and must, say in his discussion of the kingdom of ends formulation that a commitment to moral principles is what qualifies a being to be an end in herself, and a member of the kingdom of ends. The mere capacity for morality is not enough. If we suppose that some or all members of the kingdom of ends have the capacity for morality but do not in fact regulate their choices with moral principles, then the whole point of the kingdom of ends discussion is lost. The kingdom of ends could not be used as a device to discern what kinds of choices are consistent with and demanded by the moral principle of treating one another as ends. To use the concept of the kingdom of ends in the way Kant intends, one must suppose that in the kingdom of ends formulation, possessing the (unrealized) capacity for morality is not enough to qualify a being as an end in herself. So if the humanity formulation claims that the mere capacity for morality does make someone an end in herself, then the two formulations are inconsistent in their use of the idea of an end in itself.

The second version of the minimal reading of 'humanity' forces the same kind of inconsistency between the humanity and kingdom of ends formulations. What is conceptually required for the kingdom of ends formulation is that to qualify as an end and gain membership in the kingdom, one must be committed to regulating one's actions by moral principles. Just possessing some other features of rationality, even possessing *Wille*, is not enough. If the humanity formulation says that anything less than an actual commitment to morality is sufficient to qualify a being as an end in herself, then the humanity formulation is using a different concept of an end in itself from the kingdom of ends formulation.

If this is so, then it is only more obvious that reading 'humanity' as the power to set ends is inconsistent with the kingdom of ends formulation. To imagine a union of beings who set ends does not by itself provide any moral guidance. So to say that *Willkür* is an end in itself must be inconsistent with the way Kant uses the idea of an end in itself in the kingdom of ends formulation.

Only the good will reading of humanity allows the humanity formulation to be closely tied to the kingdom of ends formulation, or even consistent with it.

The good will reading of the humanity formulation also allows close connections with each of the other formulations of the Categorical Imperative. If humanity is taken to be a good will, the idea of making moral law a sufficient incentive for action plays a prominent role in each formulation.

The universalizability formulation provides a moral standard with which all agents must comply, the humanity formulation says that accepting this moral standard confers incomparably high value on the agent, the autonomy formulation explains why this acceptance of moral principles makes her so valuable, and the kingdom of ends is an aid to seeing what duties follow from recognizing the incomparably high value of every agent who is committed to morality.

The first version of the minimal reading, which takes humanity to be *Willkür*, fails to provide strong links to any of the other formulations. And while taking humanity to be the capacity for morality, or to be the possession of several features of rationality including *Wille*, does provide links to the universalizability and autonomy formulations, it forces on Kant an inconsistency between his concept of the end itself in the humanity formulation and the kingdom of ends formulation.

So, to the extent that one wishes to trace a unified thematic progression throughout the different formulations of the Categorical Imperative, one has reason to accept the good will reading over any minimal reading of 'humanity'.

6. Summary

Kant is not infallibly consistent, of course, and perhaps even some of his major ideas cannot be made to fit together satisfactorily. But charity seems to dictate that if one way of interpreting a philosopher's ideas does a better job of unifying his ideas than alternative interpretations, this is a strong reason in favour of the more unifying interpretation. I have argued in this chapter that the good will reading of 'humanity' does a better job than any of the minimal readings of rendering the humanity formulation of the Categorical Imperative more consistent with some of Kant's other major ethical ideas.

Kant's claims about the value of humanity provide one strong reason for equating humanity, in Kant's technical sense, with good will. Kant says that only humanity has a dignity, and that only a good will does. He says that only humanity has absolute, non-relative value in every circumstance, and that only a good will has unconditional value in every possible circumstance. All of these basic claims about value suggest the equivalence of humanity and good will.

But, for Kant, all value claims are a shorthand for capturing the conceptually prior idea of what rational agents would choose. To call something valuable is just to say that it is the object of choice of a being who regulates her choices with rational principles, and to say something has incomparably high value is to say that rational beings would choose to seek it or preserve it at all costs. So if humanity has an incomparably high value, then we should expect Kant to say that we should strive toward humanity at all times. And he does say this. This seems to dictate that humanity is not something that all rational beings necessarily possess, for it does not make sense to speak of striving to attain something that cannot be lost. And in fact Kant makes clear that the humanity toward which we should strive is an ideal of moral perfection, not something that every rational being necessarily possesses.

If one fails to strive for this ideal, then one fails to have an adequate commitment to morality, and lacks a good will. If a being places higher priority on her own desires than on living up to the demands of morality, then her will is defective, imperfectly rational. And the exercise of this defective will does not confer value on her contingent ends, the ends that she sets at the cost of ignoring moral principles. This is why we do not have a duty to aid others in the pursuit of their immoral ends, and also why Kant maintains that the highest good consists not of happiness alone, but of happiness in proportion to virtue.

The thematic unity that the good will reading of 'humanity' makes possible can also be seen in the relation between the different formulations of the Categorical Imperative. The universalizability formulation imposes a requirement with which an agent must comply, then the humanity formulation says that the commitment to live up to this moral requirement is the characteristic that confers the highest sort of value on an agent. The autonomy formulation explains why obedience to moral law confers such an incomparable value, instead of making one a slave. It is because the agent herself is the legislator, who possesses such power that her decrees command obedience regardless of all other considerations. Then the kingdom of ends formulation tries to work out the details of the specific moral requirements that are entailed as part of respecting the value of agents who are committed to morality. To accomplish this task, the kingdom of ends formulation must imagine a union of beings who are in fact committed to morality, in order to see how they would treat one another.

The overall picture given above is consistent, I think, and I have argued that the good will reading is what makes this picture possible. If so, this seems to be a good reason to accept the good will reading.

4

The Textual Dispute, and Arguments in Favour of Minimal Readings

I have argued that the good will reading of 'humanity' fits well with some other main ideas of Kant's ethics, and that this counts strongly in favour of the good will reading. But proponents of the minimal readings are certainly no fools, so they must also have reasons to think that humanity is something other than a good will.

No doubt one reason other commentators have disavowed the good will reading is that it seems prima facie repugnant, since it appears to exclude many competent adult humans from the fullest sort of moral consideration. But, of course, the commentators have not merely cited the apparent repugnance of the good will reading as a sufficient reason to reject the view. A repugnant interpretation of Kant's views could be the correct one, after all. So in support of one version or other of the minimal reading, philosophers writing on Kantian humanity have offered both textual support and independent arguments.

In this chapter, I will examine the Kantian texts, and the arguments that other commentators have offered for their favoured readings of 'humanity'.[1] In the next chapter, I will explain why the good will reading need not be implausible or morally repugnant, despite first impressions.

1. The Texts

It would be unfair to expect a philosopher to be completely consistent in his use of a term that is both a common everyday word and an important technical term, in a set of texts as sprawling and imaginative as Kant's works. And Kant

[1] I should state in advance that I will mention some particular textual passages that I have already cited in earlier chapters. I do not do this in order to create a distorted impression of the bulk of text that supports the good will reading, but to examine different interpretative questions. Some passages in G 428–40, in particular, are central in so many ways that visiting them more than once seems inevitable.

does a worse job than one might hope for in giving definitions and sticking to them. So there is no perfectly consistent and univocal sense that attaches to Kant's uses of the word 'humanity' ('die Menschheit').

Consequently, my aim in examining Kant's specific discussions of 'humanity' is not to show that he always and unequivocally used 'humanity' to mean 'good will'. Instead, I hope merely to show that he used it this way in the humanity formulation of the Categorical Imperative, and that if he sometimes uses it in other senses, he does not do so in order to recant the humanity formulation's claim that only a good will is an end in itself.

Defenders of other readings of 'humanity' should agree that there is not just a single meaning of the word in Kant's work. The different minimal readings of 'humanity' are not entirely compatible, and texts offered in favour of one minimal reading generally exclude other minimal readings. More basically, there are uses of 'humanity' in Kant's text that simply have little to do with the humanity that is an end in itself. In *Metaphysics of Morals* 456, Kant describes humanity as something like empathy (or Humean 'sympathy'), 'the susceptibility, given by nature itself, to feel joy and sadness in common with others'. In Third *Critique*, Kant similarly says that what distinguishes humanity from animals is the 'sociability' that consists of 'the universal feeling of sympathy, and the ability to engage universally in a very intimate communication'.[2] In *Religion* 60–1, Kant seems to alternate between using 'humanity' as the name for an ideal to be achieved, and as just a label for the human species. An example of the latter is when he talks of Jesus coming down from heaven to 'take up humanity' by 'descending into it'. In Second *Critique* 157–8, he uses 'humanity' as a label for 'human beings' and 'the individual human being',[3] and in *Anthropology from a Pragmatic Point of View*, he also seems to use 'humanity' to refer to the human species (Anth 324). His use of 'humanity' in these ways seems different from any proposed reading of the humanity formulation, and is a reminder that one should not rely too heavily on any one text as definitive.

But I do not mean to imply that it is impossible to glean any sense of how Kant means to use 'humanity' in the context of treating humanity as an end in itself. The texts, overall, strongly indicate that humanity is best taken to be a good will. Many of the passages that have been cited as evidence for one

[2] C3 355 It is admittedly not completely clear that Kant means this as a definition of humanity. He says that this sociability befits our *Menschheit*, rather than that it is equivalent to it. In the previous sentence, he has said that humanity 'means both' the sympathy and ability to communicate, but the word Kant uses there is 'Humanität', not 'Menschheit'. Overall, I think the passage is consistent with the thesis that Kant's concern in using 'humanity' is not always to describe the humanity that is an end in itself.

[3] Kant says 'auf den Menschen und auf sein Indivuum', or 'to humans and to the individual'. The 'individual human' is implied.

or another of the minimal readings are actually ambiguous when examined in context, or even tend to support the good will reading. And there are many passages that seem straightforwardly to identify good will as an end in itself. So, although no single reading unifies all of Kant's uses of the word 'humanity', the balance of textual evidence supports the good will reading of 'humanity' in the humanity formulation.

Kant's very use of the term 'humanity' might seem to suggest that he thinks all human beings are ends in themselves, regardless of whether they possess a good will. But contemporary commentators do not take it as a viable option to read 'humanity' in the humanity formulation as referring exactly to the human species.[4] There are two seemingly insurmountable obstacles to taking humanity to be simply the human species or its members. First, Kant cannot mean to pick out all members of the human species, since not all humans have even the most minimal rationality, and he means to associate 'humanity' with some kind of 'rational nature'. So being human is not a sufficient condition for possessing humanity. Second, 'humanity' does not pick out a feature that is necessarily unique to humans. It picks out a feature that any rational agent could have, whether that feature is just *Willkür,* or a good will. So being human is not a necessary condition for possessing humanity either. Given the looseness of the connection between being human and possessing humanity, Kant's misleading use of the term 'humanity' should not be taken as evidence that all humans, or only humans, must possess the feature in question.

This is, of course, not to say that Kant's use of the word 'humanity' has no intuitive connection to the human species. Whatever characteristic 'humanity' refers to, it is a trait that distinguishes most rational adult humans from all the other living beings with which we are directly acquainted. The 'humanity' that we must treat as an end in itself is some sort of rational nature.

But Kant's identification of humanity as rational nature may itself seem incompatible with the good will reading. In *Groundwork,* Kant repeatedly says that rational nature is an end in itself (G 429, 437, 439) and it may seem that rational nature is something like the power to set ends, or to set ends in accordance with principles of prudence.[5] It sounds natural to twentieth- or twenty-first-century ears to associate rationality with instrumental reason, or even with calculating the maximum personal utility of different possible

[4] See e.g. Thomas E. Hill, Jr., *Dignity and Practical Reason in Kant's Moral Theory* (Ithaca, NY: Cornell University Press, 1992), 39 or Allen Wood, *Kant's Ethical Thought* (Cambridge: Cambridge University Press, 1999), 119–20. Wood says, 'It is important to emphasize, however, [that humanity] need not belong only to our species and therefore that the dignity of rational nature and the status of being an end in itself in no way privileges us over other possible rational beings'.

[5] Korsgaard, Wood, and Cummiskey all seem to think Kant's use of the term supports their minimal readings of 'humanity', although Wood's reading is actually somewhat different from the others'.

courses of action. But Kant had no such meaning in mind. Kantian rationality, or reason, is not concerned merely with calculations of self-interest.[6] Kant divides reason into theoretical and practical aspects, and in its practical aspect reason does more than set ends and calculate how to achieve them. Practical reason also consists of *Wille*, which legislates categorical moral principles, and a being who acts in the most rational manner will take these moral principles as sufficient reasons for action. On Kant's picture, one can be more rational or less, and to be fully rational is to possess a commitment to follow the commands of morality. So when Kant says rational nature is an end in itself, his meaning is ambiguous. 'Rational nature' might mean *Willkür*, or might mean *Wille*, or might mean the ability to act on principles of prudence or the capacity to act on moral principles. But it also might mean more fully rational nature, which is possessed only by beings who accept principles of pure practical reason as decisive reasons for action, or in other words regulate their *Willkür* with the principles given by *Wille*.

The possibility that Kant may mean 'rational nature' to refer to something more than minimally rational nature, or something other than instrumental rationality, is more than a mere logical possibility. It is a perfectly natural reading of 'rational nature', given Kant's emphasis on the authority of self-legislated moral principles. A fundamental Kantian idea is that reason presents each agent with necessarily binding moral principles, and the properly functioning power of reason will acknowledge and act on the overriding force of these principles' commands. So a truly rational being will be committed to acting on moral principles.

To dissipate any remaining scepticism regarding the claim that 'humanity' could denote a feature that some functioning adult humans could lack, it is worth mentioning that the German word 'die Menschheit', more than the English 'humanity', can often carry with it a sense of something that must be achieved.[7] One example of this, roughly contemporary with *Groundwork*, comes from Mozart's opera *The Magic Flute* (*Die Zauberflöte*). A young man is undergoing various trials in order to show that he possesses the virtues necessary to become a member of a quasi-Masonic brotherhood. In the aria

See Allen Wood, 'Humanity as End in Itself', *Proceedings of the Eighth International Kant Congress*, 1/1 (1995), 306–7 and *Kant's Ethical Thought*, 118–22; Christine Korsgaard, *Creating the Kingdom of Ends* (Cambridge: Cambridge University Press, 1996), 17, 110; and David Cummiskey, *Kantian Consequentialism* (Oxford: Oxford University Press, 1996), 85 ff.

[6] The German 'Vernunft' is translated either as 'reason' or 'rationality', and the phrase usually translated as 'rational nature' is 'vernünftige Natur'.

[7] I thank Arnulf Zweig for pointing this out to me, and for the musical example. This is exactly the kind of subtle nuance of German language that my poor, graduate-school German would be insufficient to reveal.

'In diesen heiligen Hallen' ('In These Hallowed Halls'), the character Zarastro sings that in these hallowed halls, one learns to be a man ('ein Mensch zu sein'). Along these same lines, many Americans are familiar with the use of 'Mensch' in Yiddish to mean, not just any human being, but a decent, reliable, or upstanding human. In light of these points, it does not seem too much of a stretch to treat Kantian 'Menschheit' or 'rational nature' as something that one can gain or lose.

But this only opens the door for the good will reading. It is a further question whether the texts actually favour that reading.

Some have pointed to texts that they believe support reading 'humanity' as 'the power to set ends'. The most commonly cited pieces of textual evidence for this reading are two passages from *Metaphysics of Morals*.[8] In *Metaphysics of Morals* 392, Kant says, 'The capacity to set an end—any end whatsoever—is what characterizes humanity', and in 387 he speaks of man's duty to raise himself from animality 'more and more toward humanity, by which he alone is capable of setting himself ends'.

While these passages seem to identify humanity as the power to set ends, both passages are in fact far from decisive, given their contexts. In both cases, Kant is concerned with distinguishing humans from animals, or humanity from animality, so it is natural to emphasize one clear difference between them, that humans can set ends rather than having their behaviour dictated by instinct. In 392, he clarifies the claim that end-setting characterizes humanity, specifying 'as opposed to animality'. In 387, he says man has a duty to 'raise himself from the crude state of his nature, from his animality (*quoad actum*), more and more toward humanity'. In both cases, he is concerned with saying that man first has a duty to cultivate the powers that distinguish him from animals, but in both cases he immediately adds that man then has a further duty to seek to accept the motive of duty as a decisive reason for action. And Kant says *both* of these types of self-perfection are based on the 'duty for a man to make his end the perfection belonging to man as such (properly speaking, to humanity)' (MM 386). The duty to act on moral motives cannot be based on the duty of perfecting humanity unless humanity in a full sense includes a commitment to duty. So even in these passages often used as evidence for the *Willkür* reading of humanity, there is the suggestion that humanity is something more like a good will.

I do not claim this clearly renders the passages useless to the defender of the *Willkür* reading. They do, after all, sound as if they identify humanity as the power to set ends. But they are shaky support, when considered in their context.

[8] See Korsgaard, *Creating the Kingdom of Ends*, 110, 346; Cummiskey, *Kantian Consequentialism*, 85.

There is also a passage from *Groundwork* 438, in which Kant says that the end in itself can only be 'the subject of all possible ends himself', which is best taken to mean a being who sets ends. But here too, the context makes Kant's claim poor evidence for the 'power to set ends' reading of 'humanity'. This is because Kant immediately says that the reason the subject of all ends must be an end in himself is 'because this subject is also the subject of a will that may be absolutely good; for such a will cannot without contradiction be subordinated to any other object'. The passage then looks more like support for either the good will reading or (because of the 'may be') the capacity reading of 'humanity'. Kant often adds such qualifications to his claims about what has value. This again urges caution in relying too heavily on the exact wording of any one sentence, since chances are good that he qualifies the words elsewhere, perhaps even in the same paragraph.

Overall, there seems to be only ambiguous textual support for the 'power to set ends' reading of 'humanity'. And this support must be balanced against a passage from *Critique of Practical Reason*, in which Kant specifically denies that the power to set ends gives someone a special worth. Kant says, 'that he has reason does not at all raise him in worth above mere animality if reason is to serve him only for the sake of what instinct accomplishes for animals', that is, the satisfaction of his wants (C2 61). Instead, what gives him special value is making the demands of morality the 'supreme condition' of the setting of ends. And again in *Metaphysics of Morals* 435–6, Kant seems explicitly to deny that the mere power to set ends makes someone an end in herself. He says first that, as a natural being, man like 'the rest of the animals' has only 'an ordinary value'. This is so 'although man has, in his understanding, something more than they and can set himself ends, even this gives him only an extrinsic value ... that is, a price'. Then what gives a person dignity? Not the power to set ends. Instead,

> man regarded as a person, that is, as the subject of a morally practical reason, is exalted above all price; for as a person (*homo noumenon*) he is not to be valued merely as a means to the ends of others or even to his own ends, but as an end in himself, that is, he possesses a dignity.

The power to set ends is not the distinguishing feature of an end in itself.[9] In light of these passages, the texts can only be said to provide very dubitable support for taking humanity as the power to set ends.

[9] In this passage, it may not appear that a good will is the end in itself either. Rather, this passage is one of the stronger bits of evidence in favour of the 'capacity' reading of humanity. I consider that reading in more detail below, both in this section and in section 2 of this chapter.

Allen Wood proposes a somewhat more expansive definition of 'humanity'. He thinks humanity most fundamentally consists of the power to set ends, but also includes all our rational capacities except those having to do with morality. Although 'put most generally, humanity is the capacity to set ends through reason',[10] humanity also includes 'our conscious, rational capacities to manipulate things as means to our arbitrary ends', and 'to compare the ends we set and organize them into a system' of 'well-being as a whole'. As evidence justifying his reading of 'humanity', Wood cites passages from *Anthropology from a Pragmatic Point of View* 322–4 and *The Critique of Judgment* 426–7.[11] But the texts seem problematic support, each for different reasons.

In *Anthropology*, Kant does say that humankind possesses the ability to use reason to figure out how to satisfy its ends. But he is just describing an ability that humans have, he is not defining (or even discussing) 'humanity' in the technical sense in which it is used in the humanity formulation. In fact, the *Anthropology* passage also says that humans have the ability to see themselves as subject to the moral law (Anth 424), and Wood does not want to include this in his concept of 'humanity'.[12] Wood specifically denies that humanity includes features of rational nature that have 'specific reference to morality'.[13]

The Third *Critique* passage is even more problematic for Wood. Kant does say that humans have the power to set ends, and in Third *Critique* 434, he even says the setting of ends that are not determined by inclination is part of 'the development of our humanity'.[14] But this is part of an overall line of discussion that goes on to undermine Wood's reading of 'humanity'. Kant is trying to discover what it is about man that makes him an 'ultimate purpose' or 'final purpose' of nature.[15] The word translated here as 'purpose' is the German word 'der Zweck', the same word Kant uses to talk about 'ends', and the same word used in saying that humanity is an end in itself. While Kant does say that setting ends is part of humankind's development, this is not his final answer to the question of what makes man an ultimate purpose or ultimate end. The power to set ends is just the gift that nature gives us 'that makes us receptive

[10] Wood, *Kant's Ethical Thought*, 118–19. The other quotations in this paragraph are from the same paragraph. He makes roughly the same claims in 'Humanity as End in Itself'.

[11] Wood cites no particular translation, presumably having translated them himself from the Academy Edition in German.

[12] My point here is not that the *Anthropology* text supports the good will reading. Rather it is that the text does not really support Wood's reading (and, further, that Kant is not trying to define 'humanity' here).

[13] Wood, *Kant's Ethical Thought*, 118.

[14] Kant may be using 'humanity' here just to mean the human species, but I will focus on the more serious difficulties for Wood's use of the text.

[15] Kant uses each phrase several times in his sections 83 and 84 (C3 429–37).

to purposes higher than those nature can provide'.[16] The power to set ends is not itself the final end of nature, but instead only makes it possible for man to be the final end of nature by allowing man to act on moral laws. Man is only the final end of nature because 'in man, and only in him as a moral subject, do we find unconditioned legislation regarding purposes'. Kant concludes that human happiness cannot be the final end of nature, and instead 'it is only as a moral being that man can be the final purpose [end] of creation, with man's state of happiness connected with that [end] only as its consequence, and as dependent on the degree to which man is in harmony with that [end], the [end]of his existence' (C3 437). To call something a final end is not to say in so many words that it is an end in itself, or has absolute value, but it implies roughly that. Kant says that to think of ends is to suppose that there is an intellect that aims at those ends, so to think that there is a final or ultimate end is to think that this end is the ultimate or 'unconditioned' end at which such an intellect must aim.[17] In other words, an ultimate end is the object of the choice of a rational being, and is properly chosen above all other things. Given Kant's general concept of value, this means it has unconditional value, and an incomparably high value. In other words, it is an end in itself.

If this seems a stretch, it should be noted that Kant puts the same point in terms of value and good will a few pages later in Third *Critique*. Kant says,

> Hence the only thing that can give man's existence an absolute value, and by reference to which the existence of the world can have a final purpose, is the power of desire. But I do not mean here that power of desire which makes man dependent on nature (through impulses of sense), i.e. not the one according to which the value of man's existence depends on what he receives and enjoys. I mean the value that he can only give himself, and that consists in what he does, how and on what principles he acts, not as a link in nature, but in the freedom of his power of desire; in other words, I mean a good will (C3 443).

This passage does not lend support to taking humanity, the only thing with absolute value, to be just the power to set ends and organize them into a whole. Instead it says that the only thing with absolute value is a good will.

Then neither the Third *Critique* passage nor the *Anthropology* passage seems to provide adequate evidence for Wood's minimal reading, which takes humanity as the power to set ends, to follow rules of prudence, and to organize one's ends into a consistent whole.

There is one more passage cited by both Korsgaard and Wood as evidence for their respective readings of 'humanity'. Korsgaard takes it to identify

[16] C3 433. The next quotation is from the same source.

[17] The word is Kant's, in German 'unbedingt' (C3 434–5).

humanity as the power to set ends, Wood takes it to be identifying humanity as a wider set of rational abilities related to the power to set ends. The passage on which Korsgaard and Wood rely comes from *Religion*. In the passage Kant distinguishes between the predispositions to animality ('die Tierheit'), humanity ('die Menschheit'), and personality ('die Personlichkeit') (R 26–8). Personality is 'respect for the moral law as in itself a sufficient incentive of the will', which sounds like roughly the characteristic of a good will. Since Kant distinguishes between personality and humanity, Korsgaard suggests, he cannot also mean humanity to be a good will. He must instead mean 'humanity' to denote 'a more general capacity for choosing, desiring or valuing ends'.[18] Similarly, Wood says, 'The point of characterizing the end in itself as humanity rather than as personality is simply to emphasize that this end is rational nature, in all its functions, and not merely in its moral function'.[19] They take the *Religion* passage to support reading 'humanity' as 'the power to set ends', or as this power plus the power to organize those ends and find means to the ends.

But it does not support these readings. 'Humanity' in this passage does not denote *Willkür*. Kant says the 'predisposition to humanity' is 'based on practical reason', which suggests that it is not identical with a component of practical reason such as *Willkür*. Instead the predisposition to humanity, and so also humanity itself, are conceptually dependent on the existence of functioning practical reason, including *Willkür*. 'Humanity' in this passage means a particular kind of exercise of *Willkür*. Kant says the predisposition to humanity is 'a self-love that is physical yet compares' one's lot with others'. If the predisposition to humanity is self-love, then humanity, as the fruition of that predisposition, must be action that springs from self-love. Humanity is specifically the setting of ends in order to satisfy the demands of self-love. End-setting that is determined by moral principles is personality, not humanity. This sort of 'humanity' surely is not what defenders of the minimal reading want to say should be treated as an end in itself. They want to say that *Willkür* is an end in itself regardless of whether it is exercised under the guidance of moral principles, but not that it loses its value when it is exercised in ways demanded by moral principles. So 'humanity' in this passage is not consistent with the minimal readings that Wood or Korsgaard want to endorse.

But neither does 'humanity' in the passage denote a good will. The correct conclusion to draw about Kant's use of 'humanity' in the *Religion* passage is that he does not mean it to be used univocally with 'humanity' in the

[18] Korsgaard, *Creating the Kingdom of Ends*, 113–14.

[19] Wood, 'Humanity as End in Itself', 307. He says the same thing in *Kant's Ethical Thought*, 120.

humanity formulation of the Categorical Imperative. This is not surprising, given that in the passage he is concerned with picking out the predispositions in human nature, rather than discussing the value of exercising different rational powers. He is not trying to draw a systematic distinction between humanity and personality, but just looking for labels for the different features of human nature that lead to virtue and vice. Certainly his point is not to exclude 'personality' as something similar to his use of 'humanity' in the humanity formulation. This should become obvious when, at the end of the passage in question, he describes personality as 'the idea of humanity considered quite intellectually'.

This is consistent with his willingness elsewhere to use the two terms interchangeably. In the Second *Critique*, he first says, 'Man is certainly unholy enough, but humanity in his person must be holy to him', then 'This idea of personality awakens respect' (C2 87). In the same passage, he speaks of 'the personality of these beings, whereby alone they are ends in themselves'. And in *Metaphysics of Morals* he says 'humanity itself is a dignity', and then that dignity is personality (MM 462). He does not seem concerned, in *Religion* or elsewhere, to try to contrast humanity with personality in a way that undermines the good will reading of the humanity formulation.

In fact, if 'personality' is the quality of making moral principles a sufficient reason for one's actions (which, if it is a policy or commitment, is the same as a good will), the passages cited in the previous paragraph support equating good will with humanity.

Of the passages examined so far, none seem to provide powerful reasons to think that humanity is the power to set ends, nor that power plus the rational abilities associated with it.

But there are texts that provide support for some minimal readings, and particularly for reading 'humanity' as 'capacity for morality'.

As evidence that humanity is something that every human has, some minimal feature of rationality, Hill cites *Lectures on Ethics*.[20] Kant says, 'If I distinguish between his humanity and the man himself I can contemplate even the rogue with pleasure', because 'there is still some core of the good will in him'. This suggests that humanity is some feature that even a villain possesses, and further implies that humanity is some sort of capacity for morality. If *Lectures on Ethics* were the only source for such a claim, it would be tempting to dismiss it. The work is not a book Kant wrote for professional

[20] Immanuel Kant, *Lectures on Ethics*, trans. Louis Infield (New York: Harper & Row, 1963), 197. A more complete collection of Kant's lectures on ethics is Immanuel Kant, *Lectures on Ethics*, ed. Peter Heath and Jerome Schneewind (Cambridge: Cambridge University Press, 1997).

distribution, but rather consists of students' transcriptions of his class lectures,[21] and the views expressed in it are generally less developed than in his major ethical works.

But Kant says much the same thing in *Metaphysics of Morals* 441, as Hill also points out. Kant says, 'It is only through the noble predisposition to the good in us, which makes man worthy of respect, that one can find a man who acts contrary to it contemptible (the man himself, but not the humanity in him)'. This passage, like the one from *Lectures on Ethics*, seems to say that humanity is some minimal feature of rationality possessed by even the most immoral person, and to identify that feature specifically as the capacity ('predisposition') to morality. Kant also says at *Religion* 49 that the predisposition to morality is something we 'can not cease viewing with the highest wonder', and for which 'admiration is legitimate and uplifting', which is at least suggestive of the idea that the capacity for morality is worthy of respect, and possesses a dignity.

But Kant elsewhere contradicts the idea that man is *Achtungswürdich*, or worthy of respect, in virtue of having the mere capacity for morality. In Second *Critique* 76–7 he says that not everyone is worthy of respect. We admire a man for his 'jocular humor, his courage and strength, and his power of rank', but do not respect him unless he is also committed to morality. On the other hand, 'to a humble plain man, in whom I perceive righteousness in a higher degree than I am conscious of in myself, my mind bows whether I choose or not'. Respect is properly shown to those, and only to those, in whom the capacity for morality is actually realized. There seems to be conflicting evidence regarding what makes someone the proper object of respect, which makes the textual evidence regarding respect inconclusive evidence for the capacity reading.

But there are other passages, not focusing as specifically on respect, that also appear to favour the capacity reading. In *Metaphysics of Morals* 435, Kant says that a person has dignity because she is 'the subject of a morally practical reason', which may be just the ability to engage in moral thinking and action. And in *Metaphysics of Morals* 436, Kant says that

> from our capacity for internal lawgiving and from the (natural) man feeling himself compelled to revere the (moral) man within his own person, at the same time there comes *exaltation* and the highest self-esteem, the feeling of his inner worth (*valor*), in terms of which he is above any price (*pretium*) and possesses an inalienable dignity (*dignitas interna*), which instills in him respect for himself (*reverentia*).

[21] I think it is fair to say that most university teachers sometimes sacrifice a completely accurate presentation of their own views, for the sake of clarity or dramatic effect (or just unintentionally).

The most natural reading of this passage seems to be that the capacity for morality is what possesses dignity.

But these quotations offer dubitable support for the capacity reading. To say that 'morally practical reason' is what confers dignity may mean that a being has dignity if she simply has the ability to deliberate about right and wrong, and the capacity to act on moral reasons. But it may also mean that she only has dignity if she succeeds in employing morally practical reason correctly, by making moral reasons the sufficient reasons for her actions. Consistent with this interpretation, Kant says elsewhere that he has confidence that people will act rightly, because 'human nature' is 'animated by respect for right and duty', and so 'I therefore can not and will not see it [human nature] as so deeply immersed in evil that practical moral reason will not triumph in the end, after many unsuccessful attempts, thereby showing that it is worthy of admiration after all'.[22] Here Kant is both using the phrase 'practical moral reason' in a non-minimal sense, and saying that only this successful employment of moral practical reason is worthy of admiration. The passage in which Kant speaks of the capacity for morality and of 'the moral man within' (MM 436) is also less clear evidence for the capacity reading than it may appear. What Kant says is that the feeling of being compelled to obey moral law (the moral man within) is what makes one feel inner worth, dignity, and self-respect. But it would be most peculiar if Kant meant that *simply* the feeling of being compelled was sufficient to produce these feelings, unless one also actually complied with the moral demands imposed by one's own will. What produces the feelings of 'exaltation', 'self-esteem', 'inner worth', 'dignity', and 'respect for himself' is actual compliance with the demands of morality, because by complying one shows oneself to have the power to rise above contingent impulses and inclinations, to act only on laws given by oneself. Merely to recognize the moral law but not act on it does not produce feelings of esteem and dignity, but of 'true humility' when one compares oneself to the 'holiness and strictness' of moral law.[23]

Even a quotation that seems to support the good will reading may appear to offer equally good evidence in favour of the capacity reading. The passage is from *Groundwork* 435, and says first that 'Morality is the only condition under which a rational being can be an end in himself', but then adds that 'morality, and humanity so far as it is capable of morality, is the only thing which has

[22] 'On the Common Saying: "This May be True in Theory, but it does Not Apply in Practice"' [313].

[23] The quotations are from earlier in the same paragraph, MM 436.

dignity'. Though I maintain that Kant is identifying the end in itself as good will, one might argue that it is the capacity for morality that is an end in itself, since Kant uses the word 'capable' ('fähig').[24]

But the passage actually presents the defender of the capacity reading with substantial difficulties, and no clear aid. First, a look at the paragraph in which the sentence occurs reveals considerable help for the good will reading. After saying that what has dignity is morality, and humanity in so far as it is capable of morality, Kant makes clear what he means by 'morality'. He means a certain 'attitude of mind' or 'mental attitude' that is manifested when an agent performs right actions based on principle. So by saying morality has a dignity, he seems clearly to be saying that good will has a dignity. But this leaves the problematic phrase 'and humanity, so far as it is capable of morality'. However, the mere presence of the word 'capable' ('fähig') is quite weak support for the capacity reading. This is because both the English 'capable' and 'capacity' and the corresponding German words 'fähig' and 'fähigkeit' are often used to refer to more than a mere unrealized capacity.[25] Imagine, for example, a basketball coach who says that a new player will be valuable to the team because of his 'capacity to score points' or because he is 'capable of scoring a lot of points'. What is valuable is not the mere capacity, for if the capacity remains unrealized, the player will not be valuable at all. Rather, 'capacity' is used to mean something closer to a realized capacity, or demonstrated ability. 'Fähigkeit' too can carry this meaning of a 'competence' or 'ability', rather than an unrealized capacity. So Kant's talk of the dignity of a capacity for morality does not clearly support the *unrealized* capacity as an end in itself.

Overall, the texts do provide some possible support for the claim that the capacity for morality is what has incomparably high value as an end in itself. But this evidence is not overwhelming, and must be balanced against evidence for the other minimal readings and for the good will reading.

There initially appears to be an even stronger textual case for equating humanity with just the possession of *Wille*, or the power to legislate moral laws to oneself. In several places in *Groundwork*, Kant states that the 'making of universal law' is what confers special value on a being. For example, in *Groundwork* 434, Kant says, 'the will of a rational being must always be regarded as making universal law, because otherwise he could not be conceived as an end

[24] This interpretation of the passage has been offered to me in conversation or correspondence by Robert Johnson, David Cummiskey, and Stephen Engstrom.

[25] For the points about German language, I thank several people whose German, unlike mine, is fluent. I recall discussing these points with Gucki Obler and Arnulf Zweig, at least, but probably others as well.

in himself'. In *Groundwork* 435 he repeats that a being is 'marked out in virtue of his own proper nature as an end in himself' because of 'the making of universal law'. Then in *Groundwork* 436, he adds that 'the law-making which determines all value must for this reason have a dignity', and in 440 he says that 'the dignity of man consists precisely in his capacity to make universal law'. If the making of universal law is the activity of *Wille*, of legislating universal moral principles to oneself, then these passages appear unambiguously to support taking *Wille* as the end in itself, and so taking humanity to be equivalent to the possession of *Wille*.

But this case for the *Wille* reading of humanity is actually problematic, in two ways. First, some of the texts that support the *Wille* reading are undermined by Kant's statements either immediately preceding or immediately following them, that good will is the end in itself or has the highest value. A second, and more fundamental, point counting against the textual evidence for the *Wille* reading is that Kant sometimes (surprisingly, and perhaps incoherently) uses the phrase 'making universal law' to mean acting on morally permissible maxims, instead of to mean legislating moral principles to oneself.

The first problem with the textual evidence supporting the *Wille* reading of 'humanity' is that the apparent claims that *Wille* is an end in itself are often surrounded by texts that modify these statements. Kant's statement in *Groundwork* 435 that the making of universal law is what makes a being an end in herself, and his assertion in 436 that law-making has a dignity, are both part of the same paragraph, which begins by asking what it is that entitles a good will, or 'morally good disposition' to claim an incomparably high value. The statements about universal law-giving are part of Kant's answer to that prior question. In *Groundwork* 440, Kant says that the dignity of a person consists in his capacity to make universal law, but this is part of his answer to the question of why the person who actually 'fulfills all his duties' has a dignity. The close proximity of conflicting value claims makes Kant's statements less clear evidence for any particular reading.

Moreover, the phrase 'making universal law' is actually ambiguous. A look at *Groundwork* 438 begins to point to this ambiguity, as well as providing another example of Kant modifying a claim that initially seems to support the *Wille* reading of 'humanity'. Kant first says that 'every rational being, as an end in himself, must be able to regard himself as also the maker of universal law', but then adds an initially puzzling qualification. Kant says that the reason a rational being must regard himself as making universal law is that 'it is precisely the fitness of his maxims to make universal law that marks him out as an end in himself'. It *seems* that what Kant wants to say here is that the particular maxim or 'subjective principle of action' that a being acts on in a given case must accord with the 'objective principle' or 'practical law' that she legislates through *Wille*.[26] This would suggest that actual obedience to moral principles, not just the legislation of moral principles, is necessary for being an end in oneself.

But that is not exactly what Kant says; the passage is puzzling because the terminology does not quite fit. Kant speaks of maxims 'making universal law', but this does not make sense. Maxims are the particular principles on which an agent acts, and include reference to the agent's particular ends, as in 'From self-love, I will commit suicide in order to terminate the unpleasant state I am in'.[27] Such subjective principles, which refer to an agent's contingent ends (such as the ending of an unpleasant life), cannot serve as universal laws, because they could only apply to agents who happened to have a particular contingent end. It makes sense to speak of maxims being consistent with universal law, but it is incoherent for Kant to speak of maxims being made into universal law.

Probably the talk of a maxim being made a universal law is just a slip, from a more coherent idea that is present in the universalizability formulation of the Categorical Imperative. The universalizability formulation demands that we act only on maxims (subjective principles including our motives or purposes) that *could* become universal. That is, we ask ourselves if it is possible to will that everyone would act on these maxims. This idea is coherent, because as part of the test we can imagine that everyone would have the same contingent ends, as part of their maxims. But this is different from saying that we *actually* make our maxims into universal laws when we act on permissible maxims. We do not make them into actual laws, since not everyone in fact shares our contingent purposes. So the talk of making maxims into universal laws may just be loose talk. There are perhaps more charitable explanations for Kant's claim that we make our permissible maxims into universal law when we act on them,[28] but the important point for our purposes is that Kant sometimes does use the phrase 'making universal law' to mean acting on maxims that pass the universalizability test for moral permissibility. So when Kant says that a being who is an end in herself is marked out by the fact that she makes universal law, he may mean that she is an end in herself only if she acts on maxims that are permitted by moral law. In

[26] The phrases are from Kant's definition of 'maxim', G 421.

[27] The example is a paraphrase of the maxim of Kant's 'first example' in G 422.

[28] For instance, we do make a sort of non-moral principle of skill, which says that if one wills the same contingent end as we do, they should follow the same means. Or one could say that Kant thinks that any time we act on a permissible maxim, we make the end of our action valuable, and this value creates an imperfect duty for others to assist us in attaining the end.

other words, that her commitment to morality is what makes her an end in herself.

But sometimes when Kant speaks of making universal law, he does seem to mean the activity of *Wille*, presenting an agent with universal moral principles. This is the case in the 438 quotation, in which Kant says that a rational being makes moral law 'to which he may be subjected'. Here the making of universal law is the legislation of moral principles.

The best conclusion seems to be that there is some textual support for taking humanity to be the *Wille*'s activity of legislating moral law, but that much of the support is ambiguous.

The proper preliminary conclusion at this point is that there are texts that support the 'capacity for morality' reading of 'humanity' and some that support reading humanity as the possession of *Wille*. But in neither case is the support overwhelming. There seems to be even less basis for taking 'humanity' to be the power to set ends, or that power plus the ability to organize one's ends into a whole. In addition, some of the texts that appeared to support one of the minimal readings actually lend more support to the good will reading upon closer examination. And they are far from the only textual basis for the good will reading.

Two passages in *Critique of Practical Reason* clearly identify humanity as more than a minimal feature possessed by every rational agent. By sticking to duty despite the hardships it brings, a person has 'honored and preserved humanity in his own person' (C2 88). And later Kant describes the reason why 'man (and every rational being) is an end in himself' and 'that thus the humanity in our person itself must be holy to us' (C2 131–2). The reason is that 'man is subject to the moral law and therefore subject to that which is itself holy, and it is only on account of this and in agreement with this that anything can be called holy'. Compliance (or 'agreement') with moral principles is necessary for an agent to be an end in herself.

In *Metaphysics of Morals*, Kant also associates humanity with morality. In *Metaphysics of Morals* 464, he says the respect we should show another person is 'respect for man as a moral being (holding his duty in highest esteem)'. At 420, he says that 'man's duty to himself as a moral being *only* (without taking his animality into consideration) consists in what is formal in the consistency of the maxims of his will with the dignity of humanity in his person'. To treat himself properly as a moral being is to treat his humanity appropriately. If these quotations are not convincing enough, there is Kant's explanation of why suicide is wrong. 'To annihilate the subject of morality in one's own person is to root out the existence of morality itself from the world, as far as one can, even though morality is an end in itself' (MM 422–3). 'Morality', not *Willkür*, not *Wille*, and not even the mere capacity for morality, is the end in itself. Furthermore, Kant adds that 'disposing of oneself' by destroying one's morality is 'debasing humanity in one's person'.

And these quotations only echo what Kant has said in *Groundwork*. We 'attribute a certain sublimity and dignity to the person who fulfills all his duties' (G 439–40). If an agent wishes to be an end in herself, she must remember that a 'kingdom of ends in themselves (rational beings)' is a kingdom 'to which we can belong as members only if we are scrupulous to conduct ourselves in accordance with maxims of freedom, as if they were laws of nature' (G 462–3). Any doubt that remains about what Kant meant should be removed by a statement already quoted above, that 'morality is the only condition under which a rational being can be an end in himself', where morality means the 'morally good disposition' or 'mental attitude' of a being who acts on moral principles (G 435).

Kant's use of 'humanity' in his ethical writings is somewhat equivocal. This is hardly surprising. But, on balance, the textual evidence indicates that Kant meant 'humanity' in the humanity formulation to be read as 'good will'.

2. Additional Arguments for Minimal Readings

Apart from referring directly to the texts, proponents of the minimal readings of 'humanity' have also offered more general arguments for thinking that humanity must be a property that all minimally rational beings possess necessarily.

Perhaps the most direct argument for this claim is offered by Allen Wood. Wood argues that the end in itself must be a feature possessed by all rational agents, and so cannot be 'personality' or a good will. This is because 'the end in itself must ground categorical imperatives', and 'since such imperatives must be necessarily binding on all rational beings, the end which grounds them cannot have merely contingent or even doubtful existence, as it would if it were present only in the good will or the virtuous person'.[29] The argument seems to suppose that in order to ground a categorical imperative (more specifically, the humanity formulation of the Categorical Imperative), an end must exist necessarily.

But this is not so. A contingently existing end can ground a categorical imperative. Wood is right in thinking that the existence of any good wills is a contingent matter. We can imagine a world in which all (minimally) rational

[29] Wood, 'Humanity as End in Itself', 307. Wood offers the same argument, in only slightly different wording, in *Kant's Ethical Thought*, 120.

agents placed greater priority on satisfying their inclinations than on acting morally, and so no one had a good will. But the humanity formulation of the Categorical Imperative would still bind agents in such a world, in two ways. First, it would require every agent to treat a good will as an end in itself, if such a thing as a good will ever manifested itself. The Categorical Imperative would not affect actual behaviour toward others, but it would bind every agent counterfactually. Agents in that world would, by hypothesis, ignore such an imperative, but that is irrelevant. There is a second, even more important, way in which the humanity formulation of the Categorical Imperative would impose obligations even in a world where no one had a good will. The Categorical Imperative would still demand that every agent strive to possess a good will herself. Kant says all agents have a duty, based on the humanity formulation, to seek moral perfection by adopting a maxim of both performing right actions and making the moral law a sufficient incentive of one's will.[30] A good will would still have the highest possible value (though, by hypothesis, this value would not be manifested), and every agent would still be obligated to live up to this ideal. We are imagining that in the hypothetical, corrupt world, agents would not live up to any of their obligations, including this one. But still the duty would remain. So, contrary to Wood's claim, the ground of a Categorical Imperative could be something whose existence is 'contingent'.

Kant does say that 'contingent' ends cannot ground a Categorical Imperative, but Kant is using 'contingent' in a different sense from Wood (G 428). Kant means to deny that Categorical Imperatives can be grounded on ends that are adopted just due to an agent's inclinations, because it may be rational for one agent to adopt such an end if she has the relevant inclination, but equally rational for another agent with different inclinations to ignore or abandon such an end. Kant never addresses the topic of ends which are dictated by reason alone but which may fail to be manifested in the world (which is Wood's sense of 'contingent end').

Nothing I have said is meant to imply that our world is like the counterfactual one in which no one has a good will.[31] Kant no doubt believes that ends in themselves really exist in our world, and that agents must adjust their behaviour to treat them appropriately. But there is no reason to think of the claim that ends in themselves exist as anything more than an extremely plausible empirical supposition. Wood is presumably not expressing real doubts about whether any real agents have a good will, or firm commitment to morality. Such doubts

[30] MM 392–3, 446–7. See my discussion of this in Chapter 3, section 3.

[31] In section 2 of the next chapter, I take up the topic of how common good wills are in our world.

would surely be pessimistic. Our world is a better place than the hypothetical world that completely lacks good wills.[32]

Besides Wood's argument that the end in itself must be something that exists necessarily, he and Korsgaard both rely on a certain way of presenting their (slightly different) readings of 'humanity'. Their descriptions make their minimal readings sound more appealing and natural than the good will reading, but their presentation is highly misleading. Korsgaard says,

> When Kant says that the characteristic of humanity is the power to set an end, then, he is not referring to personality, which would encompass the power to adopt an end for moral or sufficient reasons. Rather, he is referring to a more general capacity for choosing, desiring, or valuing ends.[33]

Similarly, Wood says, 'it is the whole of rational nature that constitutes such an end [an end in itself]. Preserving and respecting rational nature means preserving and respecting it in all its functions, not merely in its moral function of giving and obeying moral laws'.[34] The picture they paint is that rational nature has different functions, consisting of end-setting that is determined by moral principles and end-setting that is not (plus other features of rationality, in Wood's case). To think that a good will is the end in itself, on this picture, is to pick out just one function of rational nature, rather than saying that all of rational nature is valuable. The good will reading looks arbitrary and peculiar, given the way Korsgaard and Wood divide rational nature.

But their picture does not capture the Kantian idea of the will, in its different aspects. The will is divided into *Wille*, which gives moral law, and *Willkür*,

[32] A few pages later, on 132–3, Wood presents what looks like another, independent argument for the claim that minimally rational beings without good wills have the same value as beings with good wills. But in fact, as Wood acknowledges, it is derived from the argument described above, rather than being a separate argument. Wood says that Kant must 'regard a person with a bad will as the equal of a person with good will'. This is because 'the worst rational being (in any respect you can possibly name) has the same dignity or absolute worth as the best rational being in that respect (or in any other)'. Such conclusions would obviously undermine the good will reading, since the good will reading claims that only a good will has unique and incomparable value as an end in itself. But Wood recognizes that there is really no separate argument here. The conclusions are based on Wood's claim that 'the worth of all rational beings is equal', which is a 'corollary' of the claim that every minimally rational being 'is an end in itself with absolute worth'. And this latter claim follows from his earlier argument that the end in itself must be something that necessarily exists, because to think that the end in itself is something whose existence is 'contingent' would 'undermine the categorical status of the moral imperative'. So the ultimate ground of Wood's argument in this section is his earlier argument, which I think is unsuccessful for reasons discussed above. Wood also states that his ideas here are consistent with his claim that living up to moral demands makes one worth more in one's own eyes, but not in comparison to others. I discuss this idea of Wood's below.

[33] Korsgaard, *Creating the Kingdom of Ends*, 114. Both Korsgaard's and Wood's quotations have already been cited above, in the context of the passage from R 26–8.

[34] Wood, *Kant's Ethical Thought*, 120.

which can set ends that are consistent with moral law or ends that are not. To say that just the power to set ends, or *Willkür*, is the end in itself is to pick out just one function of the will and ignore *Wille*. But to say that the good will is an end in itself is to say the entire will is valuable, if it is a properly functioning will, meaning if the *Willkür* obeys the commands of *Wille*, as is rationally required. Then it is not just end-setting for moral reasons that is valuable, it is all end-setting of a properly ordered will. The setting of ends for non-moral reasons is also valuable, if the will that sets the ends is good. Korsgaard and Wood's picture of 'rational nature' is misleadingly non-Kantian, because it ignores Kant's own account of a rational will. Only this misleading presentation makes the good will reading look more arbitrary than Korsgaard or Wood's reading.

So far, the arguments for a minimal reading of 'humanity' have followed a strategy of trying to show that humanity must be something other than a good will. But a different strategy would be to try to show that even though a good will is what we must treat as an end in itself, a good will is actually a feature that is possessed by all minimally rational agents. This would require showing that my definition of good will is inaccurate. Henry Allison's discussion of the concept of a good will provides the material for this sort of challenge to my reading of the humanity formulation. Allison suggests that Kant sometimes uses the term 'good will' to refer to something that all minimally rational beings possess—either the capacity for morality, or the possession of *Wille*. If Allison is right, then even if it is a good will that is an end in itself, some minimal reading of the humanity formulation may be correct. The problem here for my reading of the humanity formulation would not be that humanity is not a good will, but rather that I have misunderstood what a good will is in the context of the humanity formulation.

In chapter 7 of *Kant's Theory of Freedom*, Allison begins by suggesting roughly the same sort of analysis of good will as I have proposed. The topic of Allison's chapter 7 is '*Wille*, *Willkür*, and *Gesinnung*' (*Gesinnung* means roughly 'disposition'). Allison's analysis of an agent's *Gesinnung* as both the agent's character and 'an agent's fundamental maxim with respect to the moral law'[35] is consistent with my definition of good will. The idea is that an agent must be thought of as giving priority either to the demands of morality or to the demands of self-love, and a good or evil character is a matter of these fundamental priorities.

But, while Allison does not deny that a good will could be equated with a *Gesinnung* of doing one's duty come what may, he does at one point mention

[35] Henry Allison, *Kant's Theory of Freedom* (Cambridge: Cambridge University Press, 1990), 140.

that he finds a different notion of good will in *Religion*.[36] In *Religion* 37, Kant says that an 'evil heart' may 'coexist with a will which in general is good'. And in *Religion* 44, Kant says, 'For man, therefore, who despite a corrupted heart still possesses a good will, there still remains hope of a return to the good from which he has strayed'. Allison takes good will in these passages to be the 'goodness of morally legislative reason' which every agent possesses. Good will then is something like *Wille*, which legislates moral principles, plus (though Allison does not explicitly say this) perhaps also the ever-present incentive to act on these principles.

The two passages Allison cites from *Religion* deserve two different responses.

The first passage, which says that an evil heart can coexist with a good will, need not imply that all minimally rational agents have a good will, and so does not contradict my reading of the humanity formulation. Kant has said that frailty, or weakness of will, is one type of man's 'propensity to evil', or more specifically that it is the least serious type of 'evil heart' (R 29). And of course, Kant does think that frailty, or weakness of will, is compatible with a good will.[37] A good will is distinguished by its basic and enduring commitment to regulate its end-setting with moral principles. Kant allows that this enduring commitment is compatible with some lapses in particular actions, when frailty leads one to act contrary to one's own moral principles. So Kant thinks that frailty is compatible with a good will. Then, since frailty is one variety (the least evil variety) of 'evil heart', it follows that an evil heart can sometimes be compatible with a good will. In the passage Allison cites, *Religion* 37, Kant seems to be talking about frailty, saying the evil heart's 'origin is the frailty of human nature, in not being strong enough to comply with its adopted principles'. This does not imply that all degrees of evil are compatible with a good will. An agent possesses a good will if she places a priority on regulating her choices with the requirements of moral law, even if she sometimes falls short of her commitment in some particular cases. But an agent lacks a good will if she places priority on satisfying her own inclinations, without concern for the moral permissibility of her choices. So some agents have a good will, some lack a good will, and my reading of the humanity formulation is undamaged.

The other passage that Allison cites is not just about frailty, however. In *Religion* 44, Kant is not saying just that frailty is compatible with good will, but that an agent can have good will even if she places greater priority on self-love than on morality, even if her *Willkür* 'incorporates lower incentives in its

[36] Henry Allison, *Kant's Theory of Freedom* (Cambridge: Cambridge University Press, 1990), 158–61.

[37] For a more detailed explanation of this point, see Chapter 2, section 1 of this book.

maxims and makes them supreme' (R 43). This would be plainly inconsistent with the definition I have offered of good will, and in fact does seem to imply that any minimally rational being has a good will in some sense.

But it cannot be the same sense in which Kant uses 'good will' throughout *Groundwork* (nor even the same as the prevalent use of 'good will' in *Religion*). It is clear in *Groundwork* that Kant means good will to be something that at least some agents lack. In his argument in *Groundwork* chapter 1, that only a good will is good without qualification, he examines cases in which other things lack value because they are possessed by an agent without a good will. In his claim that happiness is not good when possessed by someone without a good will, it might be argued (though not, I think, without strain) that Kant is just employing a thought experiment, which does not imply that there could actually be agents without good wills. But in the case of the 'scoundrel' who possesses qualities of temperament like moderation and sober reflection, it is clear that Kant has in mind a scoundrel who could actually exist, and who lacks a good will. So if the 'good will' that Allison finds in *Religion* 44 is something that no agent can ever lack, it must be different from the good will of *Groundwork*.[38]

Neither of the two passages from *Religion* undermines the claim that, in *Groundwork,* Kant is using 'good will' to mean something like 'the will of a being who is committed to governing her *Willkür* with *Wille*'. One of the passages is compatible with this *Groundwork* definition of good will. The other passage does seem to use 'good will' in a different sense, perhaps just to mean a will that has the potential to be morally good. But this divergent use of 'good will' cannot be taken as univocal with Kant's technical sense of 'good will' in the humanity formulation, and so does not provide reason to abandon the *Groundwork* definition.

More generally, it is clear that 'good will' in *Groundwork* is something that an agent can either possess or fail to possess. So the good will reading of the humanity formulation cannot be undermined by claiming that good will is something that all minimally rational agents possess. Instead, an argument for a minimal reading of the humanity formulation must proceed by showing that the humanity that is an end in itself is something other than a good will.

One particular minimal alternative seems to have significant appeal. This is the reading that identifies humanity as the capacity for morality, rather than as

[38] Allison is not unaware of this. He says, 'at first glance, this conception of good will might appear to be far removed from the conception originally advanced at the beginning of Groundwork 1' (*Kant's Theory of Freedom*, 161). He suggests that the two conceptions are actually 'quite close', but it is not completely clear how he means them to be close.

a will that is actually committed to acting on moral principles. Besides having some textual support as described above, this reading seems to have prima facie intuitive appeal.[39] The merits of the capacity reading are great enough to warrant careful consideration.

The intuitive appeal of the capacity reading rests partly on its place as a sort of middle ground between saying that a good will is an end in itself and saying that the end in itself is merely the power to set ends. One might grant that Kant seems to conceive of humanity, in the humanity formulation, as having some moral component beyond the mere capacity to set ends, but still baulk at the seemingly repugnant conclusion that only people with good wills are ends in themselves. The capacity reading may appear to be a good compromise. It says that the capacity for morality is what confers special status on a being who possesses it, which (given Kant's account of human nature) would imply that all normal adult humans are ends in themselves. Yet since a capacity is something that should be developed, each of us with the capacity for morality still has reason actually to accept and act on moral principles, in order to realize the capacity for morality that we possess. Each of us has Kantian humanity, according to this line of thinking, but it may be more developed or less, and each of us ought to develop it more.

The capacity reading may seem like an appealing middle ground between the claims that a good will is the end in itself and that the power to set ends is. But this middle ground is highly unstable. There is an inherent conceptual difficulty in claiming that a capacity has an incomparably high value. In general, it seems that to attribute some value to a mere capacity implies an even greater value for the realized capacity. The value of a capacity for x is conceptually dependent on the value we place on x. This is perhaps obscured by an ambiguity in the word 'capacity' which I discussed in section I of this chapter. 'Capacity' often refers to an actualized capacity, not a mere potential. So we may speak of someone's 'capacity to grade papers quickly' and not mean an undemonstrated capacity, but an actual ability. So to say that someone's capacity for x is valuable may often mean that it is an actually realized capacity that is valuable. If we clearly distinguish capacity as mere potential from capacity as actual performance or competence, it seems most peculiar to value an unrealized capacity for x without placing an even greater value on x itself. And it is especially odd to say that a mere capacity, regardless of whether it is realized, has an incomparably high value. If the mere capacity has the highest possible value even when it is unrealized, then there seems to

[39] A number of people have expressed support for something like the capacity reading, in conversation or correspondence, including Thomas Hill, Stephen Engstrom, and Robert Johnson.

be no reason to develop the capacity. So, if the capacity for a good will or the capacity for moral action has a dignity, then there seems to be no reason actually to make moral principles a sufficient incentive for one's actions. Why bother, when one already has the capacity for morality, which by hypothesis is the thing with the highest possible value? This point is not surprising. It is merely a reiteration of points I have made in Chapter 3. One point is that treating humanity as an ideal to live up to implies that humanity is not a mere capacity that everyone already possesses. The other point is that only the good will reading of the humanity formulation provides the fullest sort of reason to refrain from immoral actions, because by choosing to act immorally one is jeopardizing one's good will, which is one's most valuable possession.

It is conceptually bizarre, and possibly even incoherent, to place a higher value on an unrealized capacity for anything than on the thing itself. To claim that the capacity for morality has the highest possible value is to embrace just this sort of conceptual perversity. This alone seems sufficient to render the capacity reading untenable. When coupled with the exegetical advantages of the good will reading, described in Chapter 3, the case against the capacity reading seems even stronger.

One final point deserves attention. Wood offers another, different line of argument against the idea that a good will has a dignity and so is the end in itself. Wood is aware that some passages in Kant's ethical writings may give the reader an impression that Kant attributes the highest value to a good will, rather than to minimally rational nature,[40] but Wood counters this impression with an alternative interpretation. Wood says that while Kant does attribute a special 'inner worth' to a 'morally good person', this inner worth must be understood as arising only from a comparison that an individual makes herself, a comparison between her own actions and the 'person's own self-given moral law or idea of virtue'.[41] So a person may be aware of doing better or worse at living up to moral demands, and of having a correspondingly greater or lesser worth in comparison to her ideals. But Wood emphasizes that this does not mean that the person who has greater inner worth has higher value than a person with less inner worth. 'Differences in inner worth do not in the least disturb the absolute equality of self-worth between human beings, which is entailed by FH [the formula of humanity]'. The idea apparently is that inner worth is a concept that can only be employed by an individual to assign different degrees of worth to herself, but that this inner worth does not provide a scale for comparing different individuals to one another. Wood says,

[40] See Wood, *Kant's Ethical Thought*, 118, 133–4.

[41] Ibid. 134.

> Kant's consistent position, then, is that the inner worth of a person, measured solely by comparison to the moral law, may be greater or less according to one's virtue in fulfilling the moral law one gives oneself; but the worth of a person never varies in comparison to others, since the good and bad alike possess the dignity of humanity.[42]

So Wood proposes a scale of inner worth, for an individual to measure herself against moral ideals, but maintains that this scale does not allow interpersonal comparisons of worth.

I think this position is deeply inconsistent with some of Kant's most basic ideas about value and ethics. Wood rightly seems willing to admit that, according to Kant, each individual gives herself moral law and regards living up to the demands of moral law as an unconditional demand. So, in Wood's terms, each of us measures her inner worth by assessing the extent to which she lives up to the ideal of accepting moral demands as a sufficient reason for action. But this is just to say that each of us, to the extent that she is rational, regards a good will as an ideal toward which she must strive at all costs. Given Kant's concept of value—that to be valuable is just to be the object of rational choice—this implies that for each of us, our own good will has incomparably high value.

But Kant also thinks that what makes each of us incomparably valuable is the same thing in all of us, namely our 'humanity'. Whatever humanity is, I must regard the humanity in me as having the same incomparably high value as the humanity in you. But it has already been established what I must regard as having the highest value in me. What has greatest value for me is living up to moral principles, or, in other words, striving to possess a good will. Then I must regard the same thing, good will, as having the same incomparably high value in you and in every other person who possesses it. To suppose that humanity is something different from good will, as Wood does, and to ascribe the highest possible value to humanity, would imply that each individual has reason only to strive to possess humanity, but not a good will. This is inconsistent with Wood's own position that each person rightly measures her inner worth by comparing her actions to the unconditional demands of morality. So the attempt to separate the 'inner worth' of each individual from the worth of other individuals is untenable.

But there is certainly something right about Wood's insight here. Part of Wood's point in distinguishing inner worth from a worth that can be compared to others' is to emphasize that we generally ought not to make moral comparisons between people. This is partly because we are in no

[42] Wood, *Kant's Ethical Thought*, 135.

position to make such comparisons accurately, since we can never know another's character with certainty, a claim that Kant persistently emphasizes.[43] But Wood stresses another reason not to compare our own worth to others'. We must resist the innate human tendency to 'claim for oneself an imagined worth greater than that of others'.[44] For Wood, the humanity formulation's demand that we respect every being's humanity provides a counterbalance to our own self-conceit. We ought not to derive our sense of worth from comparing ourselves to others, but instead from recognizing that we possess the same inalienable value as every other minimally rational being. Wood says 'Self-respect ascribes no greater worth to oneself than to anyone else and involves no partiality toward oneself. It rests solely on the "dignity" of humanity, the absolute worth belonging to rational nature as such'.[45] Wood seems quite right to attribute to Kant the view that humans have strong tendencies to compete with and compare themselves to others. Indeed, Wood's emphasis on Kant's empirical claims about human nature constitutes one of the many strong points of Wood's book. And it seems reasonable as well to look for elements in Kant's theory that provide an account of how one can combat such innate tendencies.

But none of this shows that all minimally rational beings have the same value. Kant thinks we have a tendency to elevate our estimates of ourselves compared to others, but this only shows that we have reason to resist this temptation. Since Kant thinks we cannot reliably assess our own or others' characters, we ought not to base our treatment of others on our inherently unreliable estimates of their character. This is not to say that in theory there can be no difference in the worth of different minimally rational beings. Kant repeatedly states that there is such a difference, as I have pointed out in section 1 of this chapter. Kant maintains that we are not in a position to make such judgements, but he does think that God could make such judgements.[46] That is the basis of Kant's arguments that one ought to believe in a supreme being who can judge beings' worthiness to be happy, and apportion their rewards in light of their worthiness.

Kant offers several reasons for thinking that we ought to treat all minimally rational beings as if they are incomparably valuable ends in themselves, but these reasons apply even if not all minimally rational beings really are ends in themselves. If this is so, then Wood is right in saying that we ought not to base our treatment of others on our estimate of their moral worth, but incorrect in

[43] See section 1 of the next chapter for a more detailed exegesis of this point.

[44] Wood, *Kant's Ethical Thought*, 9. See also ibid. 138–9, 263–5.

[45] Ibid. 263.

[46] R 48, R 76–7, C2 123–4.

saying that humanity must be some feature that is possessed by all minimally rational beings.

So it is very important to see whether the good will reading of the humanity formulation can produce sound Kantian reasons to avoid moral snobbery and mistreatment of others, even those others who lack a good will. The next chapter turns to that question.

5

Is the Good Will Reading Just Too Hard to Swallow?

Despite the evidence for the good will reading, it may seem as if it just cannot be right. There are two main intuitive obstacles to the good will reading, and in this chapter I will try to remove those obstacles.

First, some may worry that if a good will is what should be treated as an end in itself, the humanity formulation becomes unpalatably moralistic. It might be thought that the humanity formulation, on the good will reading, grounds duties only to agents who have a good will, and does not prohibit any kind of abuse of agents who lack a good will. Several people have stated this concern in conversation,[1] and Thomas Hill, Jr., and Allen Wood have expressed at least the spirit of the worry in some of their writings.[2] I believe the desire to make Kant seem less a harsh moralist and more a gentle egalitarian is a strong, often unstated motive underlying the common attempts by commentators to avoid the good will reading.[3]

I think these concerns about moralism do not provide grounds for rejecting the good will reading. The good will reading of the humanity formulation provides strong reasons to avoid mistreating minimally rational beings, even those minimally rational beings who lack good wills. This is not because they possess Kantian 'humanity', but for other reasons that Kant discusses.

But even if the good will reading does not lead to excessive moralism, and does not license the wanton abuse of beings who lack good wills, the good will

[1] In fact, in professional correspondence, one prominent Kant scholar has stated that the good will reading of the humanity formulation is not only moralistic, but 'monstrous'.

[2] See Thomas E. Hill, Jr., 'Kant's Anti-Moralistic Strain', in *Dignity and Practical Reason in Kant's Moral Theory* (Ithaca, NY: Cornell University Press, 1992), 176–95, 'Social Snobbery and Human Dignity', in *Autonomy and Self-Respect* (Cambridge: Cambridge University Press, 1991), 155–72, and 'Must Respect be Earned?', in *Respect, Pluralism, and Justice* (Oxford: Oxford University Press, 2000), 87–118; Allen Wood, *Kant's Ethical Thought* (Cambridge: Cambridge University Press, 1999), 118–22, 132–9.

[3] See my discussion of this early in Chapter 2.

reading still faces another intuitive problem. It seems possible that very few agents in the real world have a good will, which would tend to make all the concern with the humanity formulation appear overblown. Even if there are reasons to treat beings well despite their lack of good wills, it would be strange to base a whole ethical system on the treatment deserved by a few saints. If the humanity formulation must be stretched to confer moral protection on most of us, because most of us lack good wills, then this will render the good will reading of the humanity formulation peculiar at best.

I will argue that this worry too is unfounded. Despite some troubling comments that Kant makes, there is good reason to think that good wills are not rare.

1. Is the Good Will Reading Too Moralistic?

Kant says the two main kinds of ethical duties we have toward others are duties of benevolence and of respect (MM 385–8, 462), but if the good will reading is right, it looks as though we may not have either sort of duty toward many actual humans, since many humans may lack a good will.[4]

This worry, though not completely unjustified, does not in the end provide any strong reason to reject the good will reading. We are still usually or always obligated to show benevolence toward, and respect for, other humans, even if the humanity formulation stresses the value of a good will.

One reason we have duties toward even those who lack good wills is that we cannot be sure whose will is good. We cannot even be sure what reasons an agent acts on in a particular case, let alone whether she embraces a higher-level principle of only acting in ways that are morally permitted. Kant maintains that it is impossible to know with certainty whether a right action has been performed because of its rightness, or from some inclination (G 407). He is even more explicit in *Religion* that, although we can observe an agent perform impermissible actions, 'we cannot observe maxims, we cannot do so unproblematically even within ourselves; hence the judgment that an agent is an evil human being can not reliably be based on experience'.[5] We cannot even be certain of an agent's reasons for acting in a particular case, and all the less can we know what sort of character underlies the actions. Since we cannot be sure whether an agent possesses a good will, we must give her

[4] Though I will argue, in section 2 of this chapter, that good wills are not so rare.

[5] R 20. See also R 47–8, 67, 71.

the benefit of the doubt.[6] She must be presumed to be an end in herself for roughly the same reason that a defendant in an American court is presumed innocent.

Avoiding judgements about others' overall moral character is all the more important, given the innate human tendency to elevate one's own worth in comparison to others'. Kant consistently attributes to humankind a self-love and self-conceit that leads to competition,[7] in the form of both 'an unjust desire to acquire superiority for oneself over others' and 'an inclination to gain worth in the opinion of others'.[8] This leads to a 'mania for honor', or the excessive desire for the regard of others (Anth 272), and to 'arrogance', which is 'a kind of ambition (ambitio) in which we demand that others think little of themselves in comparison with us' (MM 465). Given these tendencies, it is quite plausible to think that our comparisons of our own moral character with others' will be unreliable. So it is not just technically impossible to achieve absolute certainty in our judgements about character, it is also very likely that such judgements will be distorted.[9] This human tendency to judge others' character inaccurately provides a good reason not to base our treatment of others on judgements of their moral character.

Putting aside what Kant says, it may seem hard to believe that no amount of immoral behaviour is ever sufficient to indicate the lack of a good will. It is hard to believe that a smiling torturer or a dictator who never speaks of his citizens' hardships could possess a commitment to morality. But if we diverge from Kant here to say we can be sure that such people lack good wills, this does not make the good will reading implausible. This can be seen by looking at the two basic kinds of duties we have toward others, duties of benevolence and of respect.[10]

First, look at the duty of benevolence to others, as exemplified by the duty to further others' ends. According to the good will reading, an agent's ends have value, and so deserve to be furthered, only if the agent has a good will.[11] So if we can sometimes tell that someone lacks a good will, then we have no

[6] For a fuller discussion of this topic, see Stephen Engstrom, 'The Concept of the Highest Good in Kant's Moral Theory', *Philosophy and Phenomenological Research*, 52/4, (Dec. 1992), 747–80.

[7] See various of Kant's essays of the Critical and Post-Critical period, most notably 'Perpetual Peace', 'Idea for a Universal History with a Cosmopolitan Purpose', and 'The Contest of Faculties'.

[8] Both quotations are from R 27. In fact, this is the passage that Wood and Korsgaard rely on in support of their minimal readings.

[9] Wood believes that these considerations suggest that there in fact is no difference in moral worth between individuals, but that seems to go further than is needed to combat the tendency toward inflating one's own worth. See Wood, *Kant's Ethical Thought*, 8–9, 260–5, and 138–9, and my discussion of Wood's position in Chapter 4.

[10] These are the basic categories of duties toward others that Kant describes in MM 448–68.

[11] See Chapter 3.

reason to assist such a person in achieving her ends. This applies to both her immoral ends and her morally permissible ends, since she lacks the good will that confers value on any ends. But this is not so repugnant. The good will reading would say that we may treat another's permissible ends as valueless only in those few cases in which the person is so monstrous that we can be sure he lacks a good will. If we are sure that the smiling torturer lacks a good will, it is not implausible to say we are not obligated to help him attain the small pleasures he desires—a refreshing glass of iced tea after his hard day's work, say.

But even if the complete villain does not deserve our help in achieving her ends, many would think she still deserves at least a minimal respect in virtue of being human. So if there are some humans who clearly lack good wills, and if the good will reading demands that we withhold respect from them, then this may undercut the plausibility of the good will reading. But the good will reading does not demand this. Kant himself provides some good reasons to treat all humans with respect, even if some have not earned that respect by possessing a good will.

Kant seems to agree that respect is a more inviolable duty than benevolence, saying that 'no one is wronged if duties of love are neglected, but a failure in the duty of respect infringes upon a man's lawful claim' (MM 464). He states that respect should be given to 'human beings in general' and given to them 'as human beings' or to each person 'in his quality as a human being' (MM 462–3). This may well appear inconsistent with the good will reading.

But it is not. Kant thinks we should refrain from disrespectful actions toward other humans, but not because they all necessarily have a value that makes them worthy of respect. He is quite explicit that we should respect the vicious man 'even though by his deeds he makes himself unworthy of it' (MM 463). Why should we treat him with respect if he is unworthy of respect?

Kant offers two reasons. First, to treat any human with disrespect lessens our respect for all humans,

> so as finally to cast a shadow of worthlessness over our race itself, making misanthropy (shying away from men) or contempt the prevalent cast of mind, or to dull one's moral feeling by repeatedly exposing one to the sight of such things and accustoming one to it. (MM 466)

Beings with a different psychological make-up might not be obligated to respect someone who lacks a good will, but humans are so obligated because to disrespect any human tends to lessen their respect for all humans.

The second reason not to deny all respect to the vicious person is that to do so would undermine his chances of reforming his character. Kant compares the vicious person, who makes mistakes in his use of practical reason, to someone who makes mistakes in the use of theoretical reason. One should not ridicule the person who makes factual errors, or treat him with contempt, because if 'one denies all understanding to a man who opposes one in a certain judgment, how does one want to bring him to understand that he has erred?' (MM 463). One should instead preserve the confused person's 'respect for his own understanding' by 'explaining to him the possibility of his having erred'. In this way, he will not be discouraged from developing his understanding to avoid future mistakes. And Kant says, 'The same thing applies to the censure of vice' (MM 463). It is false to think that a vicious person 'could never be improved', since he 'can never lose entirely his predisposition to the good', or *Wille*. By treating the vicious person with contempt, we would dampen her respect for the *Wille* within her, and so discourage her from coming to embrace *Wille*'s demands. The vicious person possesses all the ingredients necessary to have a good will, so we should not do anything to interfere with her coming to acquire one.[12]

Later, Kant similarly argues for a more specific duty to avoid publicly condemning others' moral character. This duty is based on respect for others' humanity, and Kant says one reason to avoid defaming others is that to treat them with respect is more likely to inspire them to moral rectitude. Kant says we should not 'take malicious pleasure in exposing the faults of others' but instead should 'throw the veil of love of man over their faults, not merely by softening our judgments but also by keeping these judgments to ourselves; for examples of respect that we give others can arouse their striving to deserve it' (MM 466). This duty to show respect for others is not based on a supposition that all humans necessarily deserve respect. In fact it presupposes the opposite. Kant does think we should treat the vicious with respect, but not because they have made themselves worthy of it by possessing a good will.

So the good will reading of 'humanity' does not recommend moral snobbery or rampant mistreatment of other humans. The imperative to treat a good will as supremely valuable is not accompanied by an imperative to make judgements about who has and lacks a good will (since such judgements are difficult or impossible to make), nor by an imperative to mistreat those who obviously lack a good will (since there are reasons to treat them with respect even though they are not worthy of it).

[12] Kant's description of why we should treat the vicious with respect may sound as though it is compatible with the capacity reading of humanity, and perhaps it is. But for reasons discussed in Chapter 4, I think it is more compatible with the good will reading, because our concern is with the actual realization of the capacity for a good will, not with the value of the capacity in itself. And Kant's clear statement that such people are not worthy of respect is incompatible with thinking their capacity for morality makes them worthy.

2. How Rare is a Good Will?

There remains another obstacle to accepting the good will reading. I argued above that the good will reading would require us to treat all (or all but a few obviously evil) humans as ends in themselves, but this may seem silly if there are actually few agents with good wills.

If only one human in 10,000 has a commitment to do her duty no matter what, it will be peculiar if a moral theory demands that we treat the other 9,999 in the same special way as the one, on the grounds that we cannot be absolutely sure that they are not special too. If someone dug through every pile of dog dung he saw, we might well think it a foolish policy, even if he claimed to have heard that once in a rare while dogs ate diamonds. A moral theory that bases our duties to everyone on the treatment deserved by a few extraordinary specimens cannot be expected to gain much support, regardless of the theory's consistency or precision.

The good will reading does not make Kant's moral theory into this kind of novelty, because it is quite plausible to think good wills are common in humans. More precisely, given the general Kantian framework for thinking about a good will, common sense indicates that good wills may be nothing rare in humans.

Again, it should be remembered that Kant is quite consistent in maintaining that we cannot be sure of an agent's disposition—that is, whether her fundamental policy (or maxim) is of doing her duty or of satisfying her inclinations. This at least rules out our being certain that we very seldom encounter good wills.

But if that were all that could be said, it would be scant help in saving the humanity reading from ridiculousness. Fortunately, much more can be said. The epistemological difficulty with good wills does not serve as a last-ditch effort to say that maybe good wills are common, despite all the evidence that they are not. On the contrary, we have significant evidence that many humans may have good wills, and the epistemological problem primarily hinders us from declaring with certainty that good wills are no rarity.

A good way to begin to see this is to ask what sort of evidence we can expect to have regarding the scarcity or prevalence of good wills, given the Kantian idea that we cannot be sure of a person's fundamental principles. The evidence will necessarily fall short of being conclusive, given Kant's claims about the limits of human knowledge, but that does not mean there can be no evidence at all for saying that many people have good wills, or that few people do.

If no one ever seemed to give the slightest regard to moral considerations, that would be the strongest sort of evidence we could demand for the claim that no human agents have good wills. But that does not seem to be the state of things. People do act wrongly sometimes, for many reasons. They may simply be too selfish to consider other people, they may be locked into damaging habits or ways of thinking and so not even consider the moral dimension of their actions, or they may bear grudges or wounds that lead them to bitterly harmful actions. But people more often seem to act in morally permissible ways. Morally acceptable or commendable actions can also have a variety of motives. There are many reasons people refrain from doing wrong–fear of the legal or social consequences, habit, timidity—but it also seems common for them to act just because they think some action is required or forbidden by morality. Even when they feel very strongly pulled toward wrongdoing, the idea that some action is wrong seems, for most people, to be a significant reason to refrain. Although we cannot be certain of our own motives, and must be even less sure of others', it seems on the face of it that moral beliefs play a substantial motivational role in most human lives. And this is significant evidence that real humans may possess good wills. Instead of a world in which people do wrong frequently, and act rightly only for selfish reasons, we seem to live in a world in which moral reasons carry weight for many people.

And Kant recognizes this at least prima facie role that morality plays in human lives. That is why, usually, when he says that we cannot be certain of our own motives or maxims he emphasizes cases in which we seem to act from moral motives. At *Groundwork* 407, he says,

> It is indeed at times the case that after the keenest self-examination we find nothing that without the moral motive of duty could have been strong enough to move us to this or that good action and to so great a sacrifice; but we can not infer from this that it is not some secret impulse of self-love which has actually, under the show of the Idea of duty, been the genuine cause determining our will.

Although Kant at least twice emphasizes the impossibility of deducing evil motives or dispositions from evil actions (R 20, MM 474), there are many more times when he puts the epistemological problem as he does above, in terms of our good actions not being certain evidence of good maxims (R 48, 66–7, 71). There are many times when it seems people act from moral motives, and we just cannot be certain that they do.

But just noting that people often seem to act on moral motives (if this is true) is not the strongest imaginable evidence that they have good wills. The clearest test cases would be when doing the right thing required great sacrifices, and the best evidence that people had good wills would be if, in such cases, they always seemed to act as morality required, and always felt as if they were doing so simply because it was morally required. This is more or less Kant's point in *Religion* 61, when he says the only way we can clearly conceive of an ideal of 'such moral perfection as is possible to a being pertaining to this world and dependent on needs and inclinations' is by imagining someone who is willing to 'take upon himself all sufferings, up to the most ignominious death, for the good of the people of the world and even for his enemies'. Kant's point is not that one only possesses a good will if one has faced such dire choices, but rather that only such extreme cases provide the strongest evidence that the agent has a good will.[13] It may seem that cases of people acting rightly in such straits are rare.

But this is not good evidence that good wills are rare. One reason it is hard to find cases of people acting rightly despite disastrous costs is that there are not so many cases, at least in well-ordered and affluent countries, where one faces single discrete decisions in which morality demands huge sacrifices. And it is not clear that in these rare circumstances, people do generally favour inclination over moral considerations. It is often said that people are at their best when circumstances are at their worst, that people tend to live up to their obligations in terribly demanding circumstances. Though I cannot imagine a workable procedure for settling the question decisively, I think it is at least plausible to claim that thoughtlessness and habit are greater obstacles to right action than personal sacrifice is, and that people would not fare so badly in clearly framed moral decisions that required great sacrifices.

Furthermore, even when people do act counter to morality, it does not show that they lack a good will, a commitment to act as duty requires. Being committed to morality, even committed to morality above all else, is compatible with acting immorally.

This is so because of the idea, which is both Kantian and common-sensical, that humans are subject to frailty, or weakness of will. Even when they are committed to a principle of acting as duty requires, they may find the pull of inclination too strong to resist. And the stronger the pull of inclination, the more prone they are to frailty. So in cases where morality requires great sacrifice or inclination provides great temptation, one could expect divergence from morality's commands. And a significant amount of divergence would still be compatible with the idea that many people have good wills.

[13] *Groundwork* 398–400 takes a different approach to the similar (but not identical) task of isolating cases in which a person is acting solely from the motive of duty. There, Kant just proposes cases in which the agent, by hypothesis, is stripped of all motives for the right action except the motive of duty.

The image called to mind when one thinks of weakness of will may be of an agent who wills mightily to do what she thinks best, but finds herself doing something else. But Kantian frailty does not come into play only in cases like this.[14] Frailty consists of being led astray, by inclination, from one's second-order maxim of always doing what duty requires. In a particular case, an agent suffering from frailty may not even think about what duty requires, because her frailty keeps her from so much as looking further than inclination. Or she may be self-deceptive, because she so much wants to satisfy inclination that she convinces herself that some action is not really her duty. These effects of frailty seem much more common than cases in which someone is fully aware of her duty and then chooses to satisfy inclination. Taking all such cases into account, frailty could explain a great many instances in which people seem to favour inclination over duty.

The picture that emerges of a human agent with good will is not of someone who has a commitment to morality, always keeps this commitment in mind, and acts on it no matter the sacrifice required. Such agents may be conceivable, but the typical human agent would be much more fallible, even if she had a good will. She would have a commitment to do her duty even when it requires great sacrifices. But her attention might wander, because of her particular interests and desires. That is the nature of beings who are subject to inclination. She might not recognize that some particular duty is required, or even that a situation is morally loaded, because she is distracted by her own interests. If circumstances lead her to focus clearly on the moral dimensions of some situation (for instance, if another person points out some morally relevant features), she will be much more likely to see what is required of her. And if she recognizes her duties, she is much more likely to perform them. But she might refuse to acknowledge her duties, because inclination leads her to deceive herself, or she might just not do what she acknowledges is required, because she fails to resist the pull of inclination. She probably will do what duty requires most of the time, and will always retain a commitment to doing so, but she will be far from morally flawless.

This picture of the human agent as imperfect, even if she has a good will, is an unavoidable part of Kant's view of human nature. A 'holy will' would inevitably act on moral principles, but such a holy will is only possible for a being who is not subject to inclinations that can lead it astray (G 439). And humans' natures are inevitably bound up with inclinations, affections, and passions that will tempt their possessor toward wrongdoing. The initial spur to the development of rational nature is the human tendency toward competition

14 Nor does weakness of will, on other conceptions, necessarily only play a role in such cases.

and 'unsocial sociability',[15] and it is only rational nature that makes it possible to have a good will, or any will at all. We have an inescapable predisposition to seek to satisfy our own desires, even contrary to moral requirements, and so all humans, 'even the best' will have within them a 'propensity to evil' (R 30). This does not mean humans will always do evil, but just that virtue, or a commitment to morality, will always face opposition. Even someone with a good will must always struggle to live up to her commitments, due to 'human nature, which is affected by inclinations because of which virtue can never settle down in peace and quiet with its maxims adopted once and for all but, if it is not rising, is unavoidably sinking' (MM 409). A human being can be committed to morality, and so have a good will, but because of human nature, even this virtuous human will inevitably fall short of perfection in her actions.

I think this picture of the flawed human agent who yet retains a good will should be familiar. I think many humans, probably most, roughly fit this picture. If so, then human good wills are priceless but not rare. And the good will reading of the humanity formulation does not seem so peculiar.

Unfortunately, although Kant has the resources to say human good wills are not rare, he in fact sometimes says the opposite. So the most I can claim is that Kant's theory suggests that good wills are common, not that Kant himself consistently says so.

He does make at least one statement that suggests good wills are not so rare. In *Anthropology* 295, he says, 'having character [*Charakter*] is the minimum requirement that can be expected of a reasonable person', and that it 'must be possible for the most ordinary human reason'. He has earlier identified character as a good will—an agent's commitment to 'definite practical principles that he has prescribed to himself irrevocably by his own reason', which has not merely price but 'intrinsic worth' (Anth 292). So he seems to be saying that a good will is not anything out of the ordinary.

But this is not actually his overall position in *Anthropology*. If character is the least we can expect, then many agents must be failing to live up this minimum standard, because Kant says character is 'a rare thing' (Anth 292).

Later in *Anthropology*, and in other works as well, he gives some specifics about what kind of people usually lack good wills.

In *Observations on the Feelings of the Beautiful and the Sublime*, Kant says, 'I hardly believe the fair sex is capable of principles. But in the place of it

[15] Immanuel Kant, 'Idea for a Universal History with a Cosmopolitan Purpose', in *Kant: Political Writings*, ed. Klaus Reich, trans. Hans Reiss (Cambridge: Cambridge University Press, 1970, 1991), 44–5.

Providence has put in their breast kind and benevolent sensations'.[16] In *The Educational Theory of Immanuel Kant*, he says women 'have but little character'.[17] In *Anthropology* he explains that women's basic pseudo-ethical principle is that 'what the world says is true, and what it does, good'. He adds that this principle is 'hard to unite with character in the strict sense of the term' (Anth 308). There is no disputing that he thinks women generally or always lack good wills.[18]

This appears to lead to the plausibility problem with the good will reading. As applied to women, the problem would be:

1. A good will is equivalent to humanity.
2. Since we must treat humanity as an end in itself, we must treat good wills as ends in themselves.
3. But good wills are rare, since more than half of all humans (namely women) lack them.
4. But (for reasons discussed in section 1 of this chapter), we must treat most or all humans as ends in themselves, even if many are not deserving of this respect.
5. So the good will reading is bizarre, since it requires us to treat everyone as if they possess humanity even though at least half of them do not.

One could avoid the bizarre tension by abandoning the good will reading, but one could also avoid it by abandoning the claim that women lack good wills.

And the latter is clearly more justified here. I take it that no one will accuse me of an ad hoc defence of the good will reading if I suggest we abandon Kant's statements that women cannot be the same kind of fully moral beings that men are (or sometimes are). His claim is not based on any sound data or theory, but rather on the premiss that nature gives women the end of propagating and refining the species (Anth 305–6), and on generalizations based on his (dubitable) social observation. It seems exactly the kind of claim that contemporary Kantians are, and should be, eager to burn quietly, along with the ideas that men must dominate in a domestic partnership (Anth 303, 309), that English people possess 'haughty rudeness' manifesting itself as 'spiteful behavior toward every other person' (Anth 311), or that 'scholarly women'

[16] Immanuel Kant, *Observations on the Feelings of the Beautiful and the Sublime*, trans. John T. Goldthwait (Berkeley and Los Angeles: University of California Press, 1960), 229.

[17] Immanuel Kant, *The Educational Theory of Immanuel Kant*, trans. Edward F. Buckner (Philadelphia: J. B. Lippincott, 1904), 222.

[18] Jean Rumsey addresses this topic in her article 'The Development of Character in Kant's Moral Theory', *Journal of the History of Philosophy*, 27/2 (Apr. 1989). Her article brought the issue and the texts on women to my attention.

use their books only as adornment, as they might wear a broken watch (Anth 307).

Kant is also most explicit in denying good will to young people. In *Anthropology* 294, he says that character, or good will, is acquired by a 'revolution' in one's basic principles, and that 'Perhaps there will be only a few who have attempted this revolution before their thirtieth year, and fewer still who have firmly established it before their fortieth year'. If it is true that most people younger than 40 lack good wills, it will give rise to the plausibility problem in the same way as the claim about women did. And it is somewhat tempting to dismiss Kant's position on young people as quickly. But it is worth taking a closer look at his evidence that people under 40 lack good wills. Kant's conclusion is based on the fact that possessing character or good will requires a 'revolution' in one's basic principles, and the additional, crucial premiss that one must be aware of such a dramatic revolution. Kant says,

> Since the act of establishing character, like a kind of rebirth, is a certain ceremony of making a vow to oneself, we must also assume that the solemnity of the act makes it and the moment when the transformation took place unforgettable to him, like the beginning of a new epoch. (Anth 294)

He adds that this sudden change is like 'an explosion'. Since this explosion of goodness is so memorable, we can conclude that anyone who does not remember such an event in her own life must not have a good will.

The problem, then, is even more serious than it first appeared. Presumably it is not only people under 40 who have not experienced this explosion. Such an event does not seem to be part of the experience of many people of any age, or at least it is not widely depicted in literature or song, or often discussed in academic circles. If the big bang theory of good will is correct, and yet most people have not experienced the explosion, then most people must not have good wills. Then, the good will reading of the humanity formulation would be bizarre. We must treat everyone as ends in themselves, as if they have good wills, even though very few people do. Of course, this problem can be avoided if the big bang theory of good wills is wrong, and it does seem to be wrong. Kant need not, and in fact cannot consistently, adhere to the idea that the acquisition of a good will is accompanied by acute and conspicuous sensations.

It is true that Kant says some of the same things about acquiring a good will in *Religion* as in *Anthropology*, but the similarities do not support the big bang theory of moral change. In *Religion*, Kant says that acquiring a good will, or switching from 'conformity with the prized principle of happiness' to 'the maxim of holiness of disposition', requires a 'revolution in the disposition of the human being' (R 47). This is because

We can not start out in the ethical training of our conatural moral predisposition to the good with an innocence which is natural to us but must rather begin from the presupposition of a depravity of our power of choice ... and, since the propensity to this [depravity] is inextirpable, with unremitting counteraction against it. (R 51)

To overcome the pull of self-love, or the priority of one's inclinations, always requires an effort, because their natural influence is so strong. Therefore Kant says that a 'revolution' is required to put the Categorical Imperative in place of the principle of seeking one's own happiness, which otherwise would dominate.[19]

But in *Religion* he most explicitly denies that we can be sure that this revolution has occurred. He says,

Assurance of this cannot of course be attained by the human being naturally, neither via immediate consciousness nor via the evidence of the life he has hitherto led, for the depths of his own heart (the subjective ground for his first maxims) are to him inscrutable. (R 51)

This is consistent with his frequent assertions that one cannot be sure of one's own basic moral disposition or fundamental maxim. We cannot have an 'immediate consciousness' of our moral disposition, but 'must at best infer it from the consequence it has on the conduct of our life' (R 71). And if we cannot know what our disposition is, we cannot know when it has changed.

Kant has good reason to say that one cannot know the nature of one's fundamental disposition. Even the existence of such a thing as a second-order principle of giving priority to either inclination or morality is something we must infer rather than observe. Given Kant's framework for thinking about rational actions at all, these dispositions or second-order principles must exist. Any action is performed for some reason. So suppose I face a choice in which my inclinations lead me toward one possible action but morality requires a different action. Say that I must choose between carefully grading some students' papers, which I really ought to do, or watching a basketball game on television, which, all things considered, I desire to do more. If I choose to watch basketball, my reason for choosing it is that I have an inclination (in this case, a desire) to do so. If I choose to grade papers, my reason is (by hypothesis) that I think it is the right thing to do. But I must have some reason for choosing whether to make inclination my reason for action or to make morality my reason for action. So I must have a second-order principle either of giving priority to acting as duty requires or of giving priority to satisfying my

19 He uses the word 'revolution' in R 47 and R 51, but elsewhere calls the same event a 'change of heart' ('Änderung des Herzens') (R 47, R 73–4), or a 'conversion' ('Sinnesänderung') (R 73–4).

inclinations.[20] The existence of these second-order principles, or dispositions, is something we deduce, not something we perceive.

If even their existence cannot be established by observation, so much the less can we directly observe which principle is dominant over the other.

Kant seems right about this basic idea that we cannot directly observe a person's character. It is not just that we cannot be absolutely certain of our own or others' moral characters. We seldom even think we have any non-inferential insight into a person's character. Occasionally, one might think one feels one own commitment to morality (or lack of it), in situations where acting morally requires some kind of sacrifice. But usually if we think about character, we think of it as something to be inferred from actions. And if an agent's disposition is something that is inferred, then revolutions of these dispositions must be inferred as well, not perceived.

It is quite reasonable to think that revolutions in one's basic disposition are not accompanied by a sudden, perceptible jolt. Ebeneezer Scrooge may have had a moral conversion that was both explosive and genuine, with supernatural help, but his case is not typical.[21] When people acquire a commitment to morality, it is usually a matter of them gradually becoming more sensitive to other individuals' concerns, then perhaps aware of more general moral considerations. Sudden resolutions to act morally are probably less reliable indicators of true moral improvement than this kind of gradual reform. If the steady improvement ends with the person having a deep commitment to doing as duty requires, then we could certainly call the improvement a revolution. It is just not a revolution that was accompanied by sudden sensations of radical change.

This fits with Kant's own statements about moral education in *Religion*. Kant describes the best methods for ensuring that 'the predisposition to the good is cultivated', and says that with the proper training 'the predisposition gradually becomes an attitude of mind, so that duty merely for itself begins to acquire in the apprentice's heart a noticeable importance' (R 48). This account of moral development in *Religion* seems both more plausible in its own right and more firmly rooted in fundamental elements of Kant's ethical theory than the big bang theory. Kant's rejection of moral fanaticism or 'enthusiasm' in MM 408–9 also suggests a rejection of the idea that dramatic, sudden outbursts of emotion are a reliable sign of genuine change of character. Rabid

[20] If I must have a reason for any rational choice, I must also have a reason for choosing my second-order principle. This notoriously perplexing issue has not been fully resolved, even by as impressive a work as Henry Allison's *Kant's Theory of Freedom* (Cambridge: Cambridge University Press, 1990).

[21] Charles Dickens, *A Christmas Carol*.

enthusiasm for morality is only the 'apparent strength of someone feverish'. In contrast,

> The true strength of virtue is a tranquil mind with a considered and firm resolution to put the law into practice. That is the state of health in the moral life, whereas an affect, even one aroused by the thought of what is good, is a momentary, sparkling phenomenon that leaves one exhausted. (MM 409)

Overall, it seems advisable to reject the big bang theory of moral change, as an idea that is not only implausible but also incompatible with Kant's more considered positions.

And if a revolution of character need not be accompanied by any explosive feelings of change, then the fact that most people have not had these feelings is no evidence that most people lack good wills. So we need not conclude that good wills are rare. And if good wills are not rare, then the good will reading does not lead to the peculiar conclusion that we must treat all humans as ends in themselves even though most of them are not really ends in themselves.

I have argued that good wills are not rare among actual humans, and that there are sound Kantian reasons to treat every minimally rational human with respect and benevolence even if some of them lack good wills. So the main intuitive obstacles to the good will reading have been removed. In the absence of such counterintuitive consequences, the textual and theoretical evidence in favour of the good will reading seems decisive. A good will is what we must treat as an end in itself.

PART II
The Humanity Formulation as a Moral Principle

6

The Argument for the Humanity Formula

A fully satisfactory reconstruction of Kant's argument for the humanity formulation has been elusive. Some elements of the argument are clear enough, but the most fundamental moves are quite cryptic. As a result, any attempt to explain the argument will involve some reconstruction and filling in, as opposed to strict interpretation and explanation. In this chapter I will propose a reconstruction of Kant's argument which I believe is true to the text, as far as the text goes, and which also lays the foundation for a proper understanding of the duties that follow from the humanity formulation.

Kant's argument has of course received attention from other commentators, and many of their ideas are quite sound. I borrow some of these ideas, particularly Korsgaard's idea of the argument as a 'regress on the conditions of value'.[1] But I think previous reconstructions of Kant's argument have been problematic in at least two important ways. They have relied on a non-Kantian concept of value in order to arrive at the conclusion that humanity must be treated as an end in itself, and they have taken the end in itself to be some minimal form of rationality, instead of a good will.

It is important to restrict the notion of value to its proper conceptual role in the argument for the humanity formulation, both to remain true to the Kantian idea that talk about value is a kind of shorthand for talk about the choices of rational beings, and to avoid misunderstandings about the more specific duties that follow from it. In particular, I will argue in Chapter 8 that relying on a non-Kantian concept of value to justify the humanity formulation will result in a misleadingly extreme view of our duties regarding others' rational natures and others' ends.

Besides attempting to reconstruct Kant's argument for the humanity formulation and forestalling possible confusions about the duties that follow from

[1] Christine Korsgaard, *Creating the Kingdom of Ends* (Cambridge: Cambridge University Press, 1996), 119–24.

it, I have another aim. My reconstruction of Kant's argument employs the good will reading of the humanity formulation, so in so far as my account is satisfactory, it will offer further support for the good will reading. If Kant's argument is more comprehensible given one reading of humanity than another, that is indirect evidence for the more useful reading.

1. Why There Must be Something that is an End in Itself

There are two general stages in Kant's argument for the humanity formulation. Kant first argues that if there is such a thing as a basic moral principle, then there must also be something that is an end in itself, because only an end in itself could ground a Categorical Imperative (G 427–8). Then he proposes that humanity or 'rational nature' is the only satisfactory candidate for the position of end in itself (G 428–9). The reasoning that underlies Kant's latter proposal is hard to decipher. But the arguments for the former claim are relatively clear, and provide important clues for understanding the more difficult argument that the end in itself must be rational nature. So in this section, as a first step toward reconstructing the complete argument for the humanity formulation, I will explain Kant's argument for the conditional claim that if there is such a thing as a basic moral principle, there must also be an end in itself.

Kant's arguments in the first two chapters of *Groundwork*, including the arguments regarding the end in itself, are not meant to stand independently of all everyday moral beliefs. Kant says in the preface to *Groundwork* that in the first two chapters his strategy is to 'proceed analytically from common cognition [of morality] to the determination of its supreme principle', that is, to see what the content of the Categorical Imperative must be if it is to fit with basic everyday beliefs about the nature of morality (G 392). He says he will leave aside the project of establishing that there really are such things as moral principles—that morality is not a 'mere phantom of the brain'—until chapter 3 (G 445). His point in beginning with the ordinary person's views about morality is not that we should take account of supposed intuitions about what is morally right or wrong in particular cases, and then accept whatever moral 'principles' best accommodate the 'data' of these intuitions. In fact, that strategy is exactly the 'Popular Philosophy' that he denounces in chapter 2 (G 406–11). Instead, Kant's method in the first two chapters is to start from fundamental ideas about the nature of moral requirements, in order to see what a principle would have to be like in order to count as a moral principle. In his argument for the universal law formulation of the Categorical Imperative, Kant relies on the everyday notion that a moral principle must apply equally and inescapably to everyone (must bring 'with it that necessity which we require of a law'), in order to reach (supposedly) the conclusion that the content of the Categorical Imperative must be 'act only in accordance with that maxim which you can at the same time will that it become a universal law' (G 420–1).

In arguing for the humanity formulation, Kant follows a similar strategy. He provisionally assumes that there are such things as basic moral principles, and points out that the only thing that could count as a moral principle or 'supreme practical principle' is a Categorical Imperative, or a 'universal practical law' that unconditionally demands compliance from everyone (G 428). Kant goes on to argue that if there is such a Categorical Imperative, then there must also be something that is an end in itself.

To understand how Kant reaches this conclusion, it is necessary to look at his discussion of different types of ends. An end is a ground of the will's self-determination, or, in more common terms, a reason that a person adopts for acting. A subjective end is an end that is based on inclination. For instance, I might have a desire to see the Taj Mahal in person and so make it my end to travel to India and visit the Taj Mahal. Kant also calls such ends 'relative ends', since they can vary from person to person. Not everyone will necessarily have any given subjective end, nor is there any necessary reason a person ought to adopt such an end if she lacks the inclination that would serve as its basis. Kant contrasts these subjective or relative ends with what he calls an 'objective end' or an 'end in itself'. An objective end does not depend on a person's inclinations, but rather is 'given by reason alone' (G 427). Since this end is required by reason alone, it 'must hold equally for all rational beings', meaning it provides every rational being with a reason to act in certain ways, regardless of her inclinations (G 427). But why must we suppose that such a thing as an objective end, or end in itself, actually exists?

This is the point at which Kant relies crucially on the idea borrowed from everyday moral thought, that if there are any such things as moral principles, they must apply necessarily to every rational being (G 419–25). That is, if there are moral principles they must be Categorical Imperatives. A Categorical Imperative is a principle that tells every agent how she must act, regardless of her inclinations. Kant takes it as obvious that in every action, an agent always acts for some end.[2] So there can be a principle

[2] Kant's clearest statement of this is in MM 385, where he says, 'Every action, therefore, has its end', but it is a suppressed premiss in the argument in *Groundwork*.

that applies necessarily to every agent only if there is something that is necessarily an end for every agent. Relative ends, or 'ends that a rational being proposes at his discretion merely as effects of his actions (material ends)', cannot unconditionally demand action from every agent, because they are ends that an agent may have or not, depending on her inclinations.[3] Kant says, 'their mere relation to a specially constituted faculty of desire on the part of the subject gives them their worth, which can therefore furnish no universal principles, no principles valid and necessary for all rational beings and also for every volition, that is, no practical laws'. Therefore, if there are any genuine moral principles there also must be something that is an end in itself, an end that every agent must recognize as a reason for action regardless of her inclinations. Kant summarizes the argument again in *Metaphysics of Morals* 381, saying, 'For since men's sensible inclinations tempt them to ends (the matter of choice) that can be contrary to duty, lawgiving reason can in turn check their influence only by a moral end set up against the ends of inclination, an end that must therefore be given *a priori*, independent of inclinations'. I think Kant's argument succeeds in proving his main stated conclusion, that if there is a Categorical Imperative, there must be some end that is not dependent on inclination. But Samuel Kerstein offers a substantial objection.

Kerstein argues that the existence of a Categorical Imperative does not entail the existence of an end with absolute value (or unconditional worth).[4] I believe Kerstein's objection partially succeeds, but is not fatal to Kant's overall argument for the humanity formulation. Kerstein asks us to imagine a Categorical Imperative that says, 'Maximize your power over rational beings', a principle Kerstein calls PW.[5] This thought experiment is unobjectionable, since at this point in *Groundwork* we are examining the implications of the existence of any possible Categorical Imperative, not just a specifically Kantian formulation. PW (or any Categorical Imperative that demands fundamental competition among rational beings, such as 'seek your own happiness regardless of effects on others') seems not to give all agents one and the same end. Kerstein takes the 'agent-neutral value' of an end to be part of what Kant wants to establish by calling something an end in itself, and Kerstein seems correct to conclude that the existence of a Categorical Imperative does not by itself establish that there must be something that is an end with agent-neutral value. If PW were a Categorical Imperative, then each person would have her own power (not

[3] G 428. The longer quotation that follows is from the same page.

[4] Samuel Kerstein, *Kant's Search for the Supreme Principle of Morality* (Cambridge: Cambridge University Press, 2002), 49–54.

[5] Ibid. 49.

the existence of power as such) as an end of ultimate value, and there would not necessarily be any end they all share.

And Kerstein is correct in thinking that throughout the passage in question, *Groundwork* 427–8, Kant sounds as if he is trying to prove the existence of one single end that all rational beings must share regardless of their inclinations. Kant fails to prove this, for just the reasons Kerstein gives. But Kant is also right about something significant. Kerstein's argument does not undermine Kant's claim that if there is a Categorical Imperative, then there must be some end that is given by reason rather than being based on inclination. If we imagine Kerstein's principle PW, then we would imagine, as Kerstein himself does (for purposes of this thought experiment only), that every agent unconditionally would be given an end of pursuing her own power over other rational beings. This end would be given to each agent by her own *Wille* regardless of whether each agent felt like dominating others. Many people might wish just to acquiesce to others or to become hermits, but they would be rationally compelled to pursue power by the principle PW legislated by their own *Wille*. The end of accruing power would be unconditional and absolute in Kant's primary sense, of being given to agents unconditionally by their own reason, independently of their desires.

So, should Kant's argument here be considered a success or a failure? Kant does not establish all that he thinks he does, and in fact he does not consider the possibility of an end like the one Kerstein proposes, given by reason rather than by inclination, but not the same end for all rational beings. But Kant has softened up the reader for his important later claims. He has shown that if there is a Categorical Imperative, there must be some end or ends given by reason alone, which leads to the question of what this end could be. He has also begun to pave the way for his later distinction between autonomous and heteronomous moral theories, since heteronomous theories are distinguished by basing all reasons for moral action on contingent, inclination-based ends (G 440–4). Kant has not yet ruled out the possibility that the Categorical Imperative might be some principle of competition, like PW. But I think he does have the resources to do so. Below, in section 3, I suggest a strategy that Kant might have employed (though he did not explicitly employ it) to show that the Categorical Imperative cannot set people at odds by giving them different, rationally dictated, unconditional ends. The basic idea I propose there is that Kant is not ruling out all moral preconceptions in his search for the Categorical Imperative, but instead is arguing that if there is any Categorical Imperative, it must match our most basic everyday ideas about the nature of moral principles. One of those ideas is that morality is meant to unite us rather than to set us at each other's throats.[6] If so, the Categorical Imperative must give us an end that is one and the same for us all.

If Kant succeeds in showing that the existence of a Categorical Imperative is conceptually dependent on non-inclination-based ends (as I think he does) and if he could eventually rule out all competitive principles such as PW as candidates for a Categorical Imperative, then even if Kerstein's objection succeeds, it is not fatal. Minor extensions of Kant's arguments show that if there is a Categorical Imperative, there must be an end in itself that is not only independent of inclination, but also an end for all rational beings.

2. Kantian Background for Claims about an End in Itself

The claim that there is some non-optional end that is required by reason is subject to serious misunderstanding, if not taken in the proper Kantian context.

One potential misunderstanding may arise because when one thinks of an end, it is natural to think of something that is to be brought about or attained. To earn a college degree, to win a medal in the Olympics, to amass a million dollars, or to become a chef are all easily recognizable ends that some humans have. In each of these cases, the end is a state of affairs to be brought about, and (to the extent that one obeys the Hypothetical Imperative) to have such an end will involve taking steps to bring about the relevant state of affairs. But an objective end, or end in itself, is not like this. Kant says that instead of being something that is to be brought about, an end in itself is 'the supreme limiting condition of the freedom of action of every human being' (G 430) or 'the limiting condition of all merely relative and arbitrary ends' (G 437). Kant means here that the end in itself or objective end is not some object or state of affairs that is to be brought into existence. An end is always some sort of reason for acting, but in the case of the end in itself the action is not to bring the end into existence. An end in itself provides a reason for other types of action. Specifically, one ought never to subjugate an end in itself to one's subjective, inclination-based ends, meaning one ought never to destroy

[6] Kerstein considers Kant's claims that morality must give us an end in common and argues that the claim is unjustified. But Kerstein does not consider the justification I give. See ibid. 50–4. However, I think the framework Kerstein develops throughout much of his book rules out a fundamental moral principle like PW, mainly because it fails to meet one Kantian criterion of a satisfactory moral principle, namely that 'a plausible set of duties (relative to ordinary moral cognition) can be derived from the principle' (ibid. 161).

or compromise an end in itself in order to satisfy one's desires or passions. So Kant says the end in itself 'must here be thought not as an end to be effected but as an independently existing end, and hence thought only negatively, that is, as that which must never be acted against' (G 437).

This is important, because if all ends were goals to be brought about, then given that Kant goes on to argue that rational nature is the end in itself, he would be committed to the absurd idea that we are obligated to maximize the number of rational beings in the world. Kant denies that all ends are of this sort, goals to be brought into existence. But he later seems to reconsider the strong claim he makes in *Groundwork* that an end in itself is in no sense an end to be brought about. In *Metaphysics of Morals* he amends his position, saying that 'it is in itself a duty for a man to make his end the perfection belonging to man as such (properly speaking to humanity)' (MM 386). The duties of self-perfection, like most of the duties Kant describes in *Metaphysics of Morals*, are based on the duty of treating humanity as an end in itself, and in one sense the duties of self-perfection are duties to bring something about. They are duties to bring about a more perfect self. Kant says we have a duty to increase our 'natural perfection', or to cultivate our natural abilities, and also to increase our 'moral perfection', or our commitment to morality (MM 391–3, 444–8). But Kant is careful to clarify that these are only duties to make oneself better, not generally to bring more perfectly rational natures into the world. He says that 'it is a contradiction for me to make another's perfection my end and consider myself under an obligation to promote this' (MM 386). This is because each of us can only perfect himself, and it is 'self-contradictory to require that I do (make it my duty to do) something that only the other himself can do'. Kant is aware that one person's actions can affect another's, of course—he says we have a duty not to tempt others to immorality, and in *Metaphysics of Morals* he devotes an appendix to 'Teaching Ethics'—but he is deeply committed to the idea that each of us is fundamentally responsible for her own character, and can choose her own principles and actions.[7] So our duty to perfect ourselves is not equivalent to a general duty to bring about more perfectly rational natures, and Kant's amendment to his *Groundwork* position that the end in itself is merely a negative end does not lead to the absurd duty to maximize the number of rational beings in the world.

It may seem odd, to some, that an end can be something other than a state of affairs to be brought about. But if this seems odd, it is mainly because Kant's basic concept of value is fundamentally different from a currently prevalent

[7] Kant discusses the duty not to tempt others in MM 394. The section on moral education is MM 477–84.

concept. Kant takes rational choice as fundamentally prior to value rather than the opposite.[8] Rational agents choose to adopt some ends because of their desires, sentiments, likes, dislikes, or other psychological states. And these ends are valuable because they are chosen by rational agents, provided that the agents truly are sufficiently rational to choose in ways that are consistent with moral principles. To have value is just to be an end chosen by a rational being. In contrast, contemporary philosophers influenced by consequentialism and by decision theory will find it natural to think that value is conceptually prior to rational choice. More specifically, they will think that the rationally and/or morally required action in any given situation is the action that will bring about the most valuable state of affairs. So identifying valuable states of affairs must be conceptually prior to identifying required actions. On this latter, currently dominant, view of value, it is indeed peculiar to think of an end that is simply a limiting condition on the pursuit of subjective ends. If value is that which should be brought about, then it is natural to think that the only importance an end could have is for it to have value as something to be brought about. But Kant does not begin by supposing that this is the only importance an end could have. Subjective ends are ends that are to be brought about in order to satisfy some agent, and to call them valuable is a way to capture the idea that some agent seeks to bring about the ends. But the end in itself has a different kind of importance. It provides a reason for agents never to destroy the end in itself, never to sacrifice it for the sake of subjective ends. To say that this end in itself has value (in fact, an incomparably high value) is just a way to capture the requirements of how to act with regard to the end in itself. And these requirements do not include maximizing the number of things that are ends in themselves.

So if it appears that Kant is saying something incoherent in maintaining that the end in itself is necessarily an end for everyone and yet is not something to be brought about, the solution lies in Kant's concept of value. And keeping this concept of value clearly in mind is also the antidote to some otherwise reasonable misunderstandings of the duties that follow from the humanity formulation. In Chapter 8, I will examine these accounts of the duties that supposedly follow from the humanity formulation, and will argue that they are mistaken as interpretations of Kant, because they make moral requirements depend on a conceptually prior notion of value.

If a properly Kantian concept of value is so important, both in explaining how an end in itself can be a 'negative end' and in keeping the duties straight that follow from the humanity formulation, then it is important to make sure

[8] See my Chapter 3, section 3 for specific textual references.

that value plays only a properly Kantian role in reconstructing the argument for the humanity formulation. And this means that the argument cannot rely on claims about humanity's value in order to reach the conclusion that it must be an end in itself. Only after establishing, on other grounds, that it is rationally required to treat humanity in certain ways (as an end in itself) is it then legitimate to paraphrase these requirements in terms of value. So the claims that humanity has 'absolute value', or 'objective value', or incomparably high value must follow from independent arguments for the humanity formulation, rather than being premisses in the argument that shows humanity must be treated always as an end in itself.

Kant himself may appear to flout this requirement. He uses the word 'Wert' (translated sometimes as 'value' and sometimes as 'worth') eight times in the paragraph immediately prior to the paragraph containing his statement of the humanity formulation, and once each in the two paragraphs before that (G 427–8). This makes it seem that either Kant's argument is flawed or (more likely) my claim that the argument must not depend on appeals to value is misguided. But I think there is no serious difficulty here. Kant's atypical concept of value is vital to many of the arguments of *Groundwork*, including the argument for the humanity formulation, but Kant is still struggling to articulate the concept, and does not explicitly and forcefully do so until the later *Critique of Practical Reason* (C2 57–63). But despite the fact that Kant's concept of value as conceptually dependent on the choices of rational agents is still emerging in *Groundwork*, he does embrace the concept in some passages (G 414, 436), and I think all the major arguments can be reconstructed in ways consistent with it.

This includes the arguments for the claims that there must be an end in itself and that humanity is that end. In *Groundwork* 428, the paragraph leading up to the humanity formulation, Kant's talk of value could all be translated into talk about subjective and objective ends, without losing his point. Kant says that subjective ends, ends based on inclination, have conditional value, or relative value. This means such ends only have value for an agent with the relevant inclination. In contrast, Kant says an end in itself or objective end has absolute value. This means it is valuable to every rational agent. Kant argues that if nothing is an end in itself, then 'nothing of absolute worth would be found anywhere' and so there could not be a Categorical Imperative—'if all worth were conditional and therefore contingent, then no supreme practical principle for reason could be found anywhere' (G 428). But this is a point that Kant has already made in *Groundwork* 427–8, without relying on value terms. The idea is that no universally necessary principle of action can be based on subjective ends, since an agent adopts subjective ends because of inclination, and so a principle of action would not apply to an agent who lacked the relevant inclination. If there is a Categorical Imperative, it must be based on an objective end, an end that every agent is rationally required to recognize as a reason for acting, regardless of her inclinations. Putting the point in terms of value is Kant's way of trying to reiterate his position in a vocabulary that the reader may find more familiar. Kant's use of value terms in the paragraphs leading to the humanity formulation does not show that his argument depends fundamentally on appeals to value.[9]

And this is fortunate. A deep point of Kant's practical philosophy is that value depends on rational choice, and part of what makes choices rational is the moral principles with which the agent regulates her choices. Then it would be circular to argue that something should be treated as an end in itself because of its special value. For this reason, and to avoid misunderstandings of the more particular duties that follow from the basic moral principle, it is important to reconstruct Kant's argument for the humanity formulation in a way that does not appeal to prior claims about the value of humanity. Kant's preliminary argument, that something must be an end in itself if there is to be any Categorical Imperative, meets this criterion of not relying on claims about value (despite the fact that Kant does lapse into putting his point in terms of value in one passage). But to show that something must be an end in itself is not yet to show that 'humanity' is such an end. In the next section I will reconstruct Kant's argument for humanity as the end in itself, in a way that does not depend on appeals to the value of humanity.

3. Why is Humanity the End in Itself?

Kant says that rational beings are ends in themselves (later he amends this by saying it is rational nature, which is possessed by rational beings, that is an end in itself). He first simply asserts that a rational being is an end in itself, in *Groundwork* 428, but he then offers two arguments for this claim.

The first argument is in 428, and seems to be an argument by elimination. This is the argument that Kant puts in terms of value, but it can be paraphrased into terms of ends and action. Objects of inclination, or subjective ends, are not necessary ends for everyone, since someone without the appropriate inclinations would have no reason to seek the object. Inclinations themselves do not have absolute value, or value in every possible circumstance, Kant maintains, meaning that not everyone has a necessary reason to seek to

[9] See also G 444 and MM 385 for other statements of the argument that do not depend on claims about value.

retain any particular inclination or acquire any given new inclination.[10] Since acquiring or satisfying an inclination is not a demand of reason that applies to all rational beings, no inclination can be an end in itself. Non-rational beings are only valuable as means, so they do not provide every rational agent with reasons to treat them in any given ways. Since subjective ends, inclinations themselves, and non-rational beings are all unsuited to be ends in themselves, only rational beings can be ends in themselves.

This argument is not particularly powerful.[11] Charitably, one could take it that Kant is merely trying to bring out and reinforce views that most people will share, rather than trying to convince a determined sceptic. But even so, Kant seems to be taking too much for granted. In particular, many current champions of increased moral status for animals will deny Kant's claim that non-rational beings are mere things and can be treated solely as means to one's ends.

But Kant immediately follows the argument by elimination with a second argument for the claim that humanity, or rational nature, must be the end in itself (G 428–9). This argument avoids the obvious problems of the argument by elimination, but it does so at the cost of being so compressed as to be largely mysterious. Kant certainly gives some signs that he takes it to be a sound deductive argument, using the word 'therefore',[12] but it is difficult to see exactly what the argument is. He is talking about what the content of the Categorical Imperative or 'practical law' must be like, and says,

> The ground of this principle is: Rational nature exists as an end in itself. This is the way in which a human being necessarily conceives his own existence, and it is therefore so far a subjective principle of human actions. But it is also the way in which every other rational being conceives his existence, on the same rational ground which holds also for me; hence it is at the same time an objective principle, from which, since it is a supreme practical ground, it must be possible to derive all laws for the will. The practical imperative will therefore be the following: Act in such a way that you treat humanity, whether in your own person or in any other person, always at the same time as an end, never merely as a means.

Several things are puzzling about this argument, if it is an argument. A fully satisfactory reconstruction would need to explain the most important features

[10] Kant goes further than this, saying that every rational being must wish to be free of inclination. This seems overzealous, and Kant himself later seems to recant this claim. In *Religion* 58, he says that 'Considered in themselves, natural inclinations are good, and to try to extirpate them would not only be futile but harmful and blameworthy as well'.

[11] Allen Wood goes into some detail about which aspects of the argument are more plausible and which less plausible. Allen Wood, *Kant's Ethical Thought* (Cambridge: Cambridge University Press, 1999), 122–4.

[12] In German, 'also'.

of the argument, which are quite unclear in the original passage. It would need to explain what reason there is to suppose that every agent 'necessarily' conceives of herself as an end in herself, and what is involved in conceiving of herself in this way. And once it explained why each agent must conceive of herself that way (why treating humanity as an end in itself is a 'subjective' principle), it would still need to explain why she should also conceive of other agents as ends in themselves too (why it is an 'objective' principle). And a satisfactory reconstruction would need to do all this without relying on claims about the value of humanity. Claims about the incomparably high value of humanity should, strictly, be used only to capture conceptually prior ideas about the humanity formulation's demands that humanity be treated as an end in itself.

The argument in 429 begins with the claim that each rational agent necessarily takes her rational nature to be an end in itself. Since an agent thinks of herself in this way, treating her own rational nature as an end in itself is 'so far a subjective principle of human action'. But this claim is already puzzling. Kant's use of 'subjective' ('subjektives') here must be inconsistent with the definition he has just offered in 428. There he says 'subjective' means something like 'based on inclinations'. A subjective end is an end adopted because one has an inclination toward it. But here in 429 he cannot mean that a principle of treating one's own humanity as an end in itself is based on inclination. It would not be a *necessary* principle of action if it were based on an agent's inclinations.[13] Inclinations are all contingent, so there could at least in theory be a rational agent who lacked the inclination that led her to act on the principle. Instead of using 'subjective' here to mean 'inclination-based', I think he is using it in a more common, non-technical sense, to say that the principle has to do with one particular individual. The principle has as its content only the agent's own rational nature, and applies to the agent's own actions. That is, she thinks her own rational nature is an end in itself, but so far there is no mention of how she will regard others or how they will regard her.

Nevertheless, the principle is still empirically false. Kant rightly acknowledges throughout his writings that it is empirically possible for an agent to fail to treat her own rational nature as an end in itself. Real agents sometimes act immorally. They act contrary to the Categorical Imperative, and one of the ways to violate the Categorical Imperative is to fail to treat one's own humanity as an end in itself. Instead of being an empirical claim about how actual agents necessarily act, Kant's statement is describing the manner in which agents are rationally required to act. It could be seen as a sort of thought experiment.

[13] In G 431, Kant himself makes this point about the humanity formulation as a whole.

Kant is saying that if we imagine any *rational* agent, we will see that she would necessarily act in certain as-yet-unspecified ways with regard to her own humanity.

But even if I am correct so far, this is just to decipher the meaning of 'subjective' in Kant's claim that treating one's own humanity as an end in itself is a necessary subjective principle. It is not yet to show what is involved in treating one's own humanity as an end in itself, nor why each rational agent should take herself as having reason to accept this requirement unconditionally.

Christine Korsgaard provides a strategy that is helpful in deciphering Kant's argument for this 'subjective principle' of action. She says 'the argument is intended as a regress on the conditions' of the value of our ends.[14]

By this, she means that she will begin by asking what it is that makes one's ends valuable. At this point, she means relative ends. The search for something that serves as the necessary and sufficient condition of the value of all relative ends will lead to the end in itself as well, she believes. So if I have an end, for instance the end of acquiring a roast beef sandwich, what makes that end valuable? A first guess would be to say that it has value because of my inclination for it, in this case because of my desire to eat the sandwich. But inclination cannot be a sufficient condition for the goodness of the end. An agent can have inclinations that conflict with her happiness, where happiness is understood as a package of significant ends. A craving for a roast beef sandwich could conflict with her end of lowering her cholesterol count, and the lower cholesterol count could be much more important to her than the fleeting pleasure of consumption. In such a case, the end will lack value despite being based on an inclination. Korsgaard sees the outline of this reasoning in Kant's dismissal of inclination and objects of inclination as the condition of the value of our ends.[15] Her proposal is that since we cannot find any other plausible candidate to serve as the sufficient condition of the value of an agent's ends, we must assume that rational choice itself is this condition. She says,

> since we still *do* make choices and have the attitude that what we choose is good in spite of our incapacity to find the unconditioned condition of the object's goodness in this (empirical) regress upon the conditions, it must be that we are supposing that rational choice itself *makes* its object good.[16]

By the failure of the 'empirical regress' she apparently means that no sort of explanatory psychology can explain what it is that makes an agent's ends good.

[14] Korsgaard, *Creating the Kingdom of Ends*, 120.

[15] Ibid. 120, 121. [16] Ibid. 122.

No desire, affection, liking, or disliking can be the necessary and sufficient condition of the value of our ends. Since we are out of other options, we must conclude that it is simply our choosing that makes a chosen end good. Each rational agent must think of her rational choice of ends as the necessary and sufficient condition of the ends' value. So, as a conclusion, Korsgaard says that 'If you overturn the *source* of the goodness of your end, neither your end nor the action which aims at it can possibly be good, and your action will not be fully rational'.[17] This is because if the agent's power of choice is the necessary condition of the value of his ends, and she sacrifices it, then her other ends will all lack value. She would then be trading her power of choice for ends that will lack value.

Korsgaard has proposed a valuable strategy, when she emphasizes that it is never worthwhile to sacrifice one's rational nature to achieve subjective ends. I think this is a key element of Kant's argument for the 'subjective principle' of treating humanity as an end in itself. But Korsgaard's reconstruction seems problematic in two important ways. My first objection will no doubt be predictable. I believe her regress argument misidentifies the ultimate condition of all value. It is not simply the power to set ends (*Willkür*) but rather the entire, properly ordered will of a being who is committed to regulating *Willkür* with *Wille*. The second and more fundamental way in which Korsgaard's reconstruction is problematic is that she makes the principle of treating one's own rational nature as an end in itself depend on a claim about value, namely that an agent's own rational nature has unconditional and incomparable value for herself.

My arguments for taking the ultimate necessary condition of all value to be a good will are familiar, based on texts I have already cited and discussed extensively in Chapter 3. Kant does not think that all end-setting confers value. Instead, he thinks that the setting of (contingent) ends confers value only when the will that sets the ends is a good will. A truly immoral person's ends do not in fact have value. This idea is expressed in Kant's position throughout his moral philosophy that the highest good is happiness in proportion to virtue, and that virtue is the necessary condition of the worthiness to be happy.[18] Kant is even more explicit in *Groundwork*, when he begins the book with the claims that a good will is both the only thing good in all circumstances, and also the necessary condition of the value of all other goods (G 397). The setting of ends does not confer value in all cases, so the ultimate necessary condition of all

[17] Korsgaard, *Creating the Kingdom of Ends*, 123.

[18] See my Chapter 3, section 4 for a more thorough discussion of this. For textual references, see C1 A808–15, B 836–43, R 5, 'What is Orientation in Thinking?' 139, C2 108–20, C3 450.

value is not the power of choice, or *Willkür*. It is a good will. At one point in her regress argument Korsgaard mentions the opening claim of *Groundwork*, that a good will is the condition of the value of other goods.[19] She uses this point to show (rightly) that Kant would not regard consistency with one's own happiness to be a sufficient condition for the value of an end. But then, after dismissing happiness as a contender, she oddly takes the question of what could serve as the condition of the value of an agent's ends as still unresolved, despite the seemingly decisive quotation from *Groundwork*. She searches for another possible answer, and concludes that the only possibility left is that (minimally) rational choice, or end-setting, is what confers value.[20] In fact, the most textually justified conclusion of her regress argument would be that a good will is the necessary and sufficient condition of all value, because it is the exercise of a properly ordered will, not just any exercise of *Willkür,* that confers value on one's ends.

But there is another, even more fundamental problem with Korsgaard's presentation of the regress argument. After establishing that rational nature (whether of a more minimal or a fuller sort) is the necessary condition of the value of all other ends, she maintains that this implies that rational nature must itself have an incomparable and unconditional value. Then she concludes that since it does have this special value, you must treat it as an end 'wherever you find it (in your own person or that of another)'.[21] Korsgaard relies on a claim about the special value of rational nature in order to establish that each of us must treat all rational nature as an end in itself, and this is problematic in several ways. Most generally, it seems contrary to Kant's conception of value, that value is a way of expressing prior claims about the choices of rational agents. As a textual point, it is worth noting that in the paragraph containing Kant's statement of the humanity formulation, Kant says he is looking for a 'supreme practical principle', not a claim about absolute or unconditional value, and Kant's first move is to look for a 'subjective principle of action'. Furthermore, employing a value claim to argue for the humanity formulation leads to a problem in trying to use the humanity formulation to arrive at more particular duties. As I will argue in Chapter 8, if one employs a prior claim about humanity's value to establish the humanity formulation, then the humanity formulation leads to

[19] Korsgaard, *Creating the Kingdom of Ends*, 121.

[20] On 123. Korsgaard acknowledges that her conclusion looks inconsistent with Kant's claim that only a good will has unconditional value. But she does not provide a satisfying resolution of the apparent inconsistency. See my Chapter 2, section 2 discussion of the attempt to reconcile a minimal reading with Kant's claims about a good will.

[21] Korsgaard, *Creating the Kingdom of Ends*, 123. The parenthetical phrase is Korsgaard's.

radically overblown duties (roughly consequentialist duties, in fact) regarding rational nature and the ends set by rational agents. There is also a more specific problem with the regress argument if one takes it to establish first that rational nature has a special value and that it therefore must be treated as an end in itself. The specific problem is that it is not clear that one must attribute an unconditional value to something that is the condition of all other value. Samuel Kerstein states this worry succinctly, saying, 'Korsgaard does not explain what would be irrational in the agent's holding that though his reflective choice of an object is what confers value on it, reflective choice is not unconditionally valuable'.[22] So, for both textual and philosophical reasons, it seems preferable to arrive at the 'subjective principle' of treating one's rational nature as an end in itself without relying on an intermediate claim about rational nature's value.

And in fact, Korsgaard's regress argument seems well suited for this task. The natural conclusion of the regress argument is a point about some fundamental requirements regarding how to treat rational nature, not a point about value. Although these requirements can later be interpreted into talk about value, it is misleading to treat value as the primary concern. The basic conclusion of the regress argument is that one 'can never act against it [rational nature] without contradiction', because 'if you overturn the *source* of goodness of your end, neither your end nor the action that aims at it can possibly be good, and your action will not be fully rational'.[23] If rational nature (minimally rational nature, on Korsgaard's account, more fully rational nature according to my account) is the necessary condition of the value of all of your ends, then it does not make sense to sacrifice your rational nature in order to achieve contingent ends that will be worthless once achieved. This conclusion does not require an intermediate step making a claim about the value of rational nature. It does rely on a claim that mentions value, namely that the objects one seeks because of inclination will lack value if one compromises one's rational nature in order to gain them. But this is just to rule out one kind of supposed justification for actions that compromise one's rational nature. It is just saying that it is incoherent to appeal to the supposed value of a contingent end in order to justify undermining one's own rational nature. It is not making a substantial claim about what has value (rational nature, or contingent ends), but rather is barring a certain kind of supposed justification which makes an illegitimate appeal to the supposedly independent value of

[22] Kerstein, *Kant's Search*, 59. See also Wood, *Kant's Ethical Thought*, 130. See also Jerome Schneewind's rejection of Korsgaard's argument for the 'intrinsic goodness' of rational nature, Jerome Schneewind, 'Korsgaard and the Unconditional in Morality', *Ethics*, 109 (Oct. 1996), 39.

[23] Korsgaard, *Creating the Kingdom of Ends*, 123.

contingent ends. So the regress argument can lead to a 'subjective principle of action' without relying fundamentally on a claim about the value of the end in itself.

But more needs to be said about exactly the requirements that follow from the regress argument. I argue above that the necessary condition of the value of all ends is that they be set not just by the exercise of *Willkür*, but by a properly ordered will in which *Willkür* is regulated by the demands of *Wille*. This does not mean that, as a matter of empirical fact, agents in the real world will never set ends without concern for the moral principles legislated by their own *Wille*. We know that agents do this sometimes, because they are imperfectly rational. But since we are trying to reach conclusions about which actions would be rationally justified or required, it is appropriate, as a thought experiment, to posit a hypothetical agent who is in fact rational and so will never act in ways that are unjustified. Such an agent will not sacrifice her fully rational nature in order to achieve any amount of subjective ends. Her subjective ends only have value if she wills the ends with her fully rational nature, so if she destroys her fully rational nature, her contingent ends will lack value when she realizes them. The claim here is not that it is impossible for someone to sacrifice her rational nature in order to achieve her subjective ends, but that it is impossible to do so rationally.

It is important that a properly ordered will, in its entirety, is the end in itself which should not be sacrificed for the sake of inclinations. If this properly ordered will, or fully rational nature, is the end in itself, then there are two ways to violate the subjective principle of not destroying one's own rational nature. The most common way to give up one's fully rational nature, or good will, is to choose to act contrary to the moral law, and so lose the commitment to morality that marks off good wills from just minimally rational wills.[24] One's subjective ends have value only if set under the direction of moral principles, so it does not make sense to choose to act immorally in order to achieve ends that are worthless. Consistently with this reading of the 'subjective' component of the humanity formulation, Kant makes clear later that the humanity formulation implies a duty of moral self-perfection, to strive always to make self-legislated moral principles a sufficient reason for action (MM 387, 392–3, 446–7). The second way to sacrifice one's own rational nature is to destroy oneself or one's minimal rational nature altogether. This kind of sacrifice—cases of suicide, or placing oneself in situations that involve

[24] As mentioned earlier, in Chapters 3 and 5, it is not true from the standpoint of theoretical reason that one necessarily loses one's commitment to morality just by once choosing to act immorally. But from the deliberative viewpoint of practical reason, one must take oneself to be abandoning the unconditional commitment to morality if one chooses to act immorally.

great risk of losing one's life for inclinations' sake, or taking permanently mind-altering drugs or the like—is probably what most naturally comes to mind when one thinks of sacrificing one's rational nature, if one does not keep in mind that Kant's idea of rational nature encompasses much more than minimal rationality. Such cases do indeed seem to violate the 'subjective principle' component of the humanity formulation, since they are cases of destroying one's own rational nature. And Kant of course thinks that every rational agent has duties to herself to avoid these kinds of actions, duties based on the humanity formulation.[25] But the more pressing everyday restriction imposed by the subjective component of the humanity formulation is to avoid lapsing into irrationality, by failing to give adequate weight to morality.

So, the subjective principle that is suggested by the regress argument is to avoid sacrificing one's commitment to morality for the sake of satisfying inclination, and to avoid sacrificing oneself or one's minimal rational powers altogether for the sake of inclination. In both cases, the basis for the restriction is that to trade a fully rational will for the satisfaction of inclinations is rationally unjustified. The only apparent strategy for attempting to justify such a trade would be that the satisfaction of inclination is valuable in itself, but that strategy is not viable. It is exactly what Kant rules out by maintaining that contingent ends are only valuable if set by a properly ordered will, or in other words by claiming that a good will is the necessary condition of the value of all contingent ends. So a modified version of Korsgaard's regress argument does establish a 'subjective principle' regarding how one must treat one's own fully rational nature.

But this leaves a further step in reconstructing Kant's argument for the humanity formulation, namely establishing that treating humanity as an end in itself is an 'objective principle' as well as a subjective one. The support Kant offers for the objective principle is that in the same way that every agent must think of her own rational nature as an end in itself, 'it is also the way in which every other rational being conceives his own existence on the same rational ground which is valid also for me; hence it is at the same time an objective principle' (G 429). In one sense, Kant's reasoning here is perfectly straightforward. The thought experiment offered above is perfectly general in the sense required to say that any rational agent would necessarily have reason never to sacrifice her own good will for the satisfaction of any amount of inclinations. The thought experiment did not presuppose any particular inclinations, but rather showed that it is always illegitimate to appeal to the supposed value of contingent ends to justify compromising one's own good

[25] See MM 422–3, MM 427–8.

will. So every rational agent has reason to treat her own fully rational nature as an end in itself. But Kant means the objective principle to establish more than this, of course. The full version of the humanity formulation says that each of us must treat humanity as an end in itself, whether it is one's own humanity or someone else's. There is a large gap to be filled in the move from saying each agent must treat her own rational nature as an end in itself to saying that each agent must treat every rational nature as an end in itself.

Sometimes this move has been made too hastily in reconstructions of Kant's argument. Kant himself provides little clue about how to proceed, and commentators generally have not acknowledged fully the existence of this gap in the argument. The usual strategy has been simply to say that each agent is taking the same aspect of herself, namely her rational nature, as valuable or as an end in itself, so what she is really valuing or taking as an end in itself is rational nature as such, not just her own rational nature. So she must treat rational nature as an end in itself wherever she finds it, whether in herself or others.[26] But this seems to gloss over the crucial step. The subjective principle tells us only that each agent has reason never to sacrifice her own rational nature for the sake of satisfying her inclinations. It has not yet said anything about others' wills, or rational wills as such.[27] Of course, the desired Kantian conclusion is that every being's rational nature is an end in itself, that there are necessary requirements on how to act with regard to every rational nature. But it would be begging the question to import that result into the argument for the move from the subjective principle to the full-blown humanity formulation. I think the need to justify the move from the subjective principle to the appropriately demanding objective principle has been partly obscured by the use of value terms in the argument. If one takes it that the subjective principle says that one's own rational nature has absolute and unconditional value, then it is easy to slide to the claim that every other agent has the same reason to claim her rational nature has the same value, and then it is easy to conclude that they all have the same value and so should be given the same consideration. But the subjective principle has not yet shown that one's own rational nature has

[26] I believe this is the reconstruction offered by Korsgaard, *Creating the Kingdom of Ends*, 123, Wood, *Kant's Ethical Thought*, 131, and H.J. Paton, *The Categorical Imperative* (Philadelphia: University of Pennsylvania Press, 1947), 175–9.

[27] Paul Guyer recognizes that the usual move here is 'obviously fallacious'. But in its place he offers the seemingly implausible claim that 'it is true as a subjective—or psychological—fact about *all* human beings that they recognize the unconditional value of the freedom of rational agency in general, not just their own freedom, and that they can also recognize that all rational agents would place equal value on this end, therefore that [it] is an unconditional end for all rational agents that complies with the original requirement that the moral law and thus its source be valid for all rational beings'. Paul Guyer, *Kant on Freedom, Law and Happiness* (Cambridge: Cambridge University Press, 2000), 162–3. It is hard to accept that all human beings have such an actual belief.

an agent-neutral value. Instead, it has shown that you have reason not to sacrifice your own rational nature, regardless of your inclinations. It has not said anything about how others should treat your rational nature or how you should treat theirs. What is needed is a justification for the move from saying that each agent must treat her own rational nature as an end in itself, to saying that each agent also must treat all other rational nature as an end in itself as well.

Although Kant does not himself make clear how to proceed here, an obvious strategy does seem to be suggested by the overall strategy of *Groundwork*. Kant has supposed that if morality is to be more than fiction, there must be a principle of morality that is binding on all rational beings. Two possible candidates for this universal principle are compatible with, and suggested by, the fact that each rational agent must treat her own rational nature as an end in itself, and so must not sacrifice her own rational nature. One possible universal principle is: each agent must treat her own fully rational nature as an end in itself, but may treat others' rational natures as expendable means to the satisfaction of her own inclinations. The other possible principle is: each agent should treat her own fully rational nature and all other fully rational natures as ends in themselves, so should not trade any rational nature for the satisfaction of her own inclinations. If we limit Kant to morally neutral premisses, he could provide no reason for thinking that the second principle is the correct one.

But he does not limit himself to morally neutral premisses. In these chapters of *Groundwork*, he is analysing what morality must be like if there is any such thing as morality. While the first principle described above does provide an imperative that is in a sense universal, it is not universal in the sense required to count as a moral principle. It would give every agent a command that verbally had the same form—'treat your own rational nature as an end in itself, so never sacrifice it for the sake of inclination'—but it would not be actually demanding that each agent treat exactly the same object(s) as deserving this special consideration. The common moral idea that is being analysed demands an end that all moral beings can share, not one that will irreconcilably set them into conflict because each properly places the highest value on different objects. This is a basic idea behind saying the fundamental principle of morality must be universal. In the Second *Critique*, Kant expresses this by saying that the kind of universality required is 'a law which would govern them all [all agents] by bringing them into unison'.[28] A law will not serve as a moral principle if 'the wills of all do not have one and the same object'. He mocks the merely verbal agreement of incompatible ends in one of his rare jokes, saying that

[28] In this passage, Kant is dismissing each person's happiness as a suitable final end, rather than addressing the possibility that rational nature might just provide an agent-relative principle, but the point can be applied to the latter as well as the former.

'a harmony may result' that is 'like the pledge which is given by Francis I to the emperor Charles V, "What my brother wants (Milan), that I want too."' If morality is not a fiction, it requires an end that can be shared by all agents, and that is what justifies the move from the 'subjective principle' in the argument for the humanity formulation to the 'objective principle' that one must treat fully rational nature as an end in itself wherever one finds it.[29]

But what is involved in treating humanity as an end in itself? So far, the practical requirement of treating humanity as an end in itself only includes not sacrificing it in order to satisfy one's inclinations. Since humanity is good will, there are different ways to violate this requirement. The subjective component of the humanity formulation forbids one to sacrifice one's own good will by choosing to place higher priority on inclination than on morality, or by altogether destroying oneself and so one's will, or by permanently impairing the basic functioning of the will. The corresponding objective principle, because it must serve as a moral principle rather than a principle of strife, imposes roughly parallel requirements on the treatment of others' fully rational natures, so far as possible given the basic differences in the effects we can have on ourselves and on others. The objective principle demands that one not destroy others for the sake of satisfying one's own inclinations, and that one not permanently impair others' deliberative powers. Since you cannot control the choices another person makes, or the principles she chooses to adopt, you cannot strictly have an obligation to preserve others' commitments to morality. But you do have a 'negative' duty not to tempt them to immorality (MM 394). And I think these requirements are all that Kant's argument in *Groundwork* 428–9 can establish.

And this is enough to reach the conclusions Kant wishes to reach in arguing for the basic humanity formulation, that humanity is an end in itself, and so should never be treated merely as a means. Humanity is an end in itself, or an objective end, because each agent is rationally required not to sacrifice her own or others' humanity, or fully rational will, for the sake of her inclinations. This requirement applies to each rational agent, regardless of the inclinations she has. So humanity is an end that must be taken account of in action regardless of inclination. That is what it is to be an objective end, or end in itself. The additional claim that rational nature should not be treated as a mere means emphasizes the way that one can fail to treat it as an end in itself. The way to violate the demand of treating humanity as an objective end is to undermine or destroy it for the sake of achieving inclination-based ends. So the way to violate the humanity formulation is to treat inclination as more important than humanity, to treat

[29] This is the strategy that I think could allow Kant to respond to Samuel Kerstein's objection, which I describe in section 1 of this chapter.

oneself or another rational being as important only because of the role they play in satisfying one's inclinations. The language of 'ends' and 'means' is a little strained, but that is not a feature unique to my reconstruction of Kant's argument. The simple statement of the humanity formulation in terms of ends and means seems to apply more naturally to some of Kant's own cases than others. As teachers of introductory ethics classes know, it is fairly intuitive to describe some violations of the humanity formulation as cases of 'using someone as a means' (deceiving someone, for example, or 'using' someone in a romantic context to make another person jealous), but it is more of a stretch to make the 'treating as a means' label intuitively fit cases of suicide or non-beneficence. Kant, I think, is using the distinction between ends and means partly because it is a distinction that is readily available from the history of philosophy and seems at least roughly to capture the idea of giving the right (or wrong) kind of weight to something in one's deliberations. Though the distinction does not precisely fit ordinary language, it does seem to capture the idea of some things playing a primary role in deliberation and others playing only a secondary and contingent role.

If Kant does adopt the terminology of ends and means because they are familiar labels, then it would be odd indeed if he failed to put the basic ideas of the humanity formulation in the even more familiar language of value. He does put the ideas in terms of value, and that is not problematic, as long as the argument for the humanity formulation does not essentially rely on claims about value as conceptually prior to rational choices. What the argument for the humanity formulation has established is that every agent is rationally required to preserve her own good will, or any other rational being's good will, rather than satisfying any amount of her inclinations. To say that a rational agent wills something is just to say that it has value, on Kant's conception of value. So, since any fully rational agent wills to preserve good will or fully rational nature, we can say that fully rational nature has value to her. Since her willing to preserve fully rational nature does not depend on particular inclinations, the value of fully rational nature is absolute value, value not dependent on inclination. And since she will never sacrifice any fully rational nature for any amount of satisfaction of inclinations, fully rational nature must have an incomparable value, or dignity.

But even if everything I have said about the argument for the humanity formulation is correct, it does not settle all the duties regarding humanity. Surely the humanity formulation requires more than just not destroying oneself or others, and striving to regulate one's choices with moral principles. But not all these other duties directly play a role in the argument for the humanity formulation. Instead, they are derived from the humanity formulation once it is established. In the next chapter, I propose a strategy for deriving these more particular duties from the basic moral principle.

7

How Duties Follow from the Categorical Imperative

It is no surprise that the argument for the content of the humanity formulation does not itself specify all the duties entailed by the humanity formulation. Kant's main aims in *Groundwork* are to describe the basic content that moral principles must have if they exist (the work of chapters 1 and 2) and then show that we must take it that such categorically binding moral imperatives do exist (the work of chapter 3). Kant says, 'The present *Groundwork* aims only to seek out and establish the supreme principle of morality', and he reserves for a later day the 'application of that supreme principle to the whole system' of morals (G 392). He calls the whole system a 'metaphysic of morals', and the *Groundwork for the Metaphysics of Morals* is of course meant as a preliminary foundation for the more complete system (G 391). In the later work actually titled *Metaphysics of Morals*, he says, 'a metaphysics of morals cannot dispense with principles of application, and we shall often have to take as our object the particular nature of man, which is known only by experience, in order to show what can be inferred from universal moral principles'.[1] Although Kant does give some examples in *Groundwork* of more specific duties that follow from the different formulations of the Categorical Imperative, this is a separate task from arguing for the content of the formulations themselves. The profusion of literature on the topic of deriving duties from the Categorical Imperative is testimony to the fact that it is no trivial task to work out the practical implications of the Categorical Imperative, even if one accepts Kant's arguments for its content.[2] Accordingly, my aim in this section is not to

[1] MM 217. This is a slight modification of Kant's position in *Groundwork*, since in *Groundwork* Kant says that a metaphysics of morals cannot take into account human nature in particular, but only the nature of rational beings in general (G 388, 410, 412). But the overall picture shared by both works is that a complete account of morality includes a discussion of both basic principles and the more specific duties derived from the basic principles.

[2] Although there are many good discussions of this topic, Barbara Herman's work seems to stand out as a particularly impressive combination of philosophical rigour and attention to the texts. See

catalogue fully all the duties that follow from the humanity formulation, nor to examine in great detail the derivation of any particular duty. Instead, I will offer a general strategy for moving from the humanity formulation to more specific duties, and will argue that both this general strategy and my reconstruction of the argument for the humanity formulation itself fit with most of what Kant says about the duties implied by the humanity formulation.

1. A Basic Strategy

Both Kant and his expositors often seem to treat the transition from the humanity formulation to particular duties as more or less an intuitive matter, and I do not think this is entirely a mistake. The universal law formulation offers a formal (though difficult to apply) procedure for determining the moral permissibility of particular choices, but the humanity formulation does not. Speculatively, I suggest this may be the reason Kant says that in making moral judgements it is better if 'one proceeds always in accordance with the strict method and takes as one's basic principle the universal formula' but that the humanity and kingdom of ends formulations 'bring the moral law nearer to intuition' (G 436–7). The humanity formulation captures some compelling features of moral thought, but seems not to be designed as a precise procedure for settling all specific moral questions. Nevertheless, it would be dissatisfying to leave the transition from the humanity formulation to specific duties as a completely vague intuitive matter, if the texts provide some indications of how Kant means the derivation of particular duties to work.

Allen Wood proposes the idea of 'expressive reasons' for action as an aid to moving from the humanity formulation to more specific duties.[3] He says that humanity is not an end to be brought into existence, but rather, 'What FH [the formula of humanity] fundamentally demands of our actions is instead that they *express* proper respect or reverence for the worth of humanity'. Wood maintains that all action performed for a reason 'is based on regarding something as objectively valuable' and is 'most fundamentally an expression of esteem for that value'. So acting as morally required is fundamentally an expression of respect for the value of humanity. Wood follows up on this

especially 'Mutual Aid and Respect for Persons', and 'Murder and Mayhem', in *The Practice of Moral Judgment* (Cambridge, Mass.: Harvard University Press, 1993), 45–72, 113–31. For a comprehensive and often helpful discussion of Kant's development of the Categorical Imperative into a metaphysics of morals, see Mary Gregor, *Laws of Freedom* (Oxford: Basil Blackwell, 1963).

[3] This quotation, and the others in this paragraph, are from Allen Wood, *Kant's Ethical Thought* (Cambridge: Cambridge University Press, 1999), 141–2.

suggestion in his later examination of Kant's four examples from *Groundwork*, making the duties in each example depend on expressing proper esteem for humanity.[4]

There is a lot about Wood's suggestion that seems appealing, but some details should still be worked out or filled in. In the form it is stated, Wood's idea seems to be that the humanity formulation most fundamentally is a claim about value, and that the way to apply the humanity formulation is to ask how to express recognition of humanity's value. I have argued that the humanity formulation is not best taken as a claim about value, but as a principle describing the actions that are rationally required with regard to humanity. The fundamental idea of the humanity formulation is that humanity, in oneself or others, should never be sacrificed for the sake of satisfying inclination. It is fair enough to translate this point into terms of value, saying that humanity has unconditional value or incomparably high value. But if this value talk is asked to bear much argumentative weight, it should be remembered that it really only embodies the practical requirement that every agent, regardless of her inclinations, must refrain from destroying or undermining anyone's fully rational nature. If this is the fundamental idea of the humanity formulation, and if talk about the value of humanity just captures this requirement, then to say that one should refrain from malicious gossip or should develop one's talents because these actions express respect for the value of humanity seems too vague. Intuitively, there seems to be some connection between esteem for a rational will and these duties, but the connection is weak. The esteem would have to arise somehow from the basic moral requirement not to destroy rational nature, and then the expression of that esteem would have to involve not only refraining from destroying rational nature, but also refraining from gossip, from letting one's talents rust, from showing ingratitude, and a host of other requirements that do not seem directly related to maintaining or destroying one's own or others' rational natures (good wills).

It would be desirable to fill in more details related to this feeling of esteem or the feeling of taking humanity to be valuable. If the feeling is supposed to have humanity (in the technical sense of the humanity formulation) as its object, then a more complete account would need to explain how humanity gives rise to this feeling. And it would also need to say more about the nature of the feeling, and how particular duties are related to it. In short, a more complete account would need to say more about the role that a feeling of esteem or of 'regarding as valuable' serves in moving from the basic moral principle of humanity as an end in itself to more particular duties.

[4] Ibid. 147–9.

Luckily, Kant himself provides a description of a moral feeling that is well suited to play this role. It is the feeling of 'Achtung', which is usually translated as 'respect', sometimes as 'reverence'. In *Critique of Practical Reason* and other texts, Kant develops an account of the sources of this feeling. He also connects the feeling to our duties to other persons and to ourselves. Kant says that each rational agent experiences the feeling of *Achtung* in response to her recognition of the force of the moral law. But a rational agent also experiences this feeling of *Achtung* when she observes the instantiation of the force of the moral law, in the form of a rational being's morally motivated actions. Moral law itself and rational beings who accept the overriding force of moral law can both give rise to the moral feeling of *Achtung*. So *Achtung* holds promise as a link between the moral law, or Categorical Imperative, and the moral feelings and duties we have toward rational beings with good will. But *Achtung* is a common word in German, with many different nuances, ranging from roughly 'Attention!' as used on a sign warning of wet paint, to a description of the feeling of deep respect that is appropriately given to some institutions or persons, so the sceptical reader may suspect that it is reckless to make too much of the fact that Kant uses 'Achtung' to denote the feeling produced both by the moral law and by persons who observe the law. However, I will point out texts in which Kant himself explicitly draws this connection, and I will argue that taking the *Achtung* produced by both moral law and moral persons as the same moral feeling provides a useful interpretative concept.[5]

The most common use Kant makes of the word 'Achtung' is to refer to the feeling produced in finite rational beings by their recognition of the force of self-legislated moral law. Kant emphasizes that this feeling is not the ultimate cause of moral action. Moral law carries its own imperative power with it, and the feeling of *Achtung* arises from recognition of that independent power. 'Consequently, respect for the moral law is a feeling that is produced by an intellectual cause' (C2 73). *Achtung* is not just a feeling that most people happen to have toward moral demands, but rather it is a feeling that the moral law necessarily produces in every finite rational being. In fact, if right action were only explicable in terms of contingent motivating feelings, then there would be no such thing as morally motivated action, according to Kant.[6] Exactly how moral principles can make unconditional demands independently of feelings is

[5] Kant uses several other words that are related roughly to the concepts of respect or reverence. Among them are 'Respekt' (similar to the English 'respect' without as much contextual variation as 'Achtung') and 'verehren' (to revere). *Achtung* is the word Kant most commonly uses that is translated as 'respect' or 'reverence', however, and the passages I cite all use 'Achtung' unless otherwise noted.

[6] C2 72. The easily misconstrued passages on moral worth in G 397–400 are really making this same point.

necessarily inexplicable, on Kant's account. 'For how a law can be of itself an immediately determining ground of the will (though this is what is essential in all morality) is for human reason an insoluble problem and identical with that of how a free will is possible'.[7] We can never produce a satisfying account of the mechanics of how moral principles alone can motivate us, because such an account would rely on causal laws, whereas to take ourselves as free and so as capable of acting on moral principles involves viewing our actions as not determined by causal laws. Since we cannot have access to any explanation of how moral principles alone can unconditionally demand action, there is no conceptual space for the feeling of *Achtung*, or respect for law, to provide such an explanation.

But we can expect an explanation of how the (causally inexplicable) force of moral law produces in us a subjective feeling of *Achtung*. 'What we shall have to show *a priori* is, therefore, not the ground from which the moral law in itself supplies an incentive, but rather what it effects (or, to put it much better, must effect) in the mind insofar as it is an incentive' (C2 72). Practical reason first recognizes moral principles as unconditional demands, then this recognition of the inescapable force of moral demands gives rise to a feeling of *Achtung*. 'Moral law strikes down self-conceit' (C2 73) by showing that there is something more important than our own inclinations, and 'what in our own judgment infringes upon our self conceit humiliates' (C2 74). By showing the secondary importance of our own inclinations compared to moral requirements, the force of moral law produces 'an effect on feeling ... which on the one side is merely negative' (C2 74). But it also produces a positive feeling of *Achtung* for the moral law itself, because the 'relative weightiness of the law' is made apparent by its 'removal of the counterweight' (C2 76) of immoral desires or its power to 'move resistance out of the way' (C2 75). So although the moral law can produce a 'feeling of displeasure' by 'the lowering of pretensions to self-esteem' (C2 78–9), it is also 'an elevation of the moral' and as such there is 'so little displeasure in it that, once one has laid self-conceit aside ... one can in turn never get enough of contemplating the majesty of this law' (C2 77). *Achtung*, then, is a moral feeling, a positive feeling of respect for moral principles which is inspired by the objective normative force of such principles.

Kant says that people also can inspire this feeling of *Achtung*. In fact, in *Critique of Practical Reason* 76, the same section containing his most prolonged discussion of *Achtung* for moral law, he says that '[*Achtung*] is always directed to persons, never to things'. But can this be the same feeling that arises from the

[7] C2 72. See also G 461–2.

recognition of the Categorical Imperative's unconditional force? One might suspect that Kant is using the common word *Achtung* to label two different feelings, and this suspicion gains force from Kant's own claim in *Groundwork* 400 that 'only bare law for its own sake, can be an object of [*Achtung*] and therefore a command'. Nevertheless, Kant's attribution of *Achtung* to persons as well as to moral law is not a slip or an ambiguity. He not only repeatedly states that people can be the object of *Achtung*, but also explains the connection between *Achtung* for the law and for persons.

Achtung for moral law and for persons is the same moral feeling, because the feature of a person that inspires a feeling of *Achtung* is her obedience to moral law. In *Critique of Practical Reason* 76–7 (again, the same section in which he explains *Achtung* inspired by moral law), Kant says that traits such as a sense of humour, strength, courage, or high social status can give rise to feelings of 'love, fear, or admiration even to amazement' and yet are not objects of *Achtung* proper. Only 'uprightness of character' elicits *Achtung*, because the person with good will 'holds before me a law that strikes down my self-conceit' and so *Achtung* 'is a tribute we can not refuse to pay to merit'. This is so despite the fact that the person providing the good example is in fact not a perfect example of making morality a sufficient reason for action. Kant says, 'in humans all good is defective', yet 'the law made intuitive by an example still strikes down my pride'. In a footnote in Second *Critique* 81, Kant repeats the idea, saying, 'If one examines carefully the concept of respect for persons, as it has already been set forth, one becomes aware that it always rests on a consciousness of a duty which an example holds before us, and that, accordingly, respect can never have any but a moral ground'. A person who seems to display a good will inspires *Achtung* for the same reason as the moral law itself does, namely because each provides an example of the power to rise above material circumstances.[8] So Kant describes the feeling of *Achtung* as arising because a finite rational being 'sees the holy elevated above itself and its frail nature'. In *Metaphysics of Morals* 464 Kant draws the same connection between *Achtung* for the moral law and for persons, saying that the duty of acting with respect (*Achtung*) for a rational being, which is an expression of a subjective feeling of *Achtung*, is really based on that being's regard for moral law. Kant says, 'Respect [*Achtung*] for the law, which in its subjective aspect is called moral feeling, is identical with consciousness of one's duty. That is why showing respect [*Achtung*] for

[8] Though the source of the feeling of *Achtung* is not empirical, the fact that moral action arouses this feeling is an empirically observable claim. And there is some empirical evidence in favour of the claim that observing moral behaviour produces this type of unique moral feeling. See Jonathan Haidt, 'The Positive Emotion of Elevation', *Prevention and Treatment*, 3/3, posted 7 Mar. 2000 (it is an online journal).

man as a moral being (holding his duty in highest esteem) is also a duty that others have toward him'. This also fits with Kant's statement in *Groundwork* 435 that morally motivated actions 'exhibit the will which performs them as an immediate object of [*Achtung*]'. And in *Groundwork* 440 Kant describes a will that acts only on condition of its actions being permitted by the Categorical Imperative and says, 'this ideal will which can be ours is the proper object of [*Achtung*]'. So, Kant explicitly and consistently equates the feeling of *Achtung* for moral law with the feeling of *Achtung* that is inspired by people who display a commitment to moral law. The source of the moral feeling in each case is an awareness of the power of morality to rise above contingent circumstances.

This moral feeling of *Achtung* is well suited to play a theoretical role in the transition from the humanity formulation as a basic moral principle to the specific duties that follow from the principle. In particular, it is better suited for this role than the more general idea of esteem for the value of humanity. *Achtung*, unlike the proposed feeling of esteem for humanity's value, is not a feeling that arises from recognition of an un-Kantian, conceptually fundamental value that is supposedly possessed by humanity. Instead, Kant himself explains that the feeling of *Achtung* arises from recognition of the unconditional force of moral demands, and also from recognition of the examples of this force that are provided by people who apparently act on moral principles. No brute claim about value is required. The feeling of *Achtung*, when conjoined with the good will reading of the humanity formulation, also draws a deep connection between the content of the Categorical Imperative and the effect of the Categorical Imperative on the moral agent who is subject to it. The Categorical Imperative, in any of its formulations, gives rise to a feeling of *Achtung* in moral agents who are aware of its force. If the humanity that is an end in itself is a good will, then humanity on its own account also gives rise to the feeling of *Achtung*, because a good will is an example of the Categorical Imperative's power to outweigh all inclination. The humanity formulation does not just command each agent to treat something as an end in itself, but more profoundly says to treat as an end in itself the kind of will that arouses the same deep moral feeling of *Achtung* as the moral law itself does. In addition, I will argue that Kant gives *Achtung* a central role in his discussions of many of our duties, and even seems to say that it underlies all duties. So, overall, *Achtung* seems to hold greater promise than the more general feeling of valuing or esteeming rational nature, as an aid to filling out the account of how specific duties follow from the humanity formulation.

The most obvious category of duty that is related to the feeling of *Achtung* is the category of duties of respect (*Achtung*) for other people. Admittedly, there can be no duty to feel respect, because there can be no duty to feel anything.

Either one has a feeling or not, and though one can work at trying gradually to cultivate a given feeling, it is beyond one's control what one feels at a given moment. Since we can only have duties to do what is in our power, we cannot have a duty to have a particular feeling (MM 449). But we do have duties to act in ways that embody respect, or in other words to act in the manner of someone who actually feels respect. So Kant says every person has a duty 'to acknowledge, in a practical way, the dignity of humanity in every other man. Hence there rests on him a duty regarding the respect [*Achtung*] that must be shown to every other man' (MM 462). This practical respect for others is 'recognition of a dignity (*dignitas*) in other men, that is, a worth that has no price, no equivalent for which the object evaluated (*aestimii*) could be exchanged'. Even if the feeling of *Achtung* is not enough to move one to act respectfully, one is still obligated to act in the ways that would spring from the feeling of *Achtung*, or recognition of something that is elevated above all inclination. The feeling of *Achtung* for other rational beings would lead to a recognition that others can be as important as oneself, and so would tend to quash a feeling of arrogance. And it would lead one not to condemn or ridicule others, so as not to drag them into a position lower than they deserve, in the opinions of others. This fits with Kant's description of the vices opposed to *Achtung* for others, the vices of arrogance, defamation, and ridicule. The duties we have to act respectfully toward others, then, are duties to act in the manner of someone who feels *Achtung* for them.

The feeling of *Achtung* is even more closely bound up with the idea of duties to oneself. To be aware of any duties at all, Kant says, one must have respect for oneself. Or, more accurately, a person 'must have [*Achtung*] for the law within himself in order even to think of any duty whatsoever'.[9] This respect for law will tell each rational being to act in ways demanded by the humanity formulation, and other formulations, of the Categorical Imperative. Since the argument for the humanity formulation explicitly prohibits sacrificing good will for the sake of satisfying inclinations, it follows directly that each agent is prohibited from destroying herself merely to achieve contingent ends. Kant says that to violate this restriction by killing oneself in order to escape an unpleasant situation is 'debasing humanity in one's person', which is to fail to treat 'morality as an end in itself'.[10] But Kant acknowledges that it is a more difficult question whether killing oneself for other reasons may be permissible, when he considers the difficult cases of martyrdom, and suicide as a moral protest. Duties of moral perfection also seem to follow directly from the

[9] MM 403. See also MM 417–18.

[10] MM 423. See also Kant's discussion of suicide in G 429.

humanity formulation. In order to preserve one's good will, one is obligated to 'strive with all one's might that the thought of duty for its own sake is the sufficient incentive of every action conforming to duty'.[11] In addition, the humanity formulation would seem to lead in the most direct way possible to a duty not to damage permanently one's basic powers of rationality, since to damage one's will is also to damage one's good will.

But to derive other duties to oneself from the humanity formulation, it is necessary to look at the details of human nature, not just at the basic argument for the humanity formulation. The feeling of *Achtung* is especially useful here. The humanity formulation represents a good will as something that is not to be traded for any amount of inclination, and so gives rise to a feeling of *Achtung* for good will. Then, given this feeling which necessarily arises toward humanity in anyone who appreciates the force of the Categorical Imperative, some additional duties follow. Kant describes several duties that would most naturally be described as duties of respect for oneself. Kant hesitates to say that we have a duty to respect ourselves, but he means that we cannot properly say we have a duty to have a feeling of *Achtung*. He says, 'it is not correct to say that a man has a duty of self-esteem; it must rather be said that the law within him inevitably forces from him respect for his own being, and this feeling (which is of a special kind) is the basis of certain duties' (MM 402–3). So Kant means to rule out a duty to have a feeling of respect for oneself, but he does not rule out that one can have duties to perform the kinds of actions that express respect for oneself. A person's duty to avoid servility is a duty not to act contrary to 'his consciousness of his dignity as a rational man, and he should not disavow the moral self-esteem of such a being' (MM 435). Each of us also has a duty to avoid avarice, and this avarice consists of 'restricting one's own enjoyment of the means to good living so narrowly as to leave one's own true needs unsatisfied' (MM 432). The requirements imposed by the argument for the humanity formulation, to refrain from sacrificing one's own minimal rationality and one's good will, seem not to lead directly to this prohibition on miserliness, since one could remain an agent (and even an agent who cares about morality) while depriving oneself of the 'comforts necessary to enjoy life' (MM 433). Instead, the duty depends on consistency with the feeling of *Achtung* inspired by a will committed to morality. One of the ways in which we express *Achtung* and esteem for the will of a being committed to morality is to take satisfaction in seeing such a being made happy, not because material reward is the motive for moral commitment, but because we inevitably see

[11] MM 393. See also MM 386–7, 446–7, and my discussion of these texts in Chapter 3, section 2 of this book.

virtue as worthiness, and as material beings we see worthiness as worthiness to be happy. This is in fact the same idea expressed in Kant's discussion of the highest good as happiness in proportion to virtue.[12] So to provide for one's own material needs is indirectly a way to express respect for one's own good will.

The duties of 'natural' as opposed to moral self-perfection also seem best derived from the humanity formulation by employing the feeling of *Achtung*. This captures the spirit of Kant's claim that to develop one's natural abilities is to make oneself 'worthy of humanity' (MM 392, 387). Humanity, or good will, produces a feeling of *Achtung*, and this feeling inspires one to develop one's talents and abilities. Why is this so? Good will is not just a commitment to morality, but is an entire properly ordered will, and the end-setting of a properly ordered will results in ends that are worth pursuing. Some of these ends are based on inclination, others are moral ends given unconditionally by reason. To develop one's abilities allows one to seek a wider range of contingent ends, and also allows one to seek moral ends in a wider variety of ways. One can have a good will without possessing the ability to achieve a wide variety of ends, but the feeling of *Achtung* produced by a (fully) rational will inspires us to make it possible for our own wills to set and achieve a wide range of ends. So Kant says, 'there is also bound up with the end of humanity in our own person the rational will, and so the duty, to make ourselves worthy of humanity by culture in general, by procuring or promoting the capacity to realize all sorts of possible ends' (MM 392). This also fits with the spirit of Kant's statement in *Groundwork* 430 that although failing to develop one's talents does not 'conflict' with 'humanity in our own person' and is consistent with the 'maintenance of this end' it also does not 'harmonize with this end'. Failing to develop one's abilities does not literally destroy one's good will, but it is not consistent with fully accepting and acting on the feeling of respect and worthiness to be happy that a rational will inspires.[13]

Achtung plays a similar role in the derivation of the duty to aid others in the pursuit of their ends. The argument for the humanity formulation by itself does not establish that one must aid others in achieving their ends in general. It does seem to show that one ought to aid others when their survival or their powers of rationality are threatened, since one ought never to sacrifice

[12] See Chapter 3, section 3 of this book for a more complete discussion of this idea, and of Kant's texts. C2 110–13 is especially relevant.

[13] In one sense, of course, one must think of oneself as losing a good will by failing to develop one's talents, just as one must take every failure to fulfil one's duties as an abandonment of one's full commitment to morality. But this issue only arises after it is settled that one has a duty to develop one's talents, and so cannot be used as part of the derivation of that duty.

any being's good will for the sake of satisfying one's own inclinations. And sometimes Kant does speak of the duty to aid others 'who have to struggle with great hardships'.[14] But Kant also has in mind a more general duty of 'making others' happiness one's end' (MM 452) or 'to further the ends of others'.[15] The best way to account for this more general duty of aiding others in the pursuit of their ends is through the feeling of *Achtung*. The good will of another rational being inspires this feeling in me, which combats my natural tendency to arrogance and makes me aware that my own contingent ends are not uniquely important. Since her proper willing makes her ends worth pursuing as well, I ought to acknowledge that they are not worthless. A way to do this is to provide some aid for her in pursuing her ends, if doing so is not too great an infringement on my own pursuit of my ends. In addition, since it is her good will that inspires *Achtung*, I am also aware of her worthiness to be happy or to achieve her ends. It does not seem that the feeling of *Achtung* would lead me to treat her ends as having the same status in my deliberations as my own ends, or in other words to be indifferent between satisfying her own ends or my own. *Achtung* counters one's own arrogance, but this does not dictate that there can be no reason to give more weight to one's own ends, or the ends of people one cares about, when it comes to contingent ends that are not vital to a being's continued survival or rationality. Kant says, 'in wishing I can be equally benevolent to everyone, whereas in acting I can, without violating the universality of the maxim, vary the degree greatly in accordance with the different objects of my love (one of whom concerns me more closely than another)' (MM 452). Some commentators have argued that Kant's basic position on the duty to promote others' ends is, or ought to be for consistency's sake, that the ends of all beings have equal value and so the ends of all beings including myself should receive the same weight in my deliberations. In Chapter 8, I will argue that this reading of Kant's position mistakenly relies on a non-Kantian conception of value.

Although these are not all the duties that Kant discusses, they are sufficient to suggest the general pattern of the derivation of specific duties from the humanity formulation, and to demonstrate the usefulness of *Achtung* in reconstructing the derivation of these duties. Some duties are implied in a very direct way by the argument for the humanity formulation itself. That argument establishes

[14] G 423. See also MM 453, to be beneficent is to 'promote according to one's means the happiness of others in need'.

[15] G 430. Other commentators have noted that Kant actually seems to describe two different duties regarding others' ends, one duty to aid others in dire need and another duty to aid others in promoting their ends in general. See Herman, *The Practice of Moral Judgment*, 68–72; Thomas E. Hill, Jr., *Dignity and Practical Reason in Kant's Moral Theory* (Ithaca, NY: Cornell University Press, 1992), 54–5.

that one ought never to sacrifice good will, in oneself or others, for the sake of satisfying one's own inclinations. So one ought to strive to live up to moral obligations, and ought not to destroy oneself altogether by killing oneself, or destroy one's minimally rational nature by chemical or mechanical means. And one ought not to destroy others altogether, or damage their powers of minimal rationality, or tempt them to immorality. But in order to derive other duties from the humanity formulation, one needs to take account of the nature of finite rational beings to whom basic moral principles apply, and I have proposed that the moral feeling of *Achtung* is a key psychological feature in deriving specific duties. *Achtung* is a positive feeling of esteem or respect for moral law and for beings with good will, aroused by recognition of the example of rising above inclination. While it is different from other feelings in that its origin is a rational recognition of the force of morality, it is like other feelings in that it affects action. To think of another being's good will gives rise to a feeling of *Achtung* directed toward her, and duties of respect for others are duties to act in the ways that this feeling of *Achtung* would lead you to act. And to act with self-respect is to act in the ways that *Achtung* for one's own good will would lead one to act. To demonstrate 'practical love' or beneficence for others is also to act in a manner expressing *Achtung*, because feeling esteem for others as moral beings defeats one's self-conceit or absorption with one's own interests, and so allows one to recognize that others also deserve to achieve some of their ends. And to cultivate one's talents is an action that 'harmonizes' with the feeling of reverence and esteem for one's own good will, because to develop more talents allows one to achieve a greater variety of ends more effectively and so to achieve better the happiness that a being with good will deserves. Kant recognizes various features of human nature that play a role in deriving specific duties from the humanity formulation—our epistemological limitations, our physical needs, our need for education, our tendency to self-conceit—but one of the most important features seems to be that our recognition of the elevating power of morality produces in us a unique, positive moral feeling.

Of course, someone seeking a complete enumeration of duties, ready to guide action in every circumstance, will be disappointed by this chapter. I have proposed a general strategy for deriving some duties from the humanity formulation, but it does not settle all moral questions. There are actually two possible complaints here. The first is that only general classes of duties have been discussed, but without a guide to how and when these duties are to be fulfilled, or whether exceptions are legitimate. The second is that not all moral questions have been addressed, even at the level of general classes of duties. These two potential problems warrant different responses.

As for the question of how and when duties must be fulfilled, or which particular cases fall under a duty, there is an answer that is both Kantian and plausible. Kant himself says that a metaphysics of morals, even if completed, would still need to be applied to individual cases. Mary Gregor proposes that the best overall reading of his position is that a metaphysics of morals can take account of general human nature to derive the moral rules that apply to humans, but that the resulting moral requirements are still not ready to serve as direct guides to action, instead being 'a system of the duties which all men have merely insofar as they are men'.[16] Gregor means that even though the metaphysics of morals gives moral rules that are more specific than the Categorical Imperative, they still do not deal with all the particular characteristics of individual humans that may affect what they ought to do in a given situation. Although Kant is not perfectly consistent in what he says about a metaphysics of morals, there is explicit textual support for Gregor's reading.[17] Kant says that his metaphysics of morals consists of 'principles of obligation for human beings as such toward one another' (MM 469) and does not take account of 'differences of age, sex, birth, strength, or weakness, or even rank or dignity, which depend in part on arbitrary arrangements' (MM 468). Kant says that these points of application do not technically count as part of the system of moral rules derived from the Categorical Imperative, since the system itself must 'proceed *a priori* from a rational concept', but that nevertheless 'even this application belongs to the complete presentation of the system' (MM 469). The metaphysics of morals only moves from the basic Categorical Imperative to more specific classes of duties that humans have. But how a given human should act in a given situation always requires a further step of using judgement to apply these duties to various human conditions, such as differences in wealth, education, power, and health. This fits with Kant's practice in *The Metaphysics of Morals*, of often appending 'casuistical questions' to his discussions of different duties, without providing answers to those questions. It also fits with Kant's claim in First *Critique* that judgement is always required to apply rules (C1 A134, B173).

Even if it is reasonable to insist on a space for judgement in the application of moral rules, one might still object that I have not even discussed all the possible general classes of duties that humans may have. Nothing I have said suggests a procedure for arriving at definitive answers to moral questions about many issues on which Kant is understandably silent, such as the moral permissibility of human cloning, the responsibilities of

[16] Gregor, *Laws of Freedom*, 17.

[17] For more on Kant's inconsistency, see n. 1 of this chapter. Also see Gregor, *Laws of Freedom*, 3–6.

large corporations to their shareholders and the general public, or moral obligations to relieve famine in distant parts of the world. And of course even when Kant does attempt to derive moral duties from the Categorical Imperative, many readers find some of his positions deeply implausible. I have not claimed to offer a way to settle all such cases in which different positions seem reasonable to different people. But then other commentators have not claimed to offer such a definitive procedure either. This is not surprising, since Kant himself seems to acknowledge that the humanity formulation is more intuitive than precise. The connection between the humanity formulation and specific duties may always have a degree of looseness, and this would leave room for some disagreement about the specific duties.

But this is not to say that it is best to throw up one's hands and leave the application of the humanity formulation entirely a matter of each person's intuitions. In Chapter 9, I will take up the pragmatic issue of rendering the humanity formulation more useful in resolving moral controversies. More specifically, I will adopt a suggestion of Thomas E. Hill, Jr., that the kingdom of ends formulation can be employed as a 'moral constructivist' tool, based on the idea of treating humanity as an end in itself, for settling moral questions. I will argue that interpreting the kingdom of ends formulation in this useful manner presupposes the good will reading of the humanity formulation. But that will be the work of Chapter 9. The work of this chapter is more scholarly, attempting to explain a Kantian general strategy for deriving duties from the humanity formulation. Even so, some other potential problems remain, besides worries about the incompleteness of Kant's system of duties. I consider these problems in the next two sections.

2. Potential Problems

The strategy I have proposed for deriving more specific duties raises several possible worries. Probably the most pressing is a new instantiation of the worry about the excessive moralism of the good will reading. In its new form, the worry is that only people with good wills inspire *Achtung*, and so one has duties only toward them and not toward everyone else. It would indeed be a disastrous reading of Kant, to claim that every moral agent ought to note which beings inspire *Achtung*, and which do not, and to apportion moral consideration accordingly. But my proposal about the role of *Achtung* does not have this grossly unpalatable consequence.

To see why, it helps to notice that using judgements about others' moral character as a yardstick for the amount of respect and other dutiful treatment they deserve would not only be terribly moralistic, but terribly unreliable as well. Kant's consistent position is that we cannot determine with certainty the strength of others', or even our own, commitment to morality.[18] Even in the passages in Second *Critique* 76–7 in which he says that a virtuous person inspires *Achtung*, Kant makes clear that the person who appears virtuous may indeed contain an unknown impurity of will. This uncertainty is no disaster, given the theoretical role that good will and *Achtung* play in grounding our duties. The person with good will serves as an example of the possibility of rising above inclination in response to moral demands, but no observed example needs to be indubitable (C2 76–8, 81 n.). This is because an apparent example of good will encountered in experience serves only to remind us of 'the Idea of moral perfection' which is not supplied by observation but 'resides in reason' (G 409). Accompanying each agent's recognition of the inescapable force of the Categorical Imperative is a demand to make compliance with morality one's own most fundamental priority, and this priority of moral principles is the identifying feature of a good will. So each rational being presents herself with this idea of a good will as an ideal she must live up to. 'There is no need, therefore, of any example from experience to make the idea of a human being morally pleasing to God a model to us; the idea is present as a model already in our reason' (R 62). Kant recognizes that 'outer experience yields no example adequate to the idea' of a good will, because 'as outer, it does not disclose the inwardness of the disposition but only allows inference to it, though not with strict certainty' (R 63). But the purpose of such outer examples of apparent good will is not to serve as a differentiating mark between beings toward whom we have moral obligations and those toward whom we do not. Instead, such apparent examples inspire *Achtung* and so remind us of the power of moral law and the place a good will holds as an end in itself (regardless of whether this particular apparent example of good will is certain).

Then the role that the feeling of *Achtung* plays in the derivation of specific duties does not demand that we attempt to use this feeling as a guide for selectively granting moral status to some beings and not to others. To view the account of duties in this manner is to run together moral theory and everyday moral experience. What is important at the level of moral theory, in deriving duties from the humanity formulation, is that both moral law and the good will of a being committed to moral law elicit the moral feeling of *Achtung*. Some of the duties that humans have are duties to act in ways that express *Achtung* for

[18] R 62–3, G 406–12. See Chapter 5, section 1 of this book.

good will, the end in itself. But this is all still at the level of developing a system of duties that apply to rational human agents, or developing a metaphysics of morals. The application of this system of duties to each individual circumstance is not yet resolved.

And in fact, in each individual circumstance that a human agent faces in the real world, she will have reason to treat herself and others as ends in themselves, and part of treating people as ends in themselves is to treat them in a manner expressing the feeling of *Achtung*. So a human agent ought to treat herself and others in ways that express *Achtung*, even though in the real world she will never be certain of anyone's moral character. Kant persuasively describes several reasons for treating others as ends in themselves, given our inevitable lack of certainty about the moral character of any human (even including ourselves). I have described these reasons in Chapter 5 of this book, but will quickly summarize them here.[19] Our uncertainty about others' moral character, coupled with our tendency to inflate our own worth in comparison to others', urges extreme caution in making any judgements about others' commitment to morality. So instead of seeking out others' faults, one ought to 'throw the veil of love of man over their faults', both by 'softening our judgments' and 'by keeping these judgments to ourselves' (MM 466). Avoiding the human vice of arrogance is the main reason to refrain from making judgements about others, but Kant also says that treating people with respect (regardless of whether it appears they deserve it) can inspire them to strive to make themselves worthy of respect (MM 463–4, 466). And a final reason to refrain from making moral treatment proportionate to one's judgements of character is that to deny moral consideration to some humans, even the ones we (unreliably) judge to be morally undeserving, will have a psychological effect of diminishing our moral sensitivity to all humans. So we ought to treat all humans as ends in themselves, even if 'one cannot, it is true, help inwardly looking down on some in comparison with others' (MM 463). In our particular choices in the real world about how to treat ourselves and others, we ought to choose to act in ways that would express *Achtung* for a good will, even if we sometimes do not feel *Achtung*.

A second worry for my reading, distinct from the worry about moralism, is that some may find it natural to take Kant's discussion of *Achtung* to suggest that what inspires *Achtung* is not a good will, but just the power to legislate moral law to oneself. After all, Kant most often says that moral law is what inspires *Achtung*, and so when he speaks of *Achtung* or respect for rational beings, one might think that what inspires *Achtung* must be their own legislation of

[19] In Chapter 5, section 1, I give more detail about each of the reasons mentioned below.

moral law to themselves. This would support a minimal reading of 'humanity', since all minimally rational beings have *Wille* and so all legislate moral law. But it does not seem to fit what Kant says in his most detailed accounts of *Achtung* for persons. In the several Second *Critique* passages cited earlier, he explicitly says that the feature of a person that inspires *Achtung* is her morally motivated action, inasmuch as it provides an example of the power to rise above the commands of self-love. The person who legislates moral law to herself but then flouts it does not provide such an example. And throughout the discussion of duties of respect for others in *Metaphysics of Morals* 462–8, Kant maintains that others should be treated in ways that express *Achtung* even though the immoral do not inspire the actual feeling of *Achtung*. If merely giving oneself moral law were sufficient for inspiring *Achtung*, then every minimally rational being would in fact inspire a feeling of *Achtung*, and Kant would not need to distinguish between actually feeling *Achtung* and acting in ways that would express this feeling. So overall the best reading of Kant's position on *Achtung* is that a good will is the feature of persons that inspires *Achtung*.

3. Short Shrift to Value?

One final obstacle to my proposals in this chapter and the last is that they seem to run contrary to an appealing interpretative idea proposed by three prominent commentators on Kant's ethics, Barbara Herman, Allen Wood, and Paul Guyer. Each basically opposes the traditional claim that value does not play a fundamental role in Kant's moral theory, particularly in the humanity formulation.

Herman argues that one of the main reasons that many readers have found Kant's ethics counterintuitive is that his ethical theory has been classified as 'deontological', which implies that it is 'a moral theory without a concept of value as its fundamental theoretical concept'.[20] In opposition to this approach, Herman cites the central role of the opening claim of *Groundwork*, that only a good will is good or valuable without qualification. And, 'Without a theory of value, the rationale for moral constraint remains a mystery'.[21] Certainly the position I have proposed in the last two chapters essentially denies that any claim about value is the theoretically fundamental concept of Kant's theory. I have argued that Kant's claims about value, including the unconditional and incomparable value of a good will, are best seen as a kind of shorthand for

[20] Herman, *The Practice of Moral Judgement*, 208. [21] Ibid. 210.

the ways in which each rational agent is required to act with regard to a good will. So, contrary to Herman, I maintain that Kant's talk of the value of good will (or humanity) is 'a function of prior and independent principles of right'. Nevertheless, I think my account preserves a good bit of the intuitive force of Herman's position. The claims about requirements of reason are not ungrounded, if my arguments are correct. I have argued that there is a rationale for the requirement to treat humanity as an end in itself, but that it is just not a rationale that appeals most fundamentally to claims about value. Regardless of one's inclinations, one has sufficient reason to preserve one's own good will, as the necessary condition of the value of any contingent ends. So even if the argument for the humanity formulation is not based on a prior claim about the value of humanity, it still is, as Herman wishes it to be, 'an argument to defeat the claims of sufficiency of empirical practical reason', or 'heteronomy of the will'.[22] And even if claims about value are not the core of Kant's ethical theory, he does still have a concept of value (as being the product of rational choice) that provides 'a way between the poles of naturalism and metaphysical realism about value'.[23] So my reconstructions of the argument for the humanity formulation, and of the derivation of particular duties from the humanity formulation, are not as far from Herman's position as they may appear at first glance.

Similarly, my position regarding the role of value is not so far from Wood's. Wood seems to propose that the humanity formulation is most fundamentally a claim about the value of rational nature, and that particular duties that are derived from it are best seen as ways of expressing esteem for the value of humanity. The part of this that I deny is that the humanity formulation is at its core a claim about value. Instead, Kant's arguments for the humanity formulation establish a principle of action regarding how to treat humanity. But in a straightforward sense, the particular duties that are derived from the humanity formulation do express esteem or respect for humanity. The end in itself is good will, I have argued, and Kant himself repeatedly says that good will inspires a feeling of respect or *Achtung*. It is fine to call this a feeling of respect or esteem for the value of humanity, as long as it is kept in mind that this idea of value is a way of capturing the more fundamental Kantian point that moral principles, and beings committed to moral principles, are what really inspire this feeling of 'esteem'.

Paul Guyer also argues, at least in some texts, that value occupies a central place in Kant's ethics. But I think his main concerns, like Herman's and Wood's, may be met without giving conceptual priority to value.

[22] Herman, *The Practice of Moral Judgement*, 238. [23] Ibid. 210.

Guyer sometimes states that Kant's ethical theory is value based. In his essay 'Kant's Morality of Law and Morality of Freedom', Guyer says that, contrary to standard readings of Kant's ethics, 'I would like to argue, however, that the fundamental but indemonstrable value of freedom itself is the heart of Kant's moral theory'.[24] As one piece of support for this claim, Guyer cites a passage from 'Lectures on Ethics' in which Kant's students have recorded Kant as saying that 'Freedom is the inner value of the world'.[25] Guyer even makes a paraphrased version of this statement the title of one of his essays.[26] He also expresses agreement with Barbara Herman on her claims about the role of value in Kant's ethics.[27] Guyer makes a conspicuous point of saying in the introduction to *Kant on Freedom, Law, and Happiness* that one of the main points of the book is that 'freedom is our most fundamental value', and that a proper understanding of Kant's ethics must take this into account.[28]

It would be obviously implausible to deny that Guyer really wants to say that Kant's moral philosophy is ineliminably based on value, namely on the value of freedom or autonomy.[29] But, like Herman, I think Guyer may really be mainly concerned to discount a particular, implausible version of 'deontology', and I think this task may be accomplished without making value claims foundational. The implausible deontology that Guyer and Herman oppose would claim that one simply must follow moral rules, even though no justification can be provided for following these rules. Guyer maintains that Kant's position in the Second *Critique* does seem to be thoroughly deontological, inasmuch as it denies that moral principles can be based on the value of any end, but Guyer thinks that Kant's position there is based on a false dichotomy.[30] Kant thinks that a Categorical Imperative, which necessarily binds all agents, cannot be based on any contingent desire or inclination, so Kant apparently concludes that the Categorical Imperative must apply independently of all ends. Guyer points out that this neglects an alternative, namely that some end with non-contingent or absolute value for every agent may ground a Categorical Imperative. This creates conceptual space to say that the absolute value of freedom could be the basis of Kant's moral theory. Guyer, like Herman,

[24] Paul Guyer, *Kant on Freedom, Law, and Happiness* (Cambridge: Cambridge University Press, 2000), 131.

[25] Ibid. 56–7, 96, 129. See Immanuel Kant, *Lectures on Ethics*, trans. Louis Infield (New York: Harper & Row, 1963), 122.

[26] 'Freedom as the Inner Value of the World', in *Kant on Freedom*, 96–125.

[27] Ibid. 185 n. 12. [28] Ibid. 2.

[29] In Chapter 11, I will consider the extent to which Guyer's view that autonomy is the end in itself is compatible with the good will reading of the humanity formulation.

[30] Guyer, *Kant on Freedom*, 133. See also 141, 187–9.

argues that there must be a value claim at the core of Kant's moral theory, because without it the theory is left mysterious and intuitively unmotivated. Guyer says:

> this is what remains profoundly unsatisfying about the argument of the *Critique of Practical Reason*: it assumes that a practical law must be necessary and universal, infers from this that it must be entirely formal, and just insists that we are capable of acting not only in accordance with it but entirely out of respect for it without explaining in what sense we have any reason to do such a thing.[31]

Guyer's position that value must play a central role in Kant's theory, and the motivation for this position, then, are both similar to Herman's.

And, as with Herman, the real remedy for Guyer's concern is just to provide a rationale for treating humanity as an end in itself, not necessarily a rationale based on value. In Guyer's case, many of his arguments are actually directed toward showing that the Categorical Imperative must be based on an end, which is not really the same as saying that it must be based on a claim about value. This need for an end of action, to accompany moral principles, is finally the conclusion of the argument in which Guyer points out Kant's false dichotomy between acting on contingent ends and acting solely from concern for complying with the form of moral law.[32] Throughout the passages in which he argues that something with 'absolute value' must ground a Categorical Imperative, Guyer freely interchanges the idea of a necessary (non-contingent) end and an end with absolute value. This is exemplified most strikingly by the fact that in the introduction to *Kant on Freedom, Law, and Happiness*, he moves seamlessly between the claim that 'freedom is our fundamental value' and the claim that 'the preservation and promotion of freedom is the primary end of human action'.[33] But this is not the only place where he makes this move. In fact, in most of the key passages arguing for value's central role, Guyer treats as equivalent the ideas that the Categorical Imperative must be accompanied by a necessary end, and that it must be based on something with absolute value.[34] But these claims ought to be separated. What I think is really needed, if there is to be a Categorical Imperative, is a reason to think that something serves as an end for every rational being, an end in itself. But to base the Categorical Imperative on an end does not entail, without further argument, that a claim about this end's value is conceptually fundamental.

[31] Guyer, *Kant on Freedom*, 138. See also 143. [32] Ibid. 134. [33] Ibid. 7.
[34] Ibid. 57, 131, 134, 143–6, 185–90, 198.

This can be illustrated most clearly by considering which parts of Guyer's position would be accepted, and which rejected, by a proponent of the traditional idea that rational choice must be conceptually prior to value in Kant's practical philosophy. This proponent would admit that the humanity formulation is based on an end that all rational beings must acknowledge—presumably no one would deny this, since to deny it one would have to ignore the very terms in which Kant puts the humanity formulation. Kant also undeniably attributes special value to the end in itself, saying it has an incomparably high value, a value independent of inclinations, and the like. So the point of dispute cannot be whether Kant thinks the Categorical Imperative is based on some end, or whether he ever talks about the value of that end. Instead, the question is which part of Kant's theory is conceptually prior and fundamental—the claim that there is an end that necessarily provides a reason for acting in certain ways, or the attribution of value to such an end. I have proposed that an argument can be provided for treating humanity in special ways, an argument that does not rely on any prior claims about value. Only after these practical requirements are established, I have argued, can we express the practical requirements in terms of value. Whatever the potential problems with my account, it is not vulnerable to the charge that it gives no rationale for treating humanity as an end in itself. The real issue is whether this non-value-based (and therefore more traditional) type of account is superior or inferior to a position like Guyer's, which takes value to be conceptually prior to requirements on action.

One strong piece of evidence in favour of the non-value-based interpretation of Kant's moral philosophy is that Kant himself emphasizes that this is his position, in the Second *Critique*. As Guyer admits, Kant gives a prolonged and explicit defence in that work for the claim that moral law is conceptually prior to any concept of the good or valuable.[35] In *Groundwork*, written earlier, Kant seems to be still a little unclear about the importance of this matter of conceptual priority.[36] Sometimes he seems to emphasize the idea of an end that provides everyone with reasons to act in certain ways, but sometimes he puts the discussion in terms of the absolute value of such an end. But since I have argued that the essential points about the end in itself can be captured without resorting to value as a prior concept, it is justified to treat Kant's position in the later Second *Critique* as his more mature view.

[35] C2 57–64.

[36] See my Chapter 3, section 3, for a more thorough defence of the position that Kant's account of value in *Groundwork* is merely less developed than in Second *Critique*, not inconsistent with it.

This approach does not leave the humanity formulation's demands unexplained and unmotivating. In fact, it is the appeal to value that renders the normative force of the humanity formulation less explicable. The assertion that freedom (or anything else) is so incomparably valuable that it must be treated in special ways will no doubt convince some readers, namely those who are already sympathetic to the fundamental importance of freedom. But, although at one point Guyer endorses the idea that 'it is true as a subjective—or psychological—fact about *all* human beings that they recognize the unconditional value of the freedom of rational agency in general',[37] it seems unlikely that every reader will actually believe freedom to be the one item of supreme value, good as an end in itself. In fact, the persistence of hedonistic and preference-satisfaction versions of consequentialism seems sufficient to show that even if everyone actually grants some value to freedom, not everyone recognizes it as the one item of supreme value or the only thing valuable for its own sake. A flat assertion of value is not a convincing basis for the Categorical Imperative.

Guyer himself seems to be of two minds regarding the need for a justification of the Categorical Imperative. On the one hand, he rejects a traditional, non-value-based reading of the Categorical Imperative, because it leaves acceptance of moral principles' normative force unjustified. But, on the other hand, Guyer repeatedly states that the fundamental principle of morality can never be given a proof, according to Kant. Guyer actually regards this as a particular strength of the value-based account of the Categorical Imperative—it fits with the supposedly Kantian idea that moral principles can never be proven, and instead makes these principles depend on axiomatic claims about value. As support for this reading, Guyer gives extraordinary weight to Kant's early essay from the pre-critical period, 'An Inquiry on the Distinctness of the Principles of Natural Theology and Discourse', known also as the 'prize essay' because it was written for a competition sponsored by the Berlin Academy of Sciences.[38] In the essay, Kant maintains that fundamental moral principles are indemonstrable. On the face of it, Guyer's overall position may appear inconsistent, since he appears to be saying simultaneously that moral principles must be unprovable, that the main weakness of the deontological reading of Kant is that it leaves the Categorical Imperative unproven, and that (contrary to the claim that moral principles are indemonstrable) the value of freedom provides a compelling rationale for obeying the Categorical Imperative. The difficulties may seem to be compounded by the fact that Guyer's position is based heavily on an early

37 Guyer, *Kant on Freedom*, 162–3. The italics are Guyer's.

38 Ibid. 39–42, 58, 130, 195–6, 239 n.

essay of Kant's which in many ways is obviously incompatible with his later, critical philosophy.

A closer look, though, reveals that the overall consistency of Guyer's picture gives it more appeal than initially may be obvious. On this picture, it is not possible to prove strictly that accepting the Categorical Imperative is justified, but the (supposedly) obvious claim that freedom is of absolute value nevertheless provides an intuitively compelling, though not theoretically conclusive, basis for accepting the Categorical Imperative. Guyer says that the Categorical Imperative depends on

> the substantive claim that freedom of the will is the sole unconditional source of moral value. Yet this substantive claim, precisely because it is a claim about absolute value, cannot itself be reached by any method of analysis: it cannot be derived from any theoretical construct nor from any more elementary concept but must somehow be accepted and recognized as the only appropriate basis for moral theory.[39]

We can see how Guyer's different claims fit together. The simplistically deontological view would assert that the Categorical Imperative simply demands compliance, leaving the issue of motivation completely unexplained. But on the other hand, Guyer believes no strict argument can be given to show that one must comply with the Categorical Imperative. The best middle ground, from this perspective, is to note that all of us finitely rational humans actually regard freedom as having absolute value. So the value of freedom gives us a motivational ground for complying with the Categorical Imperative. Although the textual support for this position is scant in Kant's writings of the critical period, the earlier 'prize essay' shows that it is a position that Kant found appealing at least at some point. So a basically consistent picture can be offered in favour of Guyer's position that an axiomatic value claim must be the basis of Kant's moral theory.

But each of Guyer's points is problematic, and, added together, the consistency of Guyer's picture is not enough to overcome the greater strength of the competing picture, that requirements of rationality must be conceptually prior to attributions of value in Kant's mature moral philosophy. Guyer discounts Kant's explicit argument in the Second *Critique* that practical principles are conceptually prior to value. But Guyer's reason for opposing this position only shows that some necessary end must accompany the Categorical Imperative, not that a value claim must underlie it. Then Guyer maintains that the supreme value of freedom is a relatively uncontroversial basis for a Categorical Imperative, but he seems to underestimate how

[39] Ibid. 58. See also the other references in the previous footnote, for consistent endorsement of the view.

controversial this value claim is. Guyer also underemphasizes the extent to which Kant seems to be trying to offer an argument, not just an assertion about value, in *Groundwork* 428–9, and I have argued that a plausible reconstruction of this argument is possible.[40] An attempt at rationally justifying the Categorical Imperative seems preferable to making it rest on a highly controversial value claim. And Kant's assertion in the early 'prize essay' that moral principles can never be rationally justified may serve adequately as a clue to Kant's thinking if it forms part of an overall compelling picture, but it is not a conclusive piece of textual evidence for favouring a view that seems to run contrary to Kant's mature moral theory. The overall view that Guyer proposes in support of basing Kant's ethics on value, then, seems less compelling than the more traditional deontological alternative.

But the distinction between teleological and deontological theories deserves further attention, because of its potential to mislead. I have argued that Kant's theory is best taken as deontological, but that this does not imply that no reason can be given for following moral principles. The question of whether Kant's moral theory is teleological is even more ambiguous. In one sense, of course, Kant's ethics is teleological. Kant makes clear that morality demands that we treat rational nature as an end in itself. And Guyer argues that morality also demands that we seek to bring about the highest good, of happiness in proportion to virtue.[41] Kant's ethics undeniably gives agents ends upon which they must act. So, in a straightforward sense, it gives agents a 'telos', a purpose or end for acting, and so it is 'teleological'. But 'teleological' has also become commonly used as synonymous with 'consequentialist' or 'utilitarian', and theories that are 'teleological' in this sense really are based on conceptually fundamental value claims. Kant's theory could be teleological in the former, more etymologically exact sense, of giving agents necessary ends, without being 'teleological' in the latter sense, of being based on claims about the value of these ends. Guyer's arguments show that Kantian morality demands recognition of an end, not that claims about the value of that end are the foundation of Kant's moral theory.

It is worth considering one additional point, to see if it adds to the appeal of Guyer's position on value. Guyer, like Herman, points out that the opening passages of *Groundwork* rely on a claim about the unconditional value of a good will. Guyer says, 'The first section [of *Groundwork*] thus clearly derives the

[40] Guyer discusses the structure of this argument, in chapter 4, section III (pp. 148–55) and chapter 5, section III (pp. 191–200) but in both cases concludes that the humanity formulation is really meant as an axiomatic claim about the value of rational nature.

[41] Ibid. 93–4, 333–45, 385–99.

moral law from an antecedent conception of the intrinsic value of the good will, contrary to the argument that any conception of value must be derived from an antecedent recognition of the law'.[42] This seems to conflate order of presentation with conceptual priority—that is, it assumes that *Groundwork* must begin with the most conceptually fundamental ideas and then work out their implications. But this would be contrary to Kant's own stated intentions, since Kant takes the first two chapters of *Groundwork* to be starting from common, everyday concepts of morality, and then analysing these concepts to derive the underlying content that moral principles must have. Guyer does address this issue, but he does so by assuming uncharitably that his opponent must think that chapter 1 must be discounted as window dressing, and 'that [chapter 2] appears to replace this teleological argument from common sense with an argument that, like that of the *Critique of Practical Reason*, derives the formula for the moral law from an analysis of the concept of a practical law'.[43] No doubt Guyer is correct to take this strategy as 'superficial',[44] but to oppose his value-based reading does not require disregarding chapter 1 of *Groundwork*. The reconstruction of the argument for the humanity formulation that I have offered in my Chapter 6 does not discount, but instead relies crucially, on the opening idea of *Groundwork*, that a good will is the necessary condition of the value of any other ends. On my reading, the end-setting of a will regulated by moral principles is the necessary condition of the value of all other, contingent, ends. So it is true of my account, as Guyer says it is of his, that there is a progression in the central argument of *Groundwork*, in which 'the intuitive conception of the good will is being replaced with the more abstract notion of rational being as an end in itself'.[45]

So Guyer's arguments do not show that Kant's ethics rest at bottom on a claim about value. And his concerns, along with Herman's and Wood's, can be met without rereading Kant's ethics as value based. The insight that a satisfying moral theory must include a rationale for moral action is correct, but a deontological theory can provide such a rationale. Kant's moral philosophy is based on an end, and arguments can be provided that this end must necessarily be recognized by all rational agents. But this is not because rational agents must recognize its conceptually prior value.

The distinction between the humanity formulation as essentially either a claim about value or a claim about rational requirements may begin to seem like a mere verbal distinction, but it is not. To understand Kant properly, it is of the utmost importance to keep in mind that practical requirements regarding the treatment of humanity are conceptually prior to claims about humanity's

[42] Ibid. 139. [43] Ibid. [44] Ibid. 140. [45] Ibid. 147.

value. This is important both because it is one of the most distinctive features of Kant's moral theory and because getting this conceptual priority wrong results in quite subversive reinterpretations of Kant's ethics. In the next chapter, I will explain how such misunderstandings follow from employing a non-Kantian concept of value.

8

Kantian Value, Beneficence, and Consequentialism

Small mistakes in laying a structure's foundation inevitably lead to conspicuous problems later, and similarly I think that some accounts of particular Kantian duties are significant misinterpretations of Kant that follow naturally from a basic but subtle misunderstanding of the humanity formulation. Christine Korsgaard offers a derivation of the duty of beneficence that supports taking it as a very strong duty to give others' ends the same status as one's own. David Cummiskey adopts similar strategies for deriving particular duties, but pushes them further, and the result is 'Kantian consequentialism', or a set of consequentialist normative principles that supposedly follow from the basic idea of the humanity formulation.

The mistake that I think underlies both Korsgaard's and Cummiskey's arguments is a mistake about Kant's conception of value. I will argue that both Korsgaard and Cummiskey take value to be conceptually prior to rational requirements on action, while Kant intends demands of reason to come first. If one examines the duties that follow from the humanity formulation without prematurely introducing any non-Kantian claims about value, then these duties are not fundamentally consequentialist and do not include a duty to maximize impartially all contingent ends. But if one treats the humanity formulation as primarily a claim about value, then these duties do follow inevitably.

This misunderstanding of Kant's basic approach is largely independent of the main thesis for which I have argued, that 'humanity' is best read as 'good will'. So I think that even those who reject the good will reading may nevertheless accept the main line of argument of this chapter (and even those who accept the good will reading may reject the claim of this chapter). To avoid obscuring the main point of this chapter, about Kant's conception of value, I will leave the 'good will' issue far in the background. I will employ the terms that Korsgaard and Cummiskey use interchangeably with 'humanity', mainly the terms 'rational agency' and 'rational nature'. I do this not to retreat from the good will reading for which I have argued, but to engage the authors on their own terms.

1. The Extent of Duties of Beneficence

Christine Korsgaard's proposed strategy for deriving the duty of beneficence from the humanity formulation seems to make it a very demanding duty, a duty to give the same weight to others' contingent ends as you do to your own. Korsgaard herself does not emphasize the extreme nature of this duty, and in some of her writings she even appears to disavow the extreme conclusion.[1] But the argument she proposes nonetheless leads to this very demanding duty. And even if Korsgaard herself really has in mind a modified version of the argument, it is worth exploring the ramifications of her argument as stated. One commentator on Kant's ethics, David Cummiskey, has adopted Korsgaard's strategy in an attempt to show that the humanity formulation really leads to full-blown consequentialist demands, and if one wishes to resist this conclusion it will be useful to look at Korsgaard's argument.

Whatever Korsgaard's actual, considered position, it does appear that the derivation she offers of the duty of beneficence leads to the strong conclusion that one must give as much weight to others' ends as to one's own. Korsgaard cites Kant's discussion of the duty of beneficence from *Groundwork* 430, where Kant says, 'the ends of a subject who is an end in himself must, if this conception is to have its full effect in me, be also, as far as possible, my ends'. Korsgaard is willing to read this literally, and she accordingly says, 'To treat another as an end in itself is to treat his or her ends as objectively good, as you do your own'.[2] Her rationale for this strong requirement is that the end in itself is 'the power of rational choice', and this power of choice is the 'source of the goodness' of all contingent ends.[3] So she says, '[W]e must regard ourselves as capable of conferring value upon the objects of our choice, the ends we set', and since others also have this power of rational choice, 'we must regard others as capable of conferring value by reason of their rational choices'.[4] On Korsgaard's picture, I regard my own ends as valuable because they are set by my own rational nature, but since every other rational being has the same rational nature and power to set ends, I must also regard her ends as just as valuable as mine. Since others' ends are as valuable as mine, I

[1] Korsgaard appears to disavow the extreme version in *Creating the Kingdom of Ends* (Cambridge: Cambridge University Press, 1996), 290.

[2] Ibid. 128. [3] Ibid. 123. [4] Ibid. 260.

ought to give their ends the same consideration as my own. 'We ought to acknowledge that others are sources of value by treating their chosen ends as good, and pursuing their happiness as they see it'.[5] The result is a sort of mini-consequentialism, not with regard to all duties, but with regard to the duty of promoting others' ends.

This is a controversial interpretation of Kant's position. Barbara Herman and Thomas E. Hill, Jr., have denied that the humanity formulation grounds a duty to regard others' ends as deserving the same status in your deliberations as your own ends. Herman says,

> There are considerable grounds for skepticism about such a duty. It involves a radical conception of a community of need and action in which it does not seem to matter whose end an end is .... Although it is hard not to see Kant's words [in *Groundwork* 430] as implying such a duty, it is implausible in its own right and at odds with deeper features of Kantian ethics.[6]

Herman suggests that making another's ends my own, as Kant says we ought to in *Groundwork* 430, might best be taken 'not in the sense that I should be prepared to act in his place (I act for him; I get for him what he wants when he cannot) but rather in the sense that I support his status as a pursuer of ends'. And Thomas E. Hill, Jr., similarly says of the supposed duty of 'general beneficence' to make others' ends one's own, that 'it is hard to see how such a duty would follow from the principle to treat humanity as an end'.[7] This is because 'Valuing someone's rational pursuit of his own ends is not the same as wanting him to have what he desires, or what he will most enjoy'.[8]

There are several reasons to favour the position of Herman and Hill. Herman argues that the supposed duty of being indifferent between pursuing one's own and others' contingent ends 'would not be supportive of the expression of rational agency in one's life'.[9] This is because the duty to satisfy others' ends for them would 'be at odds with a moral conception that stressed the development of capacities for rational choice and effective action'. In addition, both Herman and Hill note that there seem to be two different kinds of duties that could be described as duties of beneficence. Hill points out that when Kant first presents the duty of beneficence in *Groundwork* 423, as an example of a duty

[5] Ibid. 17.

[6] Barbara Herman, *The Practice of Moral Judgment* (Cambridge, Mass.: Harvard University Press, 1993), 70.

[7] Thomas E. Hill, Jr., *Dignity and Practical Reason in Kant's Moral Theory* (Ithaca, NY: Cornell University Press, 1992), 54.

[8] See also Onora O' Neill, *Constructions of Reason* (Cambridge: Cambridge University Press, 1989), 116, 134, 199.

[9] This quotation and the next are from Herman, *The Practice of Moral Judgment*, 70.

that follows from the universalizability formulation, it is not a duty to satisfy just any of a rational being's ends, but rather a duty to aid others in distress.[10] Herman similarly distinguishes between 'ends that an agent could easily give up on discovering that he could not realize them without aid (going to a movie on a day I am short of cash) and ends that an agent cannot rationally abandon (true needs)'. Both Herman and Hill think it is a mistake to give all of another's ends the same moral status as her true needs.

There is also textual support for taking the general duty to promote others' ends as a limited duty.[11] Although the distinction between perfect and imperfect duties is a matter of scholarly controversy, one plausible reading of it would support the less demanding version of the duty of beneficence.[12] In *Groundwork* 421, Kant suggests that imperfect duties differ from perfect duties in that it is permissible sometimes to 'make an exception in favor of inclination' to an imperfect duty, but not to a perfect duty. Since Kant classifies beneficence as an imperfect duty, it is reasonable to think that one need not always treat others' ends as having the same importance as one's own. But in *Metaphysics of Morals*, Kant's position is murkier. On the one hand, Kant says that the doctrine of virtue 'cannot refuse some room for exceptions', and that 'imperfect duties are ... only duties of virtue. Fulfillment of them is merit ... but failure to fulfill them is not culpability'.[13] He also allows that the practical duty of beneficence is consistent with giving greater weight to the concerns of oneself and those one cares about than to the rest of humankind (MM 451–2). This fits with the idea that one is only obligated to give some weight to others' ends, not to give them weight equal to one's own. On the other hand, Kant says that 'A wide duty is not to be taken as permission to make exceptions to the maxim of actions, but only as permission to limit one maxim of duty by another' (MM 390). Then the fact that beneficence is a wide duty does not give moral permission to choose in some cases to act to satisfy one's own desires instead of others'. While this last quotation and the *Groundwork* claim that one must make others' ends one's own are suggestive of the strong duty to consider all ends impartially, regardless of whose ends they are, the support they provide is far from decisive in light of the contrary texts. Since the texts do not conclusively settle the interpretative issue, it is important to consider

[10] Thomas E. Hill, Jr., *Dignity and Practical Reason*, 54, *Human Welfare and Moral Worth* (Oxford: Oxford University Press, 2002), 212–13.

[11] Thomas E. Hill, Jr., does an outstanding job of relating the textual issues here to the duty of beneficence. Hill, *Human Welfare and Moral Worth*, 201–43.

[12] For a thorough discussion of Kant's view of perfect and imperfect duties, see Marcia Baron, *Kantian Ethics Almost without Apology* (Ithaca, NY: Cornell University Press, 1995), 21–107.

[13] The first quotation is from MM 233, the second from MM 390.

which version of the duty of beneficence fits better overall with the rest of Kant's moral theory.

The point that Herman and Hill make, about the tension between a duty to make others' ends one's own and a respect for their rational agency, is one reason to favour the weaker version of the duty of benevolence. But an even more pressing reason to accept the weaker version is that the argument for the stronger version relies on a fundamentally non-Kantian conception of value, by implicitly taking value as conceptually prior to rational requirements on action. Korsgaard's argument for the strong version begins by noting that I must regard my own rational agency as unconditionally and incomparably valuable (the conclusion of Korsgaard's regress argument).[14] But, Korsgaard points out, it is rational agency as such that has this special value, not just my own agency, so I must treat not only my own rational agency but all rational agency as an end in itself. Treating my own ends as valuable is a way of acknowledging the value of my own rational nature as an end in itself, because what makes my own ends valuable is that I set the ends through the exercise of rational agency. But since other agents' rational nature has the same value as my own, all other agents' end-setting confers the same value on their ends as my end-setting confers on my ends. Since all of everyone's contingent ends have the same value, whose ends they are does not matter in deciding whose ends to satisfy. Only the strength of some agent's desire for the end makes different ends have different value, but it is a matter of indifference who it is that desires the end.

This account relies on a non-Kantian conception of value, because it prematurely takes the value of agents' contingent ends as determined (as a direct implication of treating all rational agents equally as ends in themselves), and then demands that since these contingent ends have equal value, they should be given equal weight in everyone's deliberations. But the claim that all agents' ends are equally valuable actually does not follow directly from the basic requirement to treat all rational agents equally as ends in themselves. The proper strategy to take in deriving the duty of beneficence from the humanity formulation is to acknowledge that one ought to treat both oneself and other agents as ends in themselves, but then to ask what kind of action this dictates with regard to satisfying others' ends. If one does not introduce the idea of the value of contingent ends (prematurely) at this point, the natural answer is not that one must give others' ends the same weight as one's own. Instead, the duty seems to be a more limited, 'imperfect' duty not to be indifferent to

[14] I think my description accurately captures the account Korsgaard gives in 'Kant's Formula of Humanity', esp. 123 and 127–8, and also in the passages cited below from other works by Korsgaard.

others' ends because, as Hill puts it, 'we cannot show respect for the rational agency of others without giving some weight to the projects they choose to pursue'.[15] Hill explains that to acknowledge that others' rational nature, like our own, is an end in itself only implies that we must give the same weight to others' ends as we can expect them to give our ends. We regard our own ends as important, when they are rationally adopted, and so as 'worthy of consideration in others' deliberations as well as our own'. Then we must also regard others' ends as having some importance in our deliberations as well. But

> This argument does not imply that we value the happiness or the particular ends of others in just the same way we value our own; for even in valuing our own rational agency, as rational agents, we are not claiming that others should give equal regard to our happiness or our particular ends.

If one resists the temptation to insert a step in the argument that states that all agents' contingent ends have equal value, then the Hillian approach to acknowledging others as ends in themselves seems more natural than the Korsgaardian one. And it is best to resist the step that makes a claim about the value of contingent ends, because it is more thoroughly Kantian to reserve claims about value until after questions of rationally required actions have been settled.

If Hill's position here seems to lack detail, it can be supplemented by the argument for the humanity formulation I offered in Chapter 6, and the derivation of the duty of beneficence I proposed in Chapter 7. My account provides better support for the limited version of the duty of beneficence than for the more demanding version. The argument for the humanity formulation itself does not yet tell us anything about a general duty to promote others' ends. The 'subjective principle' of treating oneself as an end only shows that there is no reasonable justification for choosing to act immorally, or for destroying oneself or one's minimal powers of rationality just in order to satisfy inclination. The 'objective principle' then says that (if the humanity formulation is to serve as a fundamental moral principle) one must treat others in roughly analogous ways—one must not destroy others in order to satisfy one's own inclinations, nor impair their rationality, nor tempt them to immoral behaviour. This basic principle does seem to entail directly that one ought to prevent the imminent death or loss of rational powers of another rational being, even if doing so costs the satisfaction of some of one's own inclinations. In Herman's terms, one might be morally required to give up a great deal in order to satisfy another's 'true needs'. And this by itself would no doubt require some significant changes

[15] Hill, *Dignity and Practical Reason*, 144.

in the ways that humans treat one another. But this does not yet tell us what duties we have regarding others' ends more generally, since not all ends are true needs. The general duty to aid others in pursuit of their ends does not follow directly from the argument for the humanity formulation. To derive this general duty of beneficence requires invoking details of human nature, and I have proposed that one relevant fact about human nature is the moral feeling of *Achtung* that arises from contemplating either the power of moral law or the example of this power that is provided by the idea of a good will. When one thinks of a being with good will (either because of an apparent example, or as an ideal supplied by one's own power of reason), the feeling of *Achtung* strikes down one's self-conceit and forces one to acknowledge that oneself and one's own ends are not all that matters. By negating the tendency to see one's own inclinations as all-important, the feeling of *Achtung* gives rise to the idea that others' ends should not be ignored. But this does not imply that another's ends must receive the same consideration as your own ends, in your own deliberations. It only implies that others' ends deserve the same consideration in your deliberations as you can reasonably expect your own ends to carry in others' deliberations.

Then the argument that Korsgaard offers for the strong version of the duty of beneficence contains a gap. She argues that in order to express recognition of other rational beings as ends in themselves, you must regard their contingent ends as having the same value as your own. But this ignores Hill's proposal that by giving others' ends the same weight in your deliberations that you expect your ends to carry in theirs, you adequately treat others' rational nature as an end in itself. And the only apparent reason to reject Hill's proposal is to appeal to a non-Kantian conception of value. By claiming that every rational being confers equal value on her ends, and then maintaining that this implies that all agents' contingent ends have equal value, one can plausibly conclude that since all agents' ends are equally valuable, they all ought to receive the same consideration. The cost of following this strategy is that one must prematurely introduce a claim about the value of ends, and then must define reasonable action in terms of that pre-existing value. The more Kantian approach is first to settle the question of how one should act, and then use value only as a way to capture these requirements on action.

There is room to doubt whether Korsgaard really thinks that every agent's ends must carry the same weight in everyone's deliberations. At least sometimes, she seems to deny it. In 'The Reasons We Can Share', which is not primarily an exegesis of Kant, but is Korsgaard's proposal for a roughly Kantian approach to the debate about 'reasons', she says,

I am not here concerned to argue, as Nagel is in *The Possibility of Altruism*, that we are always obliged to promote everyone's ambitions, and that therefore we must find some 'combinatorial principles' for weighing up the many reasons they provide ... I do not myself believe that reasons *can* be added across the boundaries of persons. And since we cannot always act for everyone's reasons, that cannot be our duty.[16]

This suggests that she is not committed to the claim that others' ends and one's own ought to be regarded as bearing the same prima facie weight (with the degree of an agent's commitment to an end being the decisive factor that must determine action). Yet there is also contrary evidence that Korsgaard thinks it is not morally relevant whose ends are whose. Her use of the term 'objectively good' to include contingent ends based on inclination is one bit of evidence. Korsgaard says,

A thing, then, can be said to be objectively good, either if it is unconditionally good or if it is conditionally good and the condition under which it is good is met. The happiness of the virtuous, for this reason, forms the other part of the 'highest good': virtue, and happiness in proportion to virtue, together comprise all that is objectively good. A conditionally good thing, like happiness, is objectively good when its condition is met.[17]

This category of objective goodness or value is not Kant's, and that is not an accident. In fact, Kant uses the distinction between 'subjective' and 'objective' ends ('subjektiven Zwecken' and 'objektiven Zwecken') to correspond to, respectively, ends given by inclination and ends given by reason alone (G 427–8). Only ends given by reason alone are valuable equally for all rational beings, which suggests that agents' contingent ends do not all demand equal consideration in the deliberations of every rational being. Korsgaard seems to elide the distinction between objective and subjective ends, by saying that both can have 'objective goodness', if the proper conditions are met. In general outline, Korsgaard's position in 'Lecture 4: The Origin of Value and the Scope of Obligation' in *The Sources of Normativity* also appears to support the idea that others' ends at least sometimes provide equal reasons for everyone to act in certain ways.[18] This seems to be the overall point of her sections 4.2.1 to 4.2.12, a point which is perhaps best summarized by her rhetorical question, 'Why shouldn't language force us to reason together, in just the same way it forces us to think together?'[19]

[16] Korsgaard, *Creating the Kingdom of Ends*, 290.

[17] Ibid. 118–19. See also 258, where she repeats her definition.

[18] Christine Korsgaard, *The Sources of Normativity* (Cambridge: Cambridge University Press, 1996), 131–45.

[19] Ibid. 142.

But apart from the question of Korsgaard's actual position, the argument for equal consideration of all agents' ends deserves consideration on its own merits, since it is an initially plausible line of thinking that could lead to interpretative trouble. In fact, I think David Cummiskey's arguments for 'Kantian consequentialism' rely on fundamentally the same strategy as Korsgaard's arguments for the duty to promote impartially the ends of all rational beings, and fall prey to the same objections.

2. Cummiskey's Argument for Kantian Consequentialism

If Korsgaard provides an argument that might be taken to support a sort of limited consequentialism regarding consideration of one's own and others' ends, then David Cummiskey is perfectly happy to employ similar arguments to argue for a full-blown consequentialist interpretation of Kant's ethics.

In his original and challenging book *Kantian Consequentialism*, David Cummiskey argues that the central ideas of Kant's moral philosophy provide claims about value which, if applied consistently, lead to consequentialist moral duties.[20] While Kant himself was not a consequentialist, Cummiskey thinks he should have been, given his basic approach to ethics. Cummiskey believes that the cornerstone of Kant's ethics is the humanity formulation of the Categorical Imperative, and that the humanity formulation leads to consequentialism because of the special and equal value it attributes to every agent's rational nature. The non-consequentialist Kantian is 'faced with quite a challenge', Cummiskey says, because she must provide 'an explanation of the equal practical significance of each person that does not generate the consequentialist interpretation'.[21] Because of the value Kant attributes to every rational nature, 'For structural reasons alone, consequentialism should follow' from the humanity formulation.[22]

Cummiskey is right that an important element of Kant's ethics, perhaps the central point, is the claim that rational nature must be given a unique and supreme place in one's deliberations. And it is natural to take this as fundamentally a claim about value, and to think that this inevitably leads to a requirement to maximally promote this incomparable value. But this line of thinking, though natural, is mistaken. Cummiskey is misled because he takes

20 David Cummiskey, *Kantian Consequentialism* (New York: Oxford University Press, 1996).

21 Ibid. 100. 22 Ibid. 101.

for granted a concept of value that is more consequentialist than Kantian. When understood in light of a Kantian, rather than a consequentialist, concept of value, Kant's claim that rational nature is an end in itself it does not naturally generate consequentialist normative principles.

The difference between Kantian consequentialism and more standard, non-consequentialist interpretations of Kant's ethics is a difference at the level of mid-level normative principles. Cummiskey accepts Kant's basic approach to ethics and the fundamental moral principle expressed in the humanity formulation of the Categorical Imperative. But Cummiskey thinks the more specific action-guiding principles that follow from Kant's approach, and especially from the humanity formulation, are (as Kant failed to see) consequentialist. The 'Kantian consequentialism' that Cummiskey thinks follows from Kant's moral theory is 'a requirement to maximally promote two tiers of value: rational nature and happiness, where rational nature is lexically prior to happiness'.[23] A little more specifically,

> The first part of this principle does not require us to maximize rational being or our rational capacities. Rational nature is not something we are to maximize in that sense. It does, however, require the maximal promotion of the conditions that are necessary for the flourishing of rational agency. The second part of this principle may require something like the maximization of rational-desire-satisfaction or corrected-preference-satisfaction.[24]

The sense in which these principles are consequentialist is that they require maximization with regard to that which is taken to have value for every agent, namely rational nature itself and the ends set by beings with rational nature.

Cummiskey mentions several demands that Kantian consequentialism places on agents, some of which coincide with non-consequentialist Kantian duties and some of which do not. The three relevant categories of duties are duties of respecting one's own rational nature, duties of respecting others' rational natures, and duties of promoting others' ends.[25]

The Kantian consequentialist and the standard Kantian most obviously diverge in their accounts of the duty of beneficence, or the duty to promote others' ends. The standard Kantian view says we only have a duty to give some consideration to others' ends and to promote these ends at least sometimes. But

[23] David Cummiskey, *Kantian Consequentialism* (New York: Oxford University Press, 1996), 99.

[24] Ibid. 89.

[25] These categories of duties are not the same as Kant's categories of perfect and imperfect duties to one's self and to others. That is no surprise, since I am reconstructing Cummiskey's argument here and he actually thinks the perfect/imperfect duty distinction is philosophically unjustified for Kant (see ibid. 105–23).

Cummiskey follows Korsgaard's lead and argues that the duty of beneficence requires not just giving some weight to others' ends, but actually giving others' ends the same weight as one's own. Cummiskey's line of argument for this duty also resembles Korsgaard's. Cummiskey takes the argument for humanity as an end in itself to show that, since the value of my rational nature and ends has the same 'rational ground' as the value of others' rational natures and ends, 'I must recognize others and their ends as having the same value' as mine.[26] This leads to a duty to promote maximally the satisfaction of others' ends, because everyone's ends, as it were, go into the same pot, and I have no more reason to satisfy any one person's ends (including my own) than I do to satisfy another's. The maximization involved is straightforward, and so is the contrast with the more limited version of the duty, to give some weight to others' ends and help promote their ends at least sometimes.

On the other hand, Cummiskey and a conventional Kantian would apparently agree about the sorts of duties one has with regard to respecting one's own rational nature. To respect rational nature in oneself, Cummiskey thinks one should choose actions that one believes are rationally justified, seek out justifications for actions, and develop one's capacity for evaluating actions and ends.[27] Another way he puts this is that 'If I value my rational nature, then I must develop and exercise my rational capacities, then follow my best judgement'. The conventional Kantian would agree that we have this sort of duty of self-perfection, and it does not appear to involve any real maximization. I would emphasize, since I have argued that humanity denotes a more fully rational nature, or good will, that one must not only act in accordance with demands of instrumental reason but also obey the moral principles legislated by one's own *Wille*. One should act rationally in these ways, of course, but Cummiskey seems wise to deny that we are obligated to try to maximize our rational capacities or the use of rational capacities.[28] To do so might involve becoming so self-absorbed that one fails to satisfy one's other important ends. Making it one's goal to maximize the rationality of one's particular choices, if this means maximizing the extent to which one's actions will achieve a consistent set of ends, will not be rational. Obeying the moral demands of *Wille* is another story, to some extent, since one ought always to accept moral principles as a sufficient reason for acting. But Kant also says that one ought not to become a moral fanatic who tries to see moral obligation everywhere.[29] So Kant seems to be on Cummiskey's side here, in denying that one ought to seek to maximize the exercise of one's power of reason.

[26] Ibid. 54. [27] Ibid. 98. [28] Ibid. 91.

[29] MM 409. See Chapter 3, section 3 of this book for a more thorough discussion.

Although there is no maximization involved in respecting one's own rational nature, Kantian consequentialism does demand maximization in duties of respecting others' rational natures.

The Kantian non-consequentialist would think there are duties to avoid destroying other beings with rational nature, and to refrain from tempting them to act irrationally. She would also think that, since we have a duty to give some weight to others' rationality, choices, and ends, we should at least sometimes act in ways that tend to increase others' liberty, security, and subsistence—the conditions needed for them to develop and exercise their rationality. To use Herman's term, we ought to act to satisfy others' true needs, when they are imminently threatened. But Cummiskey's Kantian consequentialism would go further in each case, demanding not only that each person must refrain from destroying other rational agents or causing them to behave irrationally, but also that each person see to it that others are free, to the maximum extent possible, from being destroyed or tempted.[30] And not only must each person sometimes take some steps to ensure others' welfare and liberty, but also each must seek to ensure these maximally. The duty to 'promote the conditions necessary for forming, revising, and effectively pursuing a conception of the good' should be maximally pursued, and therefore can 'generate moral claims to liberty, to security, and to subsistence'.[31]

In sum, then, Kantian consequentialism differs from standard Kantian ethical theory in the following ways: It requires impartially and maximally promoting rationally set ends, regardless of whether these ends are one's own or someone else's, as opposed to standard Kantian ethics which demands only some consideration of others' ends; it demands maximally promoting the level of liberty, security, and subsistence in a society rather than just demanding that one take some steps to ensure these for other agents when they are most threatened; and it requires one not only to refrain from destroying other rational beings or from tempting them to irrationality, but also to maximize the extent to which they are free from destruction or temptation.[32]

Cummiskey's argument for Kantian consequentialism contains two main strategic steps. First he argues that the humanity formulation of the Categorical Imperative establishes that every rational nature has equal and incomparable value. Then he argues that Kantian consequentialism provides the only normative principles that take seriously this equal and incomparable value.

[30] Cummiskey, *Kantian Consequentialism*, 86–7. [31] Ibid. 98.

[32] The duty to see that rational agents are free from destruction might also fall under the category of providing others with as much security as possible.

Cummiskey begins by offering a 'reconstruction and defense of Kant's own derivation of the formula of humanity'. He does this because the argument for the humanity formulation is 'the central argument of (Kant's) moral theory', and 'it justifies a distinctly Kantian form of normative consequentialism'. He adds that 'The consequentialist interpretation of the conclusion is a deviation from the otherwise standard derivation'.[33]

I will argue that Cummiskey misreads Kant's argument in a fundamental way, but because the mistake (or alleged mistake) lies more in broad strategy rather than the details, I will not dwell on the details of Cummiskey's reconstruction.[34] So, briefly, Cummiskey first argues that to take one's own rational nature as supremely valuable is a 'subjective principle' to which every rational person must adhere.[35] As a reconstruction of this, the first step in the derivation, Cummiskey offers a 'regress argument' like Korsgaard's, which says rational nature must have an incomparable value for an agent because all of her other ends have value only in virtue of being adopted through her rational nature; rational nature has incomparable value for a person because it is the necessary 'condition' of the value of all her other ends. But not only does the value of her own rational nature provide a 'subjective principle' for each agent. Every agent must also recognize as an 'objective principle' the value of rational nature wherever it exists. This is because an agent must recognize that all other rational beings must also conceive of their rational natures as having incomparable value, and 'for the exact same reason' as she conceives of her own rational nature in this way.[36] So it is 'rational nature as such' that every agent should take to be incomparably valuable.

Cummiskey acknowledges that a 'rational egoist response' is possible. This response would admit that 'each rational agent must treat her own rational nature as an end in itself', but would deny 'that each rational agent must conceive of rational agency as such as an end in itself'. Cummiskey replies that 'The response that all Kantians must take in determining the weight and significance of others and their ends, however, should be clear'.[37] The position all Kantians must take is expressed in what Cummiskey calls the 'equal-value

33 Ibid. 69, 62.

34 Although I think there is a problem with the fundamental strategy of Cummiskey's reconstruction, I do think he is right that some of the details are fairly 'standard', inasmuch as Cummiskey adopts roughly the strategy that one prominent commentator, Christine Korsgaard, follows. See Korsgaard, *Creating the Kingdom of Ends*, 119–24.

35 Commiskey, *Kantian Consequentialism*, 69–73.

36 Ibid. 73–4.

37 Ibid. 73–4. I am simplifying Cummiskey's argument here, leaving out four paragraphs about Thomas Nagel that intervene between the rational egoist response and the quotation last cited. This simplification does not unfairly misrepresent Cummiskey's main point.

principle': if the values of *x* and *y* are based on the same rational ground, then they have the same value.[38] He adds that 'An argument for consequentialism, based on this principle, will be developed in the next chapter'.[39]

Cummiskey calls his main argument for Kantian consequentialism, which is based on the equal value principle, the 'equivalence argument'. He thinks that 'if one accepts the Kantian argument for the end in itself, one is committed to the equal practical significance of all rational beings and their happiness (interpreted as the satisfaction of an ordered set of rational desires)'.[40] This is because 'the actions of any person, in the final analysis, have the exact same rational basis and justification as any of my justified actions'. What justifies the actions and makes the ends of the actions valuable is that they are the products of rational choice. Since it is rationally required for each agent to regard her own rational nature as valuable, it is true that each agent has the same rational ground for valuing her own rational nature. Then the equal value principle would say that since the value of other agents and their ends are based on the same rational ground as the value of myself and my ends, the same 'value I attribute to myself and my ends, I thus must also attribute to each other agent and her ends'.[41]

Cummiskey continues the equivalence argument, saying that if 'all rational beings are equally significant in deciding what to do', then 'I must choose courses of action that reflect this equal value'. Furthermore,

> Clearly, the most straightforward way to do this is to treat the value of all such beings equally. And the most straightforward way to do that involves striving as far as I can to promote the necessary conditions for, first, reflective rational choice, and, second, the effective realization of rationally chosen ends.[42]

This is the key move in the equivalence argument. Cummiskey in effect asserts that the only way to treat each rational nature as equally valuable is to put all the rational natures into the same pool and try as far as possible to treat them identically. This must be the point of the claim that treating the value of all rational beings 'equally' is the 'most straightforward way' to 'choose actions that reflect this equal value' of all rational natures. Otherwise 'treating the value of all such beings equally' is just a repetition of the claim that one must choose actions that reflect equal value, rather than a consequence of it.

The way Cummiskey reaches the conclusion that the conditions of rational choice should be maximized is to apply a 'put them all in one pot' view of

[38] Thomas E. Hill, Jr., questions whether an equal value principle of the kind Cummiskey proposes can be consistent with Kant's ethics. See Hill, *Human Welfare and Moral Worth*, 224–5.

[39] Cummiskey, *Kantian Consequentialism*, 74.

[40] Ibid. 87. The parenthetical remark is Cummiskey's.

[41] Ibid. 88.

[42] Ibid. 89.

rational nature. He looks at rational natures and wonders what it would take to come closest to ensuring that all these equally and supremely valuable rational natures are kept intact. The natural answer, on this approach, is to see to it that the conditions for their flourishing are maximally promoted. And since that is what it would take to see that they are all preserved, that is what each agent has an obligation to try to bring about. Similarly, once we have assured the maximal preservation and flourishing of rational natures, the 'one pot' view tells us then to maximize impartially the satisfaction of rational agents' ends. These ends all go into one pool, and the question to ask is what to do with them. The natural answer, given that whose ends they are is no reason to favour some ends over others, is to consider the importance of each end to some rational being, and the number of ends one can satisfy, and to satisfy as many of the most important ends as possible. Which is straightforward consequentialism.

If Cummiskey is right that the humanity formulation is primarily meant to show that every rational nature has an equal and incomparable value, and that the only way to acknowledge this equal value is by following consequentialist principles, then he has shown that Kant should have been a consequentialist. But neither of these claims is correct in quite the sense required for Cummiskey's argument to succeed.

Cummiskey is of course right, in one sense, to say that Kant's ethics implies that each rational nature has an equal and incomparable value. But this is not the fundamental point of the humanity formulation. Instead, the humanity formulation establishes 'principles of action' or ways in which rational nature must be treated. After these principles are established, and after they are applied to human conditions to arrive at more specific duties, then one can express these moral requirements in terms of value. But to treat the primary task of Kant's ethics as establishing claims about value is implicitly to assume a concept of value that is more at home in a consequentialist ethical theory than in a non-consequentialist Kantian ethical theory. The humanity formulation does not first of all make a claim about value, so it does not lead to the 'one-pot' view of rational natures' value, and does not support Kantian consequentialism.

Cummiskey distances himself from one non-Kantian view of value, which he calls the 'stuff' view. In order to avoid a possible *reductio ad absurdum* objection to Kantian consequentialism, Cummiskey explicitly renounces the view that value is some 'stuff' out in the world.

> The stuff view of value is a familiar view, but it does not capture the Kantian conception of value ... The idea [of the Kantian view] is that each existing person in virtue of his

rational nature (or humanity) has a claim to equal consideration. The idea is not that rational nature is an intrinsic value from the point of view of the universe, so the more of it the better. The idea is that all persons, in virtue of the value they place on their own rational nature, are committed to the equal value of other persons.[43]

Cummiskey disavows the stuff view of value because he believes that if he accepted that value is some stuff, and that rational nature has the highest sort of value, he would be saddled with the implausible conclusion that we have a duty to maximize the number of rational beings in the world.

While Cummiskey does not quite grant a dubious ontological status to value as some stuff out in the world, he does rely on a non-Kantian way of thinking about value. Cummiskey does this when he takes the claim that rational nature has a special value as conceptually prior to the question of how rational agents should act with regard to rational nature. He says that the humanity formulation first establishes the 'subjective principle' that each agent's rational nature is incomparably valuable for her, then that it establishes the 'objective principle' that every rational nature also has the same kind of incomparable value. Only after concluding that each rational nature has special and equal value does Cummiskey turn to the question of what choices (duties) are rationally required in light of this equal and special value, and he concludes that all the rational natures must be made to flourish and the satisfaction of their ends must be maximized. In a straightforward sense, his argument treats value as primary and the choices of rational agents as derivative. This approach embodies, in a broad sense, a typically consequentialist way of thinking about value. It takes value to be conceptually prior to questions about right actions. But this is not the only way to think about value.

The alternative, Kantian approach to value is to think of talk about value as a shorthand for talk about what rational agents would choose. This is the idea Kant is expressing when he maintains that all value is determined by practical laws, or by the choices that rational agents would make. What makes something valuable is that a rational being chooses it, not vice versa. In a straightforward sense, rational beings' choices are conceptually prior to any attributions of value.[44] Employing this alternative concept of value leads one first to wonder what the argument for the humanity formulation tells us about how to treat rational nature, and only then to summarize these principles in value terms. This contrasts with Cummiskey's approach, of taking the humanity formulation's main purpose as telling us that each rational nature has a special and equal value, and leaving us to figure out how to treat rational nature in light of its value.

[43] Cummiskey, *Kantian Consequentialism*, 74.

[44] See my Chapter 3, section 3, above for a more thorough discussion of this, with textual references.

As I have argued in Chapter 6, a look at the language of Kant's argument for the humanity formulation suggests that Kant did in fact mean it primarily to be establishing principles of action, principles which we can summarize by saying rational nature should be treated as an end in itself, rather than establishing a value claim. The derivation of the humanity formulation is the search for an imperative, a 'practical law', which describes how any rational agent must treat rational nature.[45] First a 'subjective principle' is sought, and it is not a claim about value but rather a principle 'of human action' which describes the choices that each rational agent must make regarding her own rational nature. Then the derivation gives a reason for thinking there is also an 'objective principle' that requires an agent, in so far as she is rational, to make certain kinds of choices regarding others' rational natures. The conclusion of the derivation, which is Kant's statement of the humanity formulation itself, then is telling us to treat rational nature ('humanity') in certain ways, namely as an end in itself. And then, to derive more specific duties regarding rational nature, Kant considers the application of the humanity formulation to human nature, to develop a 'metaphysics of morals'. At this stage of the argument, Kant need not entertain the question of how to react to rational beings in light of their incomparable value. The question of how to treat rational beings has already been settled, and value claims are just ways of abbreviating the action-guiding principles that tell us how to treat rational nature.

Once it is clear that rational nature deserves special treatment wherever it occurs, and once the kind of special treatment is specified, one might express the idea by saying that rational nature has various kinds of special value. Since you must treat it in the specific ways that are rationally required, regardless of the self-interested incentives you have for treating it otherwise, one could say that rational nature has an incomparably higher value than the satisfaction of self-interested incentives, or, more simply, that it is incomparably valuable. And since you should give every other rational being the same kind of consideration in your deliberations that you can demand in their deliberations, one could say that all rational nature is equally valuable.

But the talk about value is not the basis of duties toward humanity. Instead, employing value terms is just a way to capture conceptually prior ideas about the content of these duties. The duties Kant wishes to convey in the imperative to treat rational nature as an end in itself do not include maximization. And there is no apparent reason to think Kant is mistaken in his beliefs about the kinds of specific normative principles involved in this imperative. The reason Cummiskey presses is that only consequentialist principles can acknowledge

[45] The quotations in this paragraph are from G 428–9.

the special and equal value of rational nature. But I have argued that, when we see what value talk amounts to for Kant, the value claims can be accommodated perfectly well by non-consequentialist action-guiding principles.

If Cummiskey wishes to show that Kant should have espoused consequentialist normative principles, Cummiskey must show that the Kantian concept of value is inferior to the consequentialist concept of value, which identifies some objects or states of affairs that have value, and then says we must act in a way that reflects that value. In the absence of such a demonstration, Cummiskey's argument constitutes something like a begging of the question, since Kant takes value terms to be merely a way to describe the ways that rational agents would choose to act. The more typically consequentialist view of value may turn out to be correct, but it is not the only possibility. Until it is shown to be superior to the Kantian account of value, Cummiskey's 'equivalence argument' for Kantian consequentialism is incomplete.

It is important, then, to keep Kant's conception of value clearly in mind when deriving duties from the humanity formulation. To take value as prior to rational choice or moral requirements is a natural approach for contemporary philosophers steeped in consequentialism and decision theory. But it is fundamentally contrary to Kant's conception of value, and small mistakes in the basic understanding of the humanity formulation can lead to large errors at the level of particular duties.

9

Non-Human Animals, Humanity, and the Kingdom of Ends

So far, my focus has been mostly on scholarly issues—the meaning of 'humanity', Kant's argument for the humanity formulation, a strategy for deriving particular duties from it, and the importance of restricting value to its proper Kantian role. But the relevance of the good will reading of the humanity formulation is not restricted to Kant scholarship. I think the idea of a good will's importance can also shed light on current moral controversies, and plays an essential role in an intriguing 'constructivist' approach to thinking about moral rules. In this chapter, I will focus particularly on one pragmatic moral issue, the moral status of non-human animals. But this will lead to some general conclusions about how Kant's ethics may help resolve other such issues.

It is often thought that Kant's ethics embodies a particular kind of mistake about non-human animals' moral status, and the humanity formulation in particular has been taken as a paradigm example of this egregious mistake. The mistake is to enshrine rationality as the sole criterion for inclusion in the realm of moral consideration. Rational beings, on this reading of Kant, are incomparably important and must never be mistreated, while all other beings are morally unimportant and deserve no moral consideration for their own sake (though there may be duties not to mistreat them because of the effect this mistreatment would have, in the long or short run, on rational beings). Someone advocating reform of our attitudes toward non-human animals might well find this 'Kantian' view offensive, and work hard to undermine it.

Many philosophers in recent years have argued against the supposedly Kantian view, and more generally against any view that denies animals inherent moral status. One plausible idea that underlies many of these arguments for reform is that it is basically arbitrary to treat humans as if they have greater moral significance than non-human animals, just because of some characteristic that humans possess and other animals lack. Different levels of rationality could not ground such a fundamental difference in moral status, and other characteristics, such as language use, capacity for moral thought, or mere biological species may seem at least as irrelevant.

This basic charge, that it is arbitrary to pick out any particular trait as a basis for difference in moral status, initially seems plausible and perhaps even compelling. But I think it is incorrect. I will argue that there is prima facie reason to regard a good will, a strongly rational nature possessed by beings who are committed to morality, as a non-arbitrary criterion for a fundamental difference in moral status. More precisely, I will argue that anyone who participates in a philosophical discussion about the moral status of animals is committed, at least implicitly and provisionally, to the presumption that beings who possess a commitment to morality have a higher moral status than beings who lack this commitment. Since many humans have such a commitment, and no non-humans do, there is a good prima facie reason to think many humans have a higher moral status than any non-human animals.

I emphasize that it is only a prima facie case, because my argument is intended mainly to rebut the charge that it is arbitrary to grant creatures different moral status in virtue of any traits they possess. I do not take my arguments to show conclusively that most humans have a higher moral status than any non-humans that we know of, but just that the most reasonable place to begin the debate is with the hypothesis that they do.

To speak of a difference in moral status is vague. Many kinds of difference have been contentious issues—the distinction between beings with and without rights, for example, or between beings to whom we have direct duties and those to whom we only have indirect duties, or between beings whose lives have intrinsic value and those whose lives do not. My argument for a difference in moral status will suggest more specifically what this difference is, and it will turn out to be more complex than any of these standard distinctions. I argue that humans who are committed to morality have a higher moral status inasmuch as they play a more central role in a constructivist account of moral duties, but that the duties that result from this moral constructivist account include duties not to mistreat animals, regardless of any effects on humans.

The particular type of moral constructivism I propose here is based on the kingdom of ends formulation of the Categorical Imperative.[1] While the use of the kingdom of ends as a device to move from basic moral principles to specific moral rules is not a position that Kant himself clearly develops, it is

[1] The interpretation of the kingdom of ends I discuss in this chapter is adopted more or less directly from the proposals of Thomas E. Hill, Jr., *Dignity and Practical Reason in Kant's Moral Theory* (Ithaca, NY: Cornell University Press, 1992), 226–50, *Respect, Pluralism, and Justice* (Oxford: Oxford University Press, 2000), 33–55, 200–36, *Human Welfare and Moral Worth* (Oxford: Oxford University Press, 2002), 61–95.

a plausible Kantian approach to arriving at particular moral rules. Since this Kantian approach leads to a moderate position regarding treatment of non-human animals, Kant's reviled position among some philosophical defenders of animals may be undeserved. And since employing the kingdom of ends as a method for settling on specific moral rules seems to depend on the good will reading of the humanity formulation, the overall consistency of the picture developed in this chapter tells in favour of the good will reading.

1. The Charge of Arbitrariness

There is not just a single point of contention in debates over the moral status of non-human animals, of course. Advocates of increased consideration for animals have sought to establish several different claims. But despite these different goals, several of the most familiar arguments share a common strategy. They rely on some version of the charge that it is arbitrary to pick out a trait that some sentient beings have and others lack, and to use the trait as a justification for assigning the beings fundamentally different moral status.

Peter Singer's argument for equal consideration of animals' interests, in chapter 1 of *Animal Liberation*, is the most prominent example of this strategy.[2] In rough outline, Singer argues that the moral requirement of granting equal consideration to all humans' interests does not depend on any (presumably false) claim that humans all have equal abilities, so the equal consideration of animals' interests likewise should not be contingent upon any (also false) claim that animals' abilities are equal to humans'. And animals, at least all but the simplest animals, do have at least one interest, namely an interest in avoiding pain. So, Singer argues, animals' interests in avoiding pain ought to be taken into account. Singer reasonably points out that even this fairly mild conclusion would require substantial reforms in the ways we treat animals. To disregard the interests of non-human animals because they are not human is an unjustified bias. It is 'speciesism', a mere preference for one's own kind that is morally objectionable for the same reasons that sexism and racism are objectionable. Singer's powerful and deservedly influential argument is one example of the charge of arbitrariness, deployed to show that animals' interests should be given consideration equal to humans' interests.

Paul Taylor more directly attacks the general idea of a difference between humans' and animals' moral status. In his article 'The Ethics of Respect for Nature', Taylor argues that 'the claim that humans by their very nature are superior to other species is a groundless claim and ... must be rejected as

[2] Peter Singer, *Animal Liberation* (New York: New York Review of Books, 1975), 7ff.

nothing more than an irrational bias in our own favor'.[3] According to Taylor, there is no legitimate reason to grant greater moral status to some sentient beings than to others. It is true that normal adult humans have some traits that other animals lack, or possess only in a lesser degree. But then, other animals have traits that normal adult humans lack. Humans have a capacity for 'rational thought, aesthetic creativity, autonomy and self-determination, and moral freedom', but on the other hand, the 'speed of a cheetah, the vision of an eagle, the agility of a monkey' are traits that humans lack.[4] It might be tempting to think that the traits possessed by rational beings are somehow more important, but Taylor thinks this is 'a begging of the question'. Features associated with rationality seem more important 'from a strictly human point of view', but the other animals' traits may be more valuable to them from the standpoint of their own good. So rationality 'does not give us a neutral (non-question-begging) ground on which to construct a scale of degrees of inherent worth'.[5] To select any characteristic possessed by humans and not other animals, and to use that characteristic as a criterion for differences in moral status, is arbitrary, according to Taylor.

Tom Regan, in *The Case for Animal Rights*, argues that moral autonomy is an arbitrary characteristic on which to base the idea that we have direct duties only to humans and not to other animals.[6] Regan grants that humans are the only animals that have 'moral autonomy', meaning they are the only animals that act for moral reasons. The fact that only humans have moral autonomy leads Regan to admit that only humans are moral agents. But non-humans can be what Regan calls 'moral patients'. Moral patients are 'conscious, sentient', and possess desires, beliefs, and memory.[7] They can be 'on the receiving end of the right or wrong acts of moral agents'.[8] And since they can be harmed or helped, the fact that they do not possess moral autonomy is irrelevant to the issue of whether we have obligations to them.

> [O]nce we have made the case that moral patients can be harmed, and can be harmed in ways that are in some cases similar to the ways moral agents can be harmed, respect for the requirement of impartiality will require that we make similar judgments about the harmful treatment of both.[9]

In other words, it is arbitrary to use moral autonomy or moral agency as a criterion for singling out the kinds of beings toward whom we have direct duties.

[3] Paul Taylor, 'The Ethics of Respect for Nature', *Environmental Ethics*, 3 (Fall 1981), 207.

[4] Ibid. 211–12. [5] Ibid. 215.

[6] Tom Regan, *The Case for Animal Rights* (Berkeley and Los Angeles: University of California Press, 1983), 84–5, 151–4.

[7] Ibid. 152–3. [8] Ibid. 154. [9] Ibid. 190.

James Rachels shares the idea that there is no characteristic that justifies attributing basically different kinds of moral status to different beings. He says, 'Humans, but not rabbits, can read; they can do mathematics; they can enjoy opera; they can drive automobiles; they can make movies. The list could go on and on'.[10] The point of this list of traits that obviously do not affect a being's basic moral status is to imply that no other trait (capacity for morality, ability to set ends, etc.) is relevant either. Of course, some differences can be relevant for some particular decisions—inability to read can be a reason not to admit someone to graduate school—but 'there is no one *big* difference that justifies all differences in treatment'.[11] It is, then, arbitrary to single out some characteristic possessed by humans and use it as a criterion for distinguishing between beings toward whom we have direct duties and those toward whom we have only indirect duties.

If my description of these authors' views is accurate, then each employs some version of the charge of arbitrariness. I do not oppose all of the conclusions of these authors. But I do deny that the accusation of arbitrariness is a sound strategy.

2. The Case for a Difference in Moral Status

Singer is right, I think, to say that the mere fact of biological species does not support a difference in moral status. That would be mere prejudice or 'speciesism'. So an appeal must be made to some morally relevant trait that humans have and animals lack. But a defender of animals would also seem right to say there is no plausible candidate that will exclude all non-humans and include all humans. If we think the use of a complex language, for instance, marks a divide in moral standing, then some non-human animals (dolphins and apes are standard examples) possess the trait to a greater extent than some humans (for example, young children and severely retarded adults). The price of denying equal moral status to non-human animals is admitting that not all humans have it either. So far, the claims made by the defender of animals' moral status are plausible. But the general strategy of the accusation of arbitrariness goes beyond this. It attacks some given distinction between human and non-human animals' moral status, by saying that there is no justification for picking out any particular trait as a criterion for this difference in moral status.

[10] James Rachels, *Created from Animals: The Moral Implications of Darwinism* (Oxford: Oxford University Press, 1990), 180.

[11] Ibid. 178.

To rebut this claim, some feature must be found that plausibly grounds a difference in moral status. Some fairly widespread intuitions would support attributing this kind of moral significance to characteristics such as the capacity for self-reflection, to 'autonomy' or the power to be self-directing, or to a capacity to employ moral reasoning and act on its conclusions. But such intuitions are not universally shared. The defender of equal moral status for animals denies that there is any feature the possession of which provides a natural and uncontroversial cleavage between higher and lower moral status.

This is where I think the advocate of equal moral status is misguided. She may be right in claiming it is arbitrary to take intelligence, or the power to set ends and be self-directing, or even the capacity for moral action as the criterion for greater or lesser moral status. But I will argue that there is a prima facie case for taking an actual commitment to moral action as a legitimate criterion. More precisely, I will argue that when she participates in any debate about what our duties are, even the philosophical defender of animals must adhere to some presuppositions that imply that a commitment to morality has special value.[12] So there is prima facie reason to think that beings with good will have a fundamentally higher moral status than beings without good will.

Any genuine moral debate proceeds from certain assumptions. By 'debate' here, I of course do not mean only a formal debate, but any exploration or discussion that has a goal of determining what is right or wrong in a particular range of cases. I do not mean a discussion of metaethics, but a discussion of the moral considerations involved in specific situations, something more like 'applied ethics'.

Any such moral debate presupposes, prima facie, that there are such things as moral reasons for acting. In the end, a participant might be led to doubt this, but to conclude that right and wrong are so much hot air is to opt out of the first-order debate. Another presupposition is that the participants in the debate can act on what they take to be reasons, or set their own ends, rather than being simply moved to different behaviours by biological or psychological mechanisms beyond their control. This is presupposed by the fact that in a moral debate we take ourselves to be offering reasons that may be accepted or rejected by the other participants (or by ourselves, if we are internally pondering a moral issue). Furthermore, we take it that the participants in the

[12] So, the claims about value here are compatible with the general Kantian picture of value that I have emphasized, in which talk about value is a shorthand for claims about the choices rational agents make. Throughout this chapter, I mean 'value' to be taken in this sense. See the text below for more details.

debate can choose to act for distinctively moral reasons, rather than just acting to satisfy their own desires. For example, we may try to establish that some practice is unfair in order to give others a reason to desist from the practice, and we would regard it as possible for them to desist even if perpetuating the practice is more profitable to them.

It may seem that I am asking our ideas about the practice of moral debate to bear a heavy philosophical burden here, but I do not think the burden is unreasonable. It is true that someone might disagree, for philosophical reasons or merely temperamental ones, with my account of the presuppositions of moral debate. For instance, a non-cognitivist might deny that participating in moral debate really involves citing compelling and distinctively moral reasons for acting. Or a determinist might deny that moral debate presupposes that participants can freely choose to accept or reject reasons for action. Everyone, including the non-cognitivist or the determinist, acknowledges that moral discussions take place, and it may seem that they simply account for the phenomenon of moral debate in a different way from me. But to accept their alternative accounts is to give up a great deal which an ardent advocate of first-order ethical positions probably would not be willing to discard. It would involve giving up the idea that she can really offer morally compelling reasons for action that her opponents can and should recognize and act on.[13] If a moral debate, including one about the moral status of animals, is to be worth her time, it must make the presuppositions I have described.

And there is a further presupposition to moral debate. In discourse about what is right or wrong in a particular case, we suppose that acting for moral reasons has priority over, or has a greater value than, acting in order to satisfy one's own preferences or propensities. This is presupposed by the goal of moral debate. Moral debate is not just an attempt to influence others (e.g. by threats or appeals to their self-interest), in order to produce a certain action. It is the attempt to give reasons that must be accepted, regardless of the agent's inclinations. By saying that this implies that moral action has higher value than other actions, I do not mean anything metaphysically extravagant or contrary to the Kantian conception of value that I have espoused in earlier chapters. As a participant in a moral debate, one is aiming to produce action that is based on moral reasons, and one will not accept others' inclination as an excuse for them to act contrary to moral reasons. As a participant in moral debate, then, one must assume that everyone always has reason to

[13] Or if some form of non-cognitivism is sufficiently sophisticated to allow us to say that there are intersubjectively compelling moral reasons for action, then it would also allow us to talk about the presuppositions of moral debate that I have described above.

choose moral action over inclination-based action, when the two conflict. This is an idea that an advocate of some first-order moral position (such as increased moral consideration for animals) cannot give up, on pain of making her own moral arguments ineffective. And since one always has reason to choose moral action over inclination-based action, a Kantian conception of value implies that moral action has higher value than action based on other motives.

The argument above does build in a Kantian idea. But it is not an assumption about the moral status of animals, nor is it an assumption about any substantial moral issue. Instead, it is a general point, about the nature of value. The value claim is a way to capture the idea that any participant in a moral debate must acknowledge a special importance to acting morally.

Moral debate, then, presupposes some commitments on the part of participants, about what is possible and what is important. Among these is a presupposition that action done for moral reasons has a higher value than actions done from inclination.

Then when a first-order moral debate turns to the topic of the moral status of different kinds of beings, these presuppositions must be taken into account. Some beings are committed to acting as morality requires, and so have good wills. Other beings, including some humans and all non-human animals that we know of, lack good wills.[14] These latter beings instead act in order to satisfy their own inclinations—their desires, affections, dislikes, sympathies, or instincts—but they do not act because of a recognition of moral reasons as compelling. Then suppose the question at issue in the first-order moral debate is which kinds of beings have special value and deserve moral consideration in all circumstances and in all senses. The possible answers are that the first kinds of beings have a special value that the latter lack, or that both have the same kind of value and so deserve the same kind and degree of moral consideration.

Given the only thing that all participants agree on in the debate, that acting from moral reasons has greater value than acting from inclination, it is natural to choose the former position instead of the latter. Some beings are committed to acting morally. Other beings, whether humans who lack a commitment to act morally or animals who cannot have such a commitment, only act to satisfy inclinations. And moral debate presupposes that acting to satisfy inclinations has a lesser value than acting from moral reasons. To assert that beings who

[14] There is of course no bar to thinking that it is possible for non-humans to act for moral reasons. Maybe there are extraterrestrials who do, and maybe members of other species on earth will be able to someday.

only act from inclination should receive the same kind of consideration as beings who act from duty seems unjustified. Instead, there is a prima facie case for thinking that beings who have a commitment to moral action, which has special value, themselves have a special value that is greater than the value of beings who act only from inclination.

This is admittedly only a prima facie argument in favour of granting a special status in our deliberations to beings that have a commitment to morality. If the question is where to draw a line between beings who always deserve full moral consideration and those who do not, then it is natural to draw a line along a boundary of value that everyone agrees upon. And the only value agreed upon by all participants in a moral debate is that acting from duty, and the commitment to so act, have a special value. To claim instead that all sentient beings have the same moral status is less justified. It extends to all creatures a special moral value, when the very point at issue is whether they all have such value. An argument must be provided, if the realm of fullest moral status is to include all animals.

It will be useful here to defuse a possible objection.[15] One might think that the argument above conflates two different sorts of beings that lack good wills. A critic could grant that it is reasonable to say that rational beings who reject moral reasons for action deserve some sort of lower moral status, but the same critic might deny that non-rational beings who are incapable of acting on morality fall into the same category. The intuitive idea here (which the critic may think is my idea) is that humans who choose to act immorally have a lower moral status as a sort of punishment for their choices, but that since non-human animals do not make choices at all, they do not share the desert. But this does not capture my idea. Instead the argument above appeals to what participants in a moral debate must grant has special status, namely moral action. The presuppositions of moral debate urge a prima facie moral importance to moral actions, but no such importance either to the chosen actions of people who disregard morality or to the (possibly unchosen) behaviour of animals who are innocent of morality. It is not that lower moral status is a punishment, but that the only value to which all participants are (at least implicitly) committed is the value of moral action.

So far, I have argued that there is prima facie reason to suppose that there is a fundamental difference in moral status between beings who are committed to morality and those who are not. In section 3, I will explain the nature of this difference.

[15] Several readers of drafts of this chapter and a related paper have wondered whether this objection applies.

3. The Difference in Moral Status

Even if there is a case for accepting a fundamental difference in moral status between beings who are committed to morality and those who are not, this does not settle what the difference is. I don't wish to argue for any of the standard distinctions. I will not argue, for instance, that we have only indirect duties to beings without good wills, or that only beings with good wills have rights. I think the best position will turn out to be more complicated. I want to say both that there is a significant difference in moral status between beings with good wills and those without, and that it can nevertheless be wrong, in some robust and straightforward sense, to treat non-human beings (which lack good wills) in certain ways, regardless of the effects on humans who have good wills.[16]

In order to see how this is possible, it is important to keep in mind two different levels of talk about morality.[17]

There is our everyday talk, which almost everyone engages in from time to time. To say that a celebrity's behaviour is immoral, that a new local ordinance is unfair, or that it is wrong for your roommate to drink your milk is to engage in this everyday moral discourse. And in just the same sense, which is our ordinary way of talking about rightness and wrongness, I think we can say that it is wrong to mistreat beings who lack a good will, even if it does no harm to any being who has a good will.

But at another level of moral discourse, it may nevertheless be perfectly correct to say that beings who are committed to morality have a higher moral status than beings who lack this commitment, that they deserve a greater and more direct consideration in our moral deliberations. The type of moral discourse I have in mind is not our everyday talk about what is right and wrong, but a more philosophical discourse about what makes anything right or wrong. One sort of answer to this question about the grounding of moral rules gives much greater weight to beings with good will than to beings without it.

[16] My suggestion in this section bears a resemblance to the view of animals' moral status presented by Peter Carruthers in *The Animals Issue: Moral Theory in Practice* (Cambridge: Cambridge University Press, 1992), especially his chapter 5, pp. 98–121. Carruthers and I both propose that moral rules consist of the set of rules that would be agreed upon by hypothetical rational deliberators in certain specified circumstances. And we both believe that such a framework for thinking about morality leaves non-human animals with less than the fullest moral standing. But I think the situation I propose for deliberating about moral rules, unlike Carruthers's, is not contractarian, since I do not suppose that the hypothetical deliberators are motivated by self-interest. In addition, Carruthers seems to take it that his approach straightforwardly leads to the conclusions that we can have no direct duties to non-human animals, that they 'lack moral standing' (ibid. 105), and that they 'have no rights' (ibid. 106). I think my account (and perhaps Carruthers's as well) leads to conclusions about animals' moral status that require more cautious elucidation, as I will explain below.

[17] I thank Thomas E. Hill, Jr., for helping to frame the issue in this way.

The view I have in mind maintains that the moral rules that determine whether any action is right or wrong are exactly those rules that would be agreed upon by hypothetical rational beings deliberating together. This view, which has been called 'moral constructivism', begins by specifying a kind of deliberator and a hypothetical situation for deliberation, and says that the resulting rules that are agreed upon are the moral principles to which we should adhere. The most familiar form of moral constructivism is 'hypothetical contractarianism', but other forms of constructivism have also been defended in some detail.[18] I specifically have in mind a non-contractarian form of constructivism, which begins by imagining a hypothetical union of deliberators that resembles Immanuel Kant's kingdom of ends (G 433–9). The beings in this union are, by hypothesis, concerned with promulgating only rules that treat every member of the union as ends in themselves, and are committed to abiding by whatever rules are agreed upon.[19]

I will not argue extensively that this is the correct view of moral rules. I am putting the view forward speculatively, as one that allows both the distinction in moral status between different beings and the idea that it is straightforwardly wrong to abuse even non-humans, who cannot possess a commitment to morality. Much more would need to be done to elaborate the view fully and render it convincing. Some of this work has been done by others, but it will not be my focus. However, I will show that there is a natural fit between the constructivist view of moral rules I have in mind and the idea that a good will deserves special consideration. The ideas are mutually reinforcing, and so lend each other at least some degree of support.

I will first show that the idea of a good will's unique importance leads naturally to a constructivist account of moral rules. I will then argue that the underlying ideas of the constructivist approach to moral rules independently suggest that a commitment to morality has special value, so the two ideas mutually imply each other.

[18] John Rawls takes his own position to be simultaneously contractarian, Kantian, and constructivist. See John Rawls, *A Theory of Justice* (Cambridge, Mass.: The Belknap Press of Harvard University Press, 1971) and 'Kantian Constructivism in Moral Theory', *Journal of Philosophy*, 77/9 (1980), 515–72. A more straightforwardly contractarian form of constructivism is developed by David Gauthier, *Morals by Agreement* (Oxford: Oxford University Press, 1986). Thomas E. Hill, Jr., and Onora O'Neill would describe some of their most substantial ideas as forms of Kantian constructivism, but not as contractarian, inasmuch as the fundamental motivation of the hypothetical deliberators is not limited to self interest. See Hill, *Dignity and Practical Reason*, 226–50, *Respect, Pluralism, and Justice*, 33–55, 200–36, and *Human Welfare and Moral Worth*, 61–95; Onora O'Neill, *Toward Justice and Virtue* (Cambridge: Cambridge University Press, 1996) and *Constructions of Reason* (Cambridge: Cambridge University Press, 1989), esp. 3–27, 206–18.

[19] This constructivist account based on Kant's kingdom of ends is basically the idea proposed by Hill (see previous footnote).

Beginning with the idea that a good will has special value leads naturally to a particular constructivist picture of a union of deliberators. Suppose it is true that beings who are committed to morality ought to be treated in a special way, as ends in themselves. Then, if I want to act as I ought, I must treat every being who is committed to morality as an end in herself. I should not destroy her, or use her merely as a means to satisfying my own interests. I should acknowledge her importance, and, as one way of doing this, should give some weight to any particular ends she has adopted. Since, by hypothesis, she is committed to acting as she ought to, she will also treat me as an end in myself if I am committed to morality. This leads naturally to an idea of all beings who are committed to morality forming a sort of union in which each of them, and all of their ends, are given some weight by all the others.[20] If we imagine the rules the hypothetical union of beings would agree upon, we can see that they would be guided by at least two substantial requirements. The rules would treat every being who is committed to morality as an end in herself, and would necessarily be consistent with giving at least some weight to others' contingent ends as well.[21]

This union of deliberators is only a hypothetical construct, of course, and it is posited to serve a specific function. It is a device that we can use to decide what rules best express the basic idea of treating beings who are committed to morality as ends in themselves. It is a way to move from the humanity formulation to the applications of that basic principle in our particular world, in all its messy details. So when one discusses the members of the moral union, or their decisions, one is not supposing that they are actual beings engaged in an activity somewhere. It is just a way of trying to answer the question of what moral rules are appropriate to our world, given some basic moral presuppositions.

If we imagined that the beings in this hypothetical union of rational deliberators were utterly ignorant of one another's ends, perhaps even of their own ends, we could only draw a few rather formalistic conclusions about the sorts of rules that would result. It is doubtful that beings in such a situation would come up with any rule regarding the treatment of non-rational beings. We would be obscuring too many of the relevant details of our world.

Luckily, there is no need to imagine that the members of the union would be completely ignorant of one another's ends or circumstances. The

[20] This does not imply that all of the others' ends must be given the same weight by each as her own ends.

[21] This is not to say that every rule would mention others' ends and how to promote them. It is just that no rule would be agreed upon that would involve indiscriminately trampling the concerns of others.

function of this hypothetical ignorance, like the function of John Rawls's veil of ignorance,[22] would be to remove the possibility of deliberations being inappropriately biased. If the union of moral deliberators is used as a device to arrive at conclusions about moral principles, we would not want members of the union to make decisions based on unbridled self-interest, nepotism, allegiance to a particular institution, or prejudice against particular groups of people. But features built into the union mitigate the worry about such biases. We begin by supposing that all the members of the union will be committed to treating all other members as ends in themselves, and will only promulgate rules that could be agreed upon by all. So they necessarily will not endorse rules that express a lack of respect for any members, or that ignore their ends.

There is still room for some worry, though. By hypothesis, the members of the union are not totally self-interested, but there seems to be latitude in how to give weight to others' concerns, and how much weight to give. It would be controversial to claim that treating others as ends would eliminate all inappropriate biases. Perhaps some degree of ignorance should be posited, in order to counter this worry. But if so, it need only be a limited ignorance of particular individuals' ends, or the aims of particular special interest groups. Introducing general psychological features of humans, or ends that any member of the union would probably have, would not lead to a skewing of the human moral principles at which the members of the union arrived. If we are seeking moral rules for human beings, we can imagine that the beings that agree upon the rules are human beings, although we must add that they are idealized humans who will necessarily acknowledge the value of other humans who are committed to morality.

Even given this partial knowledge of the members' natures, why should we think that the rules agreed upon by a union of humans who are committed to morality would prohibit mistreatment of beings who lack this commitment?

One reason is that it would be known that most members of the union care about the treatment of other sentient beings, even if these other beings lack a commitment to morality. This fact would provide a reason to prohibit the mistreatment of such beings. Members of the union would give weight to the commonly shared end of avoiding the abuse of sentient beings. So far as I can see, this would be so even if it were merely a brute psychological fact about humans that they usually had some concern for other beings' welfare. But it is more than a brute fact.

[22] Rawls, *Theory of Justice*, 136–42.

Reasons can also be given to explain why the members of the kingdom of ends should care about the treatment of sentient but non-human beings. One reason is expressed by Immanuel Kant in *Lectures on Ethics*. Kant says, 'we have duties toward animals, in that we thereby promote the cause of humanity ... for a person who already displays such cruelty to animals is also no less hardened toward men'.[23] Rational beings deliberating about rules of conduct would naturally prohibit conduct that inevitably led to unacceptable future behaviour. So if it is true that cruelty to sentient, non-human beings leads to similar treatment of even those humans who possess a commitment to morality, members of the union would formulate rules prohibiting it.

There may be an additional reason to think they would prohibit abuse of sentient beings who lack a commitment to morality. Given human psychology, each (human) member of the union would think of her own pain and other members' pain as a bad thing, something to be avoided. And they would be able to imagine the situation of other sentient beings who were in pain, to empathize enough to see a general similarity between the experiences of sentient beings in pain. Given this, and the fact that the members of the union are not entirely self-regarding, it would be peculiar if they did not regard the pain of sentient beings as something to be avoided, even if the beings lack a commitment to morality. It seems almost irrational to be aware in this way of the extreme similarity between different beings' pain and not regard the pains in a similar way. If the members of the union would, given human psychology, regard sentient beings' pain as something to be avoided, then they would agree upon a rule prohibiting the needless suffering of sentient beings.[24]

More specifically, what would count as needless suffering and what would be prohibited by the rules generated by the moral deliberators? Since they necessarily, by hypothesis, place an incomparably high value on beings who

[23] Immanuel Kant, *Lectures on Ethics*, trans. Peter Heath and Jerome Schneewind (Cambridge: Cambridge University Press, 1997), 212. If this were Kant's whole story about why it is wrong to abuse animals, as some critics have taken it to be, it would seem paltry. But several philosophers have recently argued that some basic ideas of Kant's ethics provide the resources for constructing a more complex account of our moral relations with non-human animals. Besides the account I offer here (which I take to be a Kantian approach, though not one Kant himself develops), see Lara Denis, 'Kant's Conception of Duties Regarding Animals: Reconstruction and Reconsideration', *History of Philosophy Quarterly*, 17 (2000), 405–23, or Christine Korsgaard, *The Sources of Normativity* (Cambridge: Cambridge University Press, 1996), 149–60, or Allen Wood, 'Kant on Duties regarding Nonrational Nature', *Proceedings of the Aristotelian Society*, Supplement 72 (1998), 189–210.

[24] Of course, if non-human animals' experience of pain is somehow very different from humans' experience of pain, there may be no reason for the hypothetical deliberators to regard it as something to be avoided in the same way as human pain is. Carruthers argues in chapter 8 of *The Animals Issue*, 170–93, that animals do not have conscious mental states, and that 'non-conscious mental states are not appropriate objects of moral concern', 193. But he says that such claims are 'controversial and speculative, and may well turn out to be mistaken', 192, and his caution seems justified at this point.

are committed to morality, there would not be an absolute prohibition on killing and eating non-human animals, if eating meat were the only way that the lives of moral beings could be sustained.[25] But whether this is the only way to survive depends on one's geographical and economic circumstances. Some humans, no doubt, find themselves in circumstances that make it difficult to sustain themselves physically without eating meat, and the moral deliberators in the kingdom of ends would have access to general information about such circumstances. But most of us do not face the choice of eating meat or wasting away. Singer (along with other writers, and videos produced by PETA and other groups) paints a vivid picture of the suffering that animals undergo for the sake of mass-producing meat, eggs, and milk, and he argues compellingly that this suffering outweighs the minor pleasure that residents of economically developed countries get from eating meat.[26] It seems likely then, that the moral rules resulting from the 'kingdom of ends' would not prohibit all eating of meat, but would prohibit the support of factory farming.

Cases in between are, predictably, more difficult. Recognizing animals' pain as bad would provide little reason for the hypothetical deliberators to promulgate rules forbidding raising animals for food, if the animals were raised humanely and slaughtered in the least painful ways possible. But there might be other reasons, besides the animals' pain, which the hypothetical deliberators would take into account. Psychological effects on humans of such practices, the effect on the environment of large-versus small-scale meat production, and the efficiency or inefficiency of producing meat versus producing grain are some of the empirical factors that would be directly relevant to the hypothetical deliberation in the kingdom of ends. Since my aims in this chapter are more theoretical than empirical, I will not explore these issues in detail.[27] But it seems likely that the hypothetical moral union would result in moral requirements regarding our treatment of animals that would be, for the most part, 'moderate', giving weight to animals' pain but not placing absolute prohibitions on killing them for human purposes.

If the view I have offered is even roughly correct, then there is a natural sense in which one could simultaneously maintain both that there is a significant difference in moral status between beings with good will and those without, and that it is straightforwardly wrong to mistreat even beings who lack this commitment. There is a difference in moral status because the question of

[25] I think it is not the case that this line of thought would also justify routine consumption of infants, convicted criminals, or insane humans, for reasons discussed below in section 4.

[26] Singer, *Animal Liberation*, chapter 3.

[27] And of course, there are other practical questions which I will not take up, such as medical research on animals.

what is right and wrong is answered by looking only at the hypothetical choices of beings who are committed to morality. But I have argued that when we imagine a union of such beings deliberating together about what kinds of actions should be forbidden, it seems likely that, if they are human, they would forbid the infliction of needless suffering on other beings. The wrongness of a particular instance of mistreating animals does not depend on the particular act being observed by any being with a commitment to morality, nor on the particular act's effect on the agent's future dealings with morally committed beings. It is simply wrong in virtue of the kind of act it is, because of its effect on the animals. But the reason anything is wrong, including the mistreatment of animals, refers to the choices of only beings who care about morality.

Furthermore, a presupposition of this moral union of deliberators is that when the members are reasoning together about moral rules, they will only agree on rules consistent with treating all members as ends in themselves. This is a necessary feature of any rule generated. The rules generated may also embody concern for other sentient beings—I have argued that they would—but this is not a necessary feature of the union itself. It depends on what the deliberators would decide in light of contingent facts about the world, notably that animals feel pain and that humans can empathize with and care about them. This is another sense in which the view I have developed embodies a difference in moral status between beings with good will and those without.

The strategy of this chapter so far has been to argue first that there is a prima facie reason to think there is a difference in moral status between beings who have and who lack a commitment to morality. This left open the question of exactly what the difference in moral status is, and I have now put forward an answer to that question. But why think it is the right answer?

Why could the difference not be that we have direct duties to beings who are committed to morality but not to other beings, or that only beings committed to morality have rights, or that the lives of such beings are the only lives that have intrinsic value? Any of these could be the difference, I suppose, but they are not as strongly suggested by the presuppositions of moral debate as the difference I have proposed. What is needed is some natural fit between the idea of possessing a commitment to morality and being on the high side of whatever difference in moral status is being proposed.

The sort of natural fit I have in mind is present in the connection between a commitment to morality and the constructivist idea of a union of moral deliberators. By beginning with the idea of the special value of a commitment to morality, and thinking about how this would lead morally committed beings to treat one another, one arrives at the idea of a union of moral deliberators.

And this leads to my account of the difference in moral status between beings who have a commitment to morality and those who lack it.

This idea of natural fit also can be seen by working in the opposite direction, by focusing first on the purpose of positing the hypothetical union of moral deliberators. The reason we posit this union is to arrive at particular moral rules. The only way to arrive at moral rules is by limiting membership in the union to beings who are committed to morality. To say they are committed to morality cannot mean here that they are committed to a full range of particular moral rules, because those are the very rules that have not yet been decided. But the deliberators must be committed to morality in two senses. First, they must be committed to acting upon whatever rules are eventually decided on. Second, they must deliberate in ways that embody some basic moral presuppositions. Moral constructivism is a way to move from fundamental moral intuitions or principles to more specific action-guiding rules, so a constructivist strategy must suppose that the deliberators in the moral union will deliberate in ways consistent with these basic moral ideas.

Non-human animals, and humans who lack even minimal rationality, will be unhelpful in arriving at moral rules because they cannot formulate the necessary concepts to carry out the project. Humans who are minimally rational but lack a commitment to morality could participate in arriving at some kind of rules, but there is no reason to think the resulting rules would count as moral rules. They might be egoistic rules of self-reliance, or biased rules. The only device that assures the appropriateness of the rules issuing from the union of deliberators is the nature of the members, namely their commitment to morality. The project of arriving at moral rules of behaviour can be participated in only by beings who are concerned with the goal of such a project. Other beings are not playing the same game.

So, even without the analysis of moral debate that identified the special moral status of beings who are committed to morality, the idea of a union of moral deliberators independently suggests this status.

There is no such natural correlation between a commitment to morality and being an object of direct duties. If one were trying to distinguish between beings toward whom we have direct duties and those to whom we do not, the idea of the special value of a commitment to morality would be one place to draw the line. But it is not a line that is organic to the issue of direct versus indirect duties. It is imposed as the conclusion of a separate argument, the argument in section 2, which identified the presuppositions of moral debate. Similarly, if one wonders where to draw the line singling out beings whose lives have intrinsic value, the idea of drawing the line to include only beings with a commitment to morality is imposed from without. One might think that there is more of a natural fit between having rights and having a commitment to morality, if one thinks that being subject to duties correlates with being the bearer of rights. But to say that someone is subject to duties, in the sense that she ought to act a certain way, is not the same as saying she is committed to acting that way.

So, of the several possible differences in moral status, the constructivist idea of having a role in the determination of moral laws seems to provide the most natural fit with the idea of having a commitment to morality. When searching for the difference in moral status between beings with a commitment to morality and those without, the best candidate is the one I have suggested.

If this really is the important difference in moral status, does it dictate a position on whether non-rational beings in fact are the object of direct duties? If so, it is difficult to put the more complex difference in moral status into terms of simpler ones. If the account I have given above is correct, then in one sense we could be said to have direct duties to non-rational beings. We can do wrong simply in virtue of how we treat them, independent of effects on any particular rational being. But the fact that it is wrong to mistreat them is not true independently of all reference to rational beings, inasmuch as all right and wrong depends on what rational beings would decide. It is not clear that the issue can be sensibly reduced further than this, to a simple 'yes' or 'no'.

There is of course a more general scholarly purpose for the constructivist interpretation of the kingdom of ends. In Chapter 7, I proposed a Kantian strategy for deriving specific duties from the more general principle of treating humanity as an end in itself, a strategy which gave a prominent role to the feeling of *Achtung*. While I think the proposal fits well with most of Kant's actual discussions of specific duties that follow from the humanity formulation, it falls far short of providing a method of settling all moral questions. Kant himself left many moral questions unaddressed, some of them necessarily so, because they had not yet arisen in his lifetime. And his own positions on some issues (lying, marriage, masturbation, among others) are notoriously unconvincing. Although Kant himself sometimes treats the humanity formulation and other formulations of the Categorical Imperative as complete moral guides to action, ready to be applied to particular cases, the controversies over their application are good evidence that they are not such ready-made guides.[28] And Kant's own considered view on the matter seems to be that there must be an intermediate step between the Categorical Imperative and moral decisions about particular cases. The intermediate step is to work out a 'metaphysics of morals', or a

[28] The main place he treats the Categorical Imperative as a rule ready for application is in the 'four examples' in G 421–3 and 429–30.

set of more particular moral rules that apply to human circumstances.[29] The constructivist construal of the kingdom of ends is well suited to the task of filling out this set of rules. It embodies the requirement of treating every being with good will as an end in herself, while providing at least a somewhat clearer framework for taking account of human nature and empirical facts about the world. So the constructivist model of the kingdom of ends is a promising supplement for the application of the humanity formulation.

4. An Objection

One might worry that in my zeal to demonstrate a difference in moral status between beings who possess a commitment to morality and beings who lack this commitment, I have left many humans on the wrong side of the divide. The difference in moral status that I have argued for cleaves along the line of commitment to morality, and many humans lack that commitment. Of course, any attempt to make any sort of trait a plausible marker of moral status is bound to leave out some humans. Infants, very severely retarded adult humans, and humans in permanent vegetative states seem to lack most characteristics that might plausibly accompany moral status, if non-human animals do. But my position may seem especially unpalatable because it also gives lesser moral status to some competent, adult humans who do not place sufficient priority on morality. In response, it should first be noted that most humans probably do have a significant commitment to doing what they think is right.[30] I have not proposed moral impeccability as a standard, but only a strong concern to do what is morally required. But this is not the entire response to the worry. Keeping in mind that there are two levels of moral discourse—everyday moral talk and philosophical discourse about the nature of right and wrong—further helps to mitigate the apparent implausibility of my proposal.

Humans who disregard moral obligations do not play a role in answering the philosophical question, 'What moral rules would be agreed upon by good people?' and so in a sense they are denied a central place in the constructivist moral theory I have discussed. And a concern for them is not built necessarily into the structure of the hypothetical union of moral deliberators, while a concern for humans with good will is.

But there is good reason to think the rules that result from such a union would prohibit many kinds of mistreatment of people who lack a commitment

[29] G 391–2, MM 217. Kant's overall method in *Metaphysics of Morals* seems to reflect this strategy.

[30] See my more detailed discussion in Chapter 5.

to morality. And the rules would not be limited to the same rules as the ones governing treatment of non-human animals, because members of the union of moral deliberators would take different considerations into account when deciding how humans should be treated. The main difference is that we can be sure that non-human animals lack the conceptual resources necessary for understanding moral principles, let alone being committed to them.[31] In the real world, we cannot be sure that a given human lacks moral commitment, or at least we can seldom be sure. Given this uncertainty in the real world, deliberators in the union of moral beings would agree on a rule dictating that we treat all humans (or almost all, since there may be some human monsters whose disregard for morality is apparent) with all the consideration due a being with a commitment to morality. Another consideration is that it is psychologically difficult or impossible for humans to treat some other humans with contempt while preserving respect for those who deserve it. This provides an additional reason for members of the union of moral human deliberators to agree on rules demanding respect even for humans who do not care about doing right. And because the members of the union recognize the value of a commitment to morality, they will not want to discourage scoundrels from reforming themselves and acquiring this commitment. But to treat a human with contempt weakens her belief that she can improve herself and so discourages her from attempting to adhere better to the moral demands of her own *Wille* (MM 463–4). For all these reasons, which I have discussed in more detail in Chapter 5, members of the union of rational human deliberators would agree upon rules that demand treating at least most humans as ends in themselves.

Then the difference in moral status embodied in the union of moral deliberators does not mean that humans who lack a good will should receive only the same kind of treatment as non-human animals. At the level of everyday moral discourse, it would be true to say that such humans usually ought to be given the same kind of consideration as humans who are more dedicated to acting rightly.

Of course, some humans lack not only a commitment to morality, but even minimal rationality. It might be thought that very young children or severely mentally deficient adults might, on my view, justifiably be accorded only the same status as non-humans. But this need not be especially problematic. They might have the same status in one sense, inasmuch as they cannot be included in the deliberative union of moral beings, and concern for them is not built

[31] This is a contingent fact, compatible with admitting that there may be non-humans in the universe somewhere who are concerned to do what is right.

into this union, but moral principles issuing from the union might nevertheless demand different treatment for them from that demanded for non-humans. It is true that concern for the pain of such clearly non-rational humans presumably would lead to moral rules prohibiting the pointless infliction of such pain, for the same reasons as in the case of non-humans. But in the case of children, there would be additional reasons to formulate rules demanding their proper care and development. They are, after all, future members of society, and so their proper development and education will affect the welfare and stability of society. It is plausible to suppose that members of the moral union would care about the welfare of society both for prudential reasons and for the sake of other members. It also seems natural for members to see children differently from animals in light of the fact that children have the strong potential for a commitment to morality and so are future deliberators in the union itself.

The rules governing treatment of severely retarded adult humans, as well as humans in persistent vegetative states and the like, would probably be more limited, but still not the same as the rules governing treatment of animals.[32] In some ways, the rules might demand less—someone in a persistent vegetative state would not need spacious living quarters or opportunities for frequent social interaction, while an ape or even a rabbit might. But the main consideration for deliberators in the kingdom of ends would be the psychological improbability of maintaining respect for most humans while treating some with contempt. This would lead to symbolic duties of respect for such humans, in addition to duties not to inflict needless pain on them. I believe this accords with everyday intuitions about the sorts of duties we have to permanently non-rational humans.

There is no reason to think that non-rational humans should be treated in the same ways as animals, even if they have in one sense a lesser status than fully rational humans who possess a commitment to morality. The lesser status I am proposing is at the level of philosophical examination of the source of moral rules, not at the level of everyday talk about what is right and wrong.

In the absence of further objections, the prima facie criterion I have offered for differential moral status suggests that it is not arbitrary to say that many humans have a moral status that all known non-human animals lack. But the nature of this moral difference also allows that we can have straightforward duties not to mistreat animals, or non-rational humans, or competent but

[32] I see no reason to think that humans who are only mildly retarded might not be capable of having a commitment to morality.

immoral humans. This bolsters the case that I made in Chapter 5, that the good will reading does not render the humanity formulation repugnantly moralistic. In one sense, mainly at the level of moral theorizing, the good will reading of course treats good will as having central importance. But this is consistent with the existence of a great many straightforward duties toward all humans, and also toward non-humans, regardless of whether they possess good will.

10

Would Kant Say we should Respect Autonomy?

It is routine to cite Kant as the progenitor of the multifarious conceptions of personal autonomy employed today in philosophy and other disciplines.[1] It is equally commonplace to note that, despite their Kantian ancestry, these conceptions are not identical to Kant's. Both the credit and the caution are justified, I think, but the details of the relation between Kant's conception of autonomy and any given current conception are often left murky or even mischaracterized. And often it is vaguely thought that the humanity formulation is somehow roughly equivalent to a contemporary principle of 'respecting autonomy' and that the two moral principles differ only in their details. But this is mistaken, and the good will reading of the humanity formulation helps to illuminate the extent of the gap between Kant's ethics and the contemporary principle of respect for autonomy.

My aim in this chapter is not to catalogue all the uses of 'autonomy' in contemporary moral philosophy, political philosophy, psychology, and other areas. Many authors have helpfully listed and described some of the key uses of the term, and a complete taxonomy would no doubt be useful as well.[2] But that would probably require a book in itself, and my concerns in this chapter are more specific. I will focus on the principle of respect for autonomy which has become central to contemporary bioethics, and on comparing this principle to Kant's own statements about autonomy and about humanity as an end in itself.

[1] Onora O'Neill says, of contemporary appeals to autonomy in many areas, that 'at times it seems they agree only that autonomy has a noble, Kantian pedigree that links it closely to morality'. She quickly adds that 'their claims to Kantian ancestry are greatly exaggerated'. Onora O'Neill, 'Autonomy: The Emperor's New Clothes', *Proceedings of the Aristotelian Society*, Supplement 77 (2003), 1–21.

[2] See John Christman, introduction to *The Inner Citadel* (Oxford: Oxford University Press, 1989), 3–23; Gerald Dworkin, 'The Nature of Autonomy', in *The Theory and Practice of Autonomy* (Cambridge: Cambridge University Press, 1988), 3–20; Thomas E. Hill, Jr., 'Autonomy and Benevolent Lies', and 'The Importance of Autonomy', in *Autonomy and Self-Respect* (Cambridge: Cambridge University Press, 1991), 25–51.

Bioethicists who discuss autonomy often acknowledge that the bioethical principle of respect for autonomy is only a remote descendant of Kant's claims, but there is no real unanimity or consistency about this. A close relationship between Kant's ethics and the contemporary principle of respect for autonomy is posited not only in some standard bioethics textbooks,[3] but also in professional reference books[4] and articles in bioethics journals.[5] The tendency to assume a substantial connection between Kant and the bioethics principle of respect for autonomy is widespread enough that Rosamond Rhodes recently wrote, 'Because Kant's account is the most frequent point of reference for discussions of autonomy in the bioethics literature, I employ Kantian terms in my account'.[6] But I think it is a mistake to draw any close connection between Kant's ethics and contemporary 'respect for autonomy'. And it is not entirely a harmless mistake. If one assumes that Kant must espouse some principle similar to 'respect for autonomy', it leads to distortions of his view, by stretching his conception of autonomy out of any recognizably Kantian form or by twisting the content and role of the humanity formulation. The mistaken association of Kant with 'respect for autonomy' also tends to lend a false historical lustre to current approaches to bioethics that Kant would disavow, and to distract attention away from genuinely important conceptual questions about bioethical principles. Explaining the differences between Kant's ethics and bioethical respect for autonomy will lead to a clearer view of both Kant and the bioethics principle.

In this chapter, I am pursuing this clarification. I will argue that Kant's moral theory contains no normative principle resembling the bioethics principle of respect for autonomy. His concept of autonomy is not only different in its details from the concept current in bioethics, it also plays a fundamentally different role. For Kant, autonomy plays a role in the deep justification of moral theory, but is not specified as a direct object of moral concern by any normative principle. And the humanity formulation of the Categorical Imperative, which does of course prescribe humanity as an object of moral concern, does not significantly resemble the bioethical principle of respect for

[3] Ronald Munson, *Intervention and Reflection: Basic Issues in Medical Ethics* (Belmont, Calif.: Wadsworth/Thomson Learning, 2000), 105; Thomas A. Mappes and David DeGrazia, *Biomedical Ethics*, 5th ed. (New York: McGraw-Hill, 2001), 43.

[4] Bruce Miller, entry for 'Autonomy', in Warren Thomas Reich (ed.), *Encyclopedia of Bioethics* (New York: Macmillan, 1995), 216–17; Thomas L. Beauchamp and James F. Childress, *Principles of Biomedical Ethics*, 5th edn. (Oxford: Oxford University Press, 2001), 63–4.

[5] Candace Cummins Gauthier, 'Philosophical Foundations of Respect for Autonomy', *Kennedy Institute of Ethics Journal*, 3/1 (1993), 23–4, and 'The Virtue of Moral Responsibility in Healthcare Decisionmaking', *Cambridge Quarterly of Healthcare Ethics*, 11/3 (2002), 273–81; Rosamond Rhodes, 'Rethinking Research Ethics', *American Journal of Bioethics*, 5/1 (2005), 7–28, esp. 11.

[6] Rhodes, 'Rethinking Research Ethics', 11 n.

autonomy. The two principles would be similar, if some minimal readings of the humanity formulation were correct, but these minimal readings are not correct and the two principles are radically different.

Beyond arguing that Kant's ethics provides only indirect and contingent support for the bioethics principle of respect for autonomy, I will argue that it is unjustified to dismiss Kant's humanity formulation as a less sound moral principle than the currently influential bioethical principle. Many of the reasons that bioethicists cite for rejecting a more Kantian ethical approach are based on uncharitable misinterpretations of Kant's ethics. In addition, there are cases in which it is counterintuitive to say that we have even prima facie obligations to 'respect autonomy' in the sense demanded by the bioethics principle, and the humanity formulation handles such cases more satisfactorily.

1. The Bioethics Principle of Respect for Autonomy

The word 'autonomy' is derived from the Greek for 'self' and 'rule', and denotes a kind of freedom or independence in which one controls oneself rather than being controlled. The word was long used to describe political states that were independent of foreign rule, but Kant seems to be the first to apply the word (in German, *die Autonomie*) to individuals. Kant's use of the term pre-dates any English use of 'autonomy' applied to individuals, and the earliest philosophical talk in English about the 'autonomy' of individuals appears in discussions of Kant's work.[7] The word 'autonomy' has had a remarkably diverse career since then, and now serves as a label for a variety of conceptions which are central to issues in political philosophy and political science, moral philosophy, and psychology. Although these conceptions of personal autonomy often differ significantly from one another, there is a shared core concept that is captured by the word's etymology. Autonomy is always in some sense a matter of ruling oneself, as opposed to being controlled by something or someone else.

Sometimes in bioethics, the principle of respect for autonomy amounts to little more than a demand to let patients make choices about their medical care. This emphasis on choice, sometimes to the exclusion of any other aspect of respect for autonomy, is understandable, given the original role of the principle. Authors familiar with the early years of the discipline of bioethics suggest that the principle of respect for autonomy originated mainly as a moral

[7] *Oxford English Dictionary* (Oxford: Oxford University Press, 1989), 807.

justification for requirements of informed consent.[8] Paternalistic decisions by physicians about patients' treatments were routine until recent decades. The moral requirement of respecting patients' autonomy was a way to capture what is wrong with excluding patients from decisions about their treatments, namely that control of their own fates is taken out of their hands. Since the alleged defect in previous medical decision-making was that patients often were given no choice at all, it was natural to emphasize the most pressing remedy for that defect, namely to let patients make choices about their own treatment. Given these origins of the principle of respect for autonomy, it is understandable if it is often treated mainly as a demand to allow people to make choices.

But a more sophisticated notion of respect for autonomy is required for pursuing many projects in bioethics, and underlies even the basic requirement of informed consent. The principle 'respect patients' choices' would ground a requirement of consent, but not informed consent. The rationale for requiring that physicians give adequate information before obtaining consent is to allow patients to make choices that fit with their overall desires, goals, and attitudes. This is the real requirement and intuitive force of the principle of respect for autonomy, and it accords with most explicit formulations of that principle. Tom Beauchamp and James Childress, in the virtually canonical *Principles of Biomedical Ethics*, state, 'To respect an autonomous agent is, at minimum, to acknowledge that person's right to hold views, to make choices, and to take actions based on personal values and beliefs'.[9] Textbooks generally offer a definition of the principle that resembles Beauchamp and Childress's.[10] And when bioethicists appeal to a principle of respect for autonomy in discussions of controversial issues, the default assumption is that they are relying on something like Beauchamp and Childress's principle, a requirement to allow patients to make choices in accord with their own goals and values.

This is not to say that the principle of respect for autonomy, in its standard formulation, is universally embraced. Many authors have argued that the principle should be modified, clarified, or replaced, and there seems to be a

[8] Robert Veatch, 'Autonomy's Temporary Triumph', *Hastings Center Report*, 14 (Oct. 1984), 38–40 and 'Which Grounds for Overriding Autonomy are Legitimate?', *Hastings Center Report*, 26/6 (Nov.–Dec. 1996), 42–3; Onora O'Neill, *Autonomy and Trust in Bioethics* (Cambridge: Cambridge University Press, 2002), 16–27, 34–42; Albert R. Jonsen, 'Future Challenges to Medical Ethics and Professional Values', in Robert B. Baker, Arthur L. Caplan, Linda L. Emanuel, and Stephen R. Latham (eds.), *The American Medical Ethics Revolution* (Baltimore: Johns Hopkins University Press, 1999), 267–8. O'Neill points out that issues of women's reproductive rights also played a large role in developing the idea of respect for choices in a medical context.

[9] Beauchamp and Childress, *Principles of Biomedical Ethics*, 63.

[10] Munson, *Intervention and Reflection*, 40–3; Mappes and DeGrazia, *Biomedical Ethics*, 39–42; Tom Beauchamp and LeRoy Walters, *Contemporary Issues in Bioethics*, 6th edn. (Belmont, Calif: Wadsworth-Thomson Learning, 2003), 22–3.

consensus that it at least has been overemphasized in comparison to other moral considerations in medical ethics. Bioethicists have long expressed misgivings about the dominance of the principle of autonomy in their field, and cautioned that it should not be allowed to eclipse other moral principles.[11] For almost as long, serious objections also have been raised to the principle's basic suitability as a guiding moral ideal. Some critics have argued that the ideal of respect for autonomy emphasizes a typically male ideal of independence,[12] or that the principle of respect for autonomy embodies ideals of self-sufficiency and individuality typical of the English-speaking countries in which the field of bioethics originated, but does not do as good a job of capturing other cultures' ideals.[13] But none of these criticisms undermines the claim that there is a more or less stable and dominant conception of the principle in the field of bioethics. Instead, they are reactions to that dominant principle and its perceived shortcomings. It is fair to say that there is rough consensus that, for better or worse, the standard bioethical principle of respect for autonomy demands that people be allowed to control their own lives by making decisions that reflect their overall plans, goals, and values.

If one is searching for a conception of autonomy that most naturally accompanies or grounds the principle of respect for autonomy, an obvious candidate suggests itself. Since respect for autonomy is a demand to allow individuals to make choices based on their own plans, ends, and values, it is

[11] Daniel Callahan, 'Autonomy: A Moral Good, Not a Moral Obsession', *Hastings Center Report*, 14/5 (Oct. 1984), 40–2 and 'Can the Moral Commons Survive Autonomy?', *Hastings Center Report*, 26/6 (Nov.–Dec. 1996), 41–2; Veatch, 'Autonomy's Temporary Triumph', 38–40; Carl Schneider, *The Practice of Autonomy: Patients, Doctors, and Medical Decisions* (New York: Oxford University Press, 1998); Willard Gaylin and Bruce Jennings, *The Perversion of Autonomy* (Washington, DC: Georgetown University Press, 2003), esp. 213–50; James Childress, 'The Place of Autonomy in Bioethics', *Hastings Center Report*, 20/1 (Jan.–Feb. 1990), 12–16.

[12] Susan Sherwin, *No Longer Patient: Feminist Ethics and Health Care* (Philadelphia: Temple University Press, 1992), 133–57; Catriona Mackenzie and Natalie Stoljar, *Relational Autonomy: Feminist Perspectives on Autonomy, Agency, and the Self* (New York: Oxford University Press, 2000); Anne Donchin, 'Understanding Autonomy Relationally: Toward a Reconfiguration of Bioethical Principles', *Journal of Medicine and Philosophy*, 26/4 (Aug. 2001), 365–86; Susan Sherwin, *The Politics of Women's Health* (Philadelphia: Temple University Press, 1998), esp. chapter 2 'A Relational Approach to Autonomy in Health Care', 19–47, chapter 6 'Agency, Diversity, and Constraints:Women and their Physicians, Canada, 1850–1950', 122–49, and chapter 10 'Reframing Research Involving Humans', 234–59.

[13] Leslie J. Blackhall, Sheila T. Murphy, and Gelya Frank, 'Ethnicity and Attitudes toward Patient Autonomy', *Journal of the American Medical Association*, 274/10 (13 Sept. 1995), 820–5; Joseph A. Carrese and Lorna A. Rhodes, 'Western Bioethics on the Navajo Reservation: Benefit or Harm?', *Journal of the American Medical Association*, 274 (13 Sept. 1995), 826–9; Michael D. Fetters, 'The Family in Medical Decision-Making: Japanese Perspectives', *Journal of Clinical Ethics*, 9/2 (Summer 1998), 132–46; H. Eugene Hern, Jr., Barbara A. Koenig, Lisa Jean Moore, and Patricia A. Marshall, 'The Difference that Culture Can Make in End-of-Life Decisionmaking', *Cambridge Quarterly of Healthcare Ethics*, 7/1 (Winter 1998), 27–40; Farhat Moazam, 'Families, Patients, and Physicians in Medical Decisionmaking: A Pakistani Perspective', *Hastings Center Report*, 30/6 (Nov.–Dec. 2000), 28–37.

natural to think that autonomy is the power to make such choices, based on one's own plans, ends, and values. To respect this power is to allow people to exercise it, by providing them with accurate information, listening to their decisions, and refraining from gratuitous interference. This allows them to live, to a significant extent, according to their own plans of life. Beauchamp and Childress appear to propose this conception of autonomy in their most explicit definition of the term, saying, 'Personal autonomy is, at a minimum, self-rule that is free from both controlling interferences by others and from limitations, such as inadequate understanding, that prevent meaningful choice'.[14] The reference to 'meaningful choice' suggests choices that reflect an agent's own goals, in contrast to mere choice that may be exercised even when coercion is involved or false information is provided. When some bioethicists use the phrase 'self-determination' instead of 'autonomy', they also seem to have in mind a capacity to choose in accord with overall goals and values.[15]

But this conception of autonomy as a capacity to make choices in accord with goals and values is not unequivocally accepted, even by those who espouse the orthodox principle of respect for autonomy. Beauchamp and Childress, though they seem to define autonomy as roughly self-determination in accord with one's values, show signs of ambivalence in other passages about whether this is the sort of autonomy that should be respected. They explicitly reject Gerald Dworkin's conception of autonomy, which identifies autonomy as 'a second-order capacity of persons to reflect critically upon their first-order preferences, desires, wishes, and so forth and the capacity to accept or change them in light of higher-order preferences and values'.[16] The main concern which leads them to reject Dworkin's definition is that it 'presents an ideal beyond the reach of normal choosers'.[17] Beauchamp and Ruth Faden, in *A History and Theory of Informed Consent*, say that if authenticity (reflective endorsement of one's first-order desires) is made a necessary feature of autonomy, then 'the importance of the principle of respect for autonomy would itself be diminished, because its utility in guiding moral conduct in everyday interactions would be reduced'.[18] To avoid this result, Beauchamp and Childress, and Faden as

[14] Beauchamp and Childress, *Principles of Biomedical Ethics*, 58.

[15] Tom Beauchamp and Ruth Faden make a compelling case that 'self-determination is the legal equivalent of the moral ideal of autonomy' in law-oriented discussion of medical obligations. Tom Beauchamp and Ruth Faden, *A History and Theory of Informed Consent* (Oxford: Oxford University Press, 1986), 28.

[16] Dworkin, *The Theory and Practice of Autonomy*, 20.

[17] They also point out a more theoretical objection to Dworkin's definition, that Dworkin provides no good reason to think that second-order desires are more important or authentic than first-order desires. But they seem more concerned with the moral objection to Dworkin's definition, described here.

[18] Beauchamp and Faden, *History and Theory*, 265.

well, propose making autonomous choice the central object of concern in the principle of respect for autonomy, instead of assigning this central role to autonomy as a property of persons. And they offer an undemanding standard for what counts as autonomous choice. They say they will focus on 'non-ideal requirements' of respect for autonomy, meaning requirements that will make most typical choices count as autonomous. Specifically they say that choices are autonomous and should be respected to the extent that the choosers act intentionally, with understanding of their choice, and without controlling influences.

Contrary to their position, I think that if one accepts the standard principle of respect for autonomy, then one also ought to accept the more robust conception of autonomy, as the power to make decisions in accord with one's overall ends and plans. In most presentations of the bioethical principle of respect for autonomy, its importance and suitability as a moral principle are left an intuitive matter. If the principle is to be compelling, then the conception of autonomy that underlies it must be something that is worth preserving, pursuing, or respecting. Controlling one's own destiny by choosing in ways that reflect one's ends, plans, and values fits the bill—it sounds like something noble enough to ground a moral principle. A thinner conception of autonomy may well not. If unhindered choice is the main thing to be respected, as Beauchamp and Childress would have it, then it becomes questionable whether this is something that is sufficiently worth respecting. In the medical context in particular, it would seem to require regarding the rash choices of distressed patients, or the inconsistent decisions of someone halfway in the grip of unusual religious beliefs, as possessing such intrinsic value that they intuitively ground the important principle of respect for autonomy. In addition, many of the particular duties that are standardly supposed to follow from the principle of respect for autonomy seem to follow from the more robust conception of autonomy, but not from the Beauchamp/Childress/Faden conception of autonomous choice. The duty of respecting privacy, and more specifically of maintaining medical confidentiality, is hard to connect to their idea of autonomous choice. If the importance of respect for autonomy rests on the intuitive importance of intentional choice, then respecting autonomy would not necessarily include a requirement of maintaining confidentiality once such choices have been made. Guiding one's life in accord with one's overall plans and values connects more strongly with this duty, since revealing private information about someone can derail her plans. It is even harder to see why there is a reason to encourage others to reflect on their decisions, since unhindered and intentional choice by itself is what the principle is meant to preserve, even if that choice is unreflective.[19] So it appears that the conception of autonomy that provides the most complete and intuitively compelling foundation for the principle of respect for autonomy is autonomy as the power to control one's destiny by choosing in ways that express one's basic goals and values.

Furthermore, Beauchamp and Childress need not resist this conception of autonomy. Doing so does not imply that only carefully reflective ('fully autonomous') choosers deserve accurate information, respect for privacy, or acknowledgement of their choices. If controlling one's own destiny is important, then room ought to be given for agents to do so. Since we humans are prone to judge others by our own standards, and to regard their choices as irrational if they are based on values fundamentally different from our own, there is good reason to resist such judgements and give others the benefit of the doubt when it comes to questions about the extent to which their choices reflect their genuine ends. Given human nature, the fundamental importance of allowing people to control their own lives must be accompanied by a principle that demands respect for most of their choices, even in many cases in which one might suspect that they are not really reflecting carefully. Since the robust conception of autonomy provides the best support for the principle of autonomy, and is not liable to the problems that Beauchamp and Childress think it is, it seems justified to take it as part of a package, along with the principle.

But this issue need not be settled definitively for my purposes, of showing that Kant's conception of autonomy is fundamentally different from and possibly more satisfactory than the conception employed in the principle of respect for autonomy. I will argue that neither of the two conceptions of autonomy in bioethics is similar to Kant's. Furthermore, autonomy plays a basically different role in Kant's theory from the one it plays in bioethics.

2. Kant's Conception of Autonomy

The most natural place to begin looking for a connection between Kant's ethics and the bioethical principle of respect for autonomy is in Kant's own discussions of autonomy. But there is very little connection to be found here. At a basic level, bioethics and Kant's practical philosophy share a root idea of

[19] Ezekiel L. Emanuel and Linda L. Emanuel do a good job of comparing slightly different conceptions of autonomy and showing the type of information and guidance from physicians that would most naturally accompany each. Ezekiel L. Emanuel and Linda L. Emanuel, 'Four Models of the Physician–Patient Relationship', *Journal of the American Medical Association*, 267/16 (22–9 Apr. 1992), 2221–6.

autonomy as something like 'self-rule'. But Kant's conception is much more metaphysically laden, and he specifically treats mere choice, or even choice in accord with desires and plans, as unsuited to play the role that he assigns autonomy in his theory.

One of Kant's most important and distinctive lines of ethical argument is given in chapter 3 of *Groundwork*, and is meant to show that every rational being must accept the Categorical Imperative as a principle that demands unconditional compliance.[20] Autonomy plays an indispensable role in this argument. Kant's basic strategy is to argue that any rational being capable of deliberation and choice must take herself to be free, that the only conception of freedom robust enough to play the necessary role is the one he calls autonomy, and that the only way in which a being can be autonomous is by legislating to herself unconditionally binding moral principles. Kant begins by noting that to engage in a process of deliberating about what actions to perform, one must regard oneself as able to choose among different options. Even someone who accepts philosophical arguments for determinism cannot escape the activity of deciding what to do, so even if she thinks determinism provides an account of human action that is true for theoretical purposes, she nevertheless must accept the idea of freedom for purposes of engaging in practical reasoning. But one can only be truly free of controlling influences over one's actions, Kant maintains, if one can act on reasons that are freely given by oneself, rather than acting on causes that one passively receives as part of a causal chain leading to action. Kant argues that moral principles provide the only reasons for action that can count as being given spontaneously and freely to oneself, because they are legislated by one's own power of *Wille*, an aspect of one's own will, independently of any pre-existing inclination. In outline, then, Kant's argument says roughly:

1. Every rational being must, from the practical standpoint of deliberating about possible courses of action, take herself to be free.
2. To be free in the sense required for freely deliberating and choosing requires that one be able to act on self-given reasons, rather than just on motives that are passively received.
3. The only reasons for action that are truly self-given are the demands of morality, because only they give reasons independent of passively received inclinations.
4. So every rational being who engages in deliberation must, for practical purposes, regard herself as bound by self-given moral principles.

[20] I am specifically summarizing what I take to be Kant's main line of argument in G chapter 3 (446–63), but see also C2 29–57, and C1 A532–58, B500–86.

To be autonomous is to provide oneself with reasons for action, as described in step 2, so Kant means autonomy to play a key role in the argument that rational agents must regard themselves as bound by moral principles. Kant examines other possible conceptions of freedom, and rejects them as too weak to play this necessary role.

One conception of freedom that cannot serve Kant's purposes is freedom as just the ability to choose. Kant considers the possible existence of beings who have the power of choice (*Willkür*), but who can use this power of choice only to 'choose' exactly the actions that are dictated by their strongest desires. The will of such beings would be what Kant calls an '*arbitrium brutum*', or animal will (C1 A534, B502). Kant seems to think that non-human animals actually are such beings, but even if one rejects this claim, it is possible as a thought experiment to imagine beings that have *Willkür*, but no *Wille*. A rational being's own *Wille* is the source of the moral principles that provide reasons for action independent of inclinations, so a being who lacked *Wille* would make choices only on the basis of desires, affections, and other psychological features with which she simply finds herself. The will of such a being would be 'pathologically necessitated', meaning that the power of choice would be employed only to make choices that are predetermined by the being's given motivational states. By imagining such a will, Kant is making a point against the doctrine currently called 'compatibilism'. Real freedom, Kant maintains, is as incompatible with determination by internal causes as with determination by external causes. If every choice is necessarily caused by pre-existing states, whether they are states of the external world or one's own psychological states, then choice would just be another mechanism playing its role in a causal scheme, and agents would not be free in a meaningful sense. Kant regards this conception of freedom (possessing a mere power of choice) as anaemic, and mocks it by saying, 'it would at bottom be nothing better than the freedom of a turnspit, which, when it is wound up, also accomplishes its movements of itself' (C2 97).

Meaningful freedom must include more than just the power of choice, Kant thinks. 'Human choice' differs from 'animal choice (*arbitrium brutum*)' because it is not 'determined by inclination', and 'Freedom of choice is this independence from being determined by sensible impulses; this is the negative concept of freedom' (MM 213). So at the beginning of chapter 3 of *Groundwork*, when Kant says, 'Will is a kind of causality of living beings so far as they are rational, and freedom would be that property of such causality that it can be efficient independently of alien causes determining it', his phrase 'alien causes' refers not only to external causes, but also to desires, aversions, and other psychological features (because one just finds oneself with these psychological features, and is not ultimately responsible for their origins). Real freedom must not only be freedom from external causes, but also from any supposedly inescapable system of internal motivational forces.

This 'negative' conception of freedom as independence from pre-existing causes is, in a sense, incomplete. Kant recognizes this, and says, 'The preceding definition of freedom is *negative* and therefore unfruitful for insight into its essence; but there flows from it a *positive* concept of freedom, which is so much the richer and more fruitful' (G 447). If we simply said that a free will is not causally determined by any pre-existing states, this would sound as if free choice were merely random, and no reasons could be provided for free choice. But this is not the view Kant proposes. A will always makes choices for some reason, not just randomly. Since external or pre-existing causes cannot be the reason for free choice, but choice (as opposed to random events) demands a reason of some kind, the only possibility left open is 'the property that a will has of being a law to itself' (G 447).[21] This 'positive freedom' is autonomy in Kant's sense. What makes a rational being free is not merely that she can choose, but that she can choose to act on reasons, in the form of moral principles, that are produced by her own will. 'Reason must regard itself as the author of its principles independently of alien influences' (G 448). To be autonomous is to be able to freely provide oneself with reasons for action, so in other words, we must suppose that we are autonomous because autonomy is a presupposition of deliberation, and we must suppose that we are bound by moral principles because moral principles provide the only sort of reasons for action that make autonomy possible.

Thus Kant's conception of autonomy is quite different from the conceptions employed in bioethics. Kant's conception of autonomy (for brevity I will call it autonomy_k) takes autonomy to be 'self-rule' in a quite strong sense. To possess autonomy_k is to be able to act on reasons that are profoundly self-given—moral reasons, provided by moral principles that one legislates to oneself as a free activity of pure reason, independently of contingent psychological influences. This is the only conception of autonomy that will do the work Kant needs, of moving from the observation that we unavoidably engage in deliberation and choices of actions to the conclusion that when we deliberate we must take ourselves to be bound by moral principles. By rejecting weaker versions of freedom as insufficient to count as meaningful freedom or autonomy, Kant is rejecting the bioethical conceptions of autonomy. The two possible conceptions of autonomy which may be central to the standard bioethical

[21] Kant follows this same structure of argumentation in C2 33, moving from negative to positive conceptions of freedom.

principle of respect for autonomy are either autonomous choice, construed merely as intentional, informed, and unconstrained choice, or else autonomy as a power of persons to make choices that reflect their overall aims, desires, or values. In the passages cited above, Kant explicitly rejects mere choice as meaningful freedom, and so is ruling it out as equivalent to his conception of autonomy. Similarly, he would rule out the more robust version of bioethics autonomy, which takes autonomy to be the power possessed by rational agents to make particular choices that reflect their desires, overall plans, and goals. This version of autonomy involves more than just choosing, but still would not serve Kant's purposes. The ends and 'values' on which someone might base her choices need not be self-legislated ends or values (they could just be the products of pre-existing inclinations, developed through one's passively received desires and environmental influences), and so would not necessarily count as truly autonomous. So neither possible bioethical conception of autonomy is very close to Kant's.

The point is not that Kant is clearly right. In fact, the argument described above is highly controversial.[22] Kant is quite aware that his conclusions are not obvious. He views the claim that moral principles must be legislated by the will of each rational agent, rather than by any external source, as a revolutionary insight in ethics, equivalent to the move in his theoretical philosophy that he describes as a Copernican revolution of viewpoint.[23] He means his claims about autonomy to be startling. But this illustrates how radically Kant's conception of autonomy differs from bioethicists'. Kant offers one of his most radical arguments in an attempt to show that each of us must be regarded as possessing autonomy_k, while bioethicists mean it to be intuitively uncontroversial and obvious to any serious moral thinker that typical moral agents possess autonomy, as the power to make choices or as the (imperfectly exercised) power to make choices that reflect their overall plans and values.

Given the deep differences between autonomy_k and bioethics autonomy (or autonomy_b), it would be surprising if Kant's claims about autonomy gave significant support to the bioethical principle of respect for autonomy. And in fact they do not. The principle of respect for autonomy makes autonomy_b a basic object of moral concern, demanding that beings with autonomy_b be treated in certain ways. Kant does not employ autonomy_k in this way. That is, Kant not only fails to endorse a principle of respect for autonomy_b, he also does not propose a principle of respect for autonomy_k. Autonomy_k is not

[22] For the most comprehensive and influential discussion of the argument, see Henry Allison, *Kant's Theory of Freedom* (Cambridge: Cambridge University Press, 1990), esp. chapter 12 214–27.

[23] In C1 Bxvi–Bxxii, Kant compares the strategy of First *Critique* to Copernicus' strategy.

specified as an object of moral concern, which must be treated in certain ways. The roles autonomy is meant to play in his moral theory are simply different.

The most significant role that autonomy$_k$ plays is the one described in the argument above, to show that rational agents must regard themselves as bound by moral principles. The point of this argument is not to establish a moral principle that says to respect rational beings because they possess autonomy. Instead, the thrust of the argument is that each rational being must regard herself as possessing autonomy$_k$, and that to possess autonomy$_k$ requires falling under the demands of self-legislated moral principles, so each of us must regard herself as bound by the demands of moral principles. Autonomy$_k$ is the source of moral principles, not necessarily the object for which moral principles demand respect or special treatment.

If Kant did mean to endorse a principle of 'respect for', or morally mandatory treatment for, autonomy$_k$, there is an obvious place where he should be expected to say so. That place is in what is usually called the 'autonomy formulation' of the Categorical Imperative. But instead a quite different idea is found there. Kant presents a 'principle of the autonomy of the will' (G 433), which he means to be a moral principle of the same status as the universalizability and humanity formulations of the Categorical Imperative. After summarizing these first two formulations of the Categorical Imperative, Kant says, 'From this there follows our third practical principle of the will: the supreme condition of the will's harmony with universal practical reason is the Idea of the will of every rational being as a will that legislates universal law'.[24] This is his first presentation in *Groundwork* of autonomy$_k$, and the point of the passage is not to specify autonomy, or beings who possess autonomy, as the objects of moral concern. Instead, he argues that autonomy is the only possible *source* of moral principles. He says that only a principle freely legislated by one's own will is 'well adapted to be a categorical imperative' because 'it is based on no interest, and consequently, of all possible imperatives, can alone be unconditional' (G 432). This is his consistent point throughout the passage—not that the Categorical Imperative says to treat beings in a certain way because they possess autonomy, but that autonomy is the only possible source of unconditionally binding moral principles. To fit this point into the overall strategy of *Groundwork*, recall that in chapter 2 Kant is still analysing ordinary ideas about moral principles, or providing a description of what a moral principle would have to be like, if there is any such thing. Then in chapter 3, he goes on to argue that in fact we all ought to accept moral principles as legitimate and inescapable reasons for action. So, in chapter 2

[24] G 431. See also G 432, where Kant calls it the 'third formulation of the principle'.

(G 431–3), when Kant first presents the idea of autonomy, he is saying that if there are such things as unconditionally binding moral principles, they must originate in an agent's own free will, not in any external source, because external authorities can only provide conditional reasons for action, which appeal to an agent's contingent desires or inclinations. Then in chapter 3, Kant argues that every rational agent does have reason to take herself to be bound by self-legislated moral principles, because she cannot escape the activity of practical reasoning or the presupposition of freedom as autonomy that accompanies this activity, and autonomy requires that one be able to act on moral principles given freely by one's own will.

Kant's main uses of autonomy$_k$, then, are as an explanation of how moral principles can unconditionally demand compliance regardless of inclinations, and as a part of the argument in chapter 3 of *Groundwork* that every rational being capable of practical reasoning must take herself to be bound by moral principles.[25] The point in both cases is to identify autonomy as the source of moral principles, not as an object of special moral treatment. Autonomy$_k$ differs from autonomy$_b$ not only in its details, but in the most basic roles it is meant to play.

This highlights the need to avoid a tempting mistake when comparing Kantian autonomy to autonomy$_b$. The mistake would be to start from the contemporary principle of respect for autonomy$_b$, then to note that autonomy$_k$ differs from autonomy$_b$, and to ask whether it makes more sense to demand respect for autonomy$_b$ or for autonomy$_k$. To force autonomy$_k$ into the Procrustean bed of the bioethical principle of respect for autonomy is not genuinely to consider Kant's own views.

The strategy also has a tendency to lead to a further mistake. If one starts from the bioethical principle of respect for autonomy, and compares various versions of the principle, which differ in the conception of autonomy on which they rely, there is a demonstrable temptation to move too hastily in dismissing some versions of the principle. This tendency is demonstrated by Beauchamp and Childress's too-quick dismissal of the version of the principle that says to respect individuals' power to make choices based on overall goals and values. This move is too hasty, I argued in section 1, because it assumes that to demand respect for this robust version of autonomy$_b$ also implies that one ought to attempt to discriminate between autonomous and non-autonomous people and choices, and to refuse to respect the insufficiently autonomous.

[25] Kant also makes a related point in G 441–4, where he contrasts his autonomy-based account of moral principles with all previous theories of morality, which make the mistake of basing morality on 'heteronomy' or some source other than the agent herself.

An analogous hasty move is tempting, if one plugs Kant's autonomy$_k$ into the principle of respect for autonomy. One might think that the principle then says to attempt to discriminate between choices that are based on moral principles and those that are not, and to apportion respect on the basis of one's judgements about the moral commitments of the choosers.[26] That this move is contrary to Kant's own ideas can be seen by the fact that Kant's arguments are meant to show that all rational agents possess autonomy$_k$. Autonomy$_k$ is not a property possessed only by the virtuous, nor does it fade in and out as one makes morally justified and morally wrong choices. Autonomy$_k$ is, and must be, a property of all rational agents, since it is the sole source of moral obligations, and these obligations apply to everyone (even when some people fail to live up to them). The idea that Kant somehow thinks agents can gain or lose autonomy depending on their actions is reinforced by some commentators' use of the phrases 'autonomous action' and 'heteronomous action' to refer to morally motivated versus non-morally motivated action. The words are not Kant's—he attributes autonomy and heteronomy to individuals and to moral theories, not to actions—and neither is the view that goes along with it, despite the common use of the terms to describe Kant's ideas.[27] Since the strategy of examining a hypothetical principle of 'respect for autonomy$_k$' is fraught with the possibility of misunderstanding, it seems that looking at Kant's own actual theory is preferable.

I am not supposing that bioethicists will all be flabbergasted to hear that the conception of autonomy that they employ is not lifted directly from Kant. It is routine to acknowledge that Kantian autonomy is only the ancestor of bioethics autonomy, not its twin. In fact, Mill is mentioned almost as often as Kant as a source for the current principle of respect for autonomy, and this attribution is eminently plausible despite the fact that Mill uses the term 'liberty' instead of 'autonomy'.[28] Nevertheless, despite routine disclaimers that respect for autonomy$_b$ is not strictly Kant's idea, there seems to be a widespread belief that the principle has an especially close connection to Kant. In this section, I have argued that such a connection does not derive from Kant's own position on autonomy.

[26] Two authors who succumb to this temptation are Eric Matthews, 'Autonomy and the Psychiatric Patient', *Journal of Applied Philosophy*, 17/1 (2000) and Barbara Seckar, 'The Appearance of Kant's Deontology in Contemporary Kantianism: Concepts of Patient Autonomy in Bioethics', *Journal of Medicine and Philosophy*, 24/1 (1999), 43–66.

[27] For example, see Beauchamp and Childress, *Principles of Biomedical Ethics*, 351.

[28] For some examples, see Beauchamp and Childress, *Principles of Biomedical Ethics*, 63–4; Mappes and DeGrazia, *Biomedical Ethics*, 43; Gauthier, 'Philosophical Foundations', 21–37. Onora O'Neill specifically argues that the bioethics principle of respect for autonomy is derived mainly from Mill, and not from Kant. See O'Neill, *Autonomy and Trust in Bioethics*, chapters 2 and 4.

3. Humanity and Autonomy

Kant's discussions of autonomy are not the only place to look in his moral theory for possible connections to the bioethical principle of respect for autonomy. I have argued that Kant does not propose any moral principle of respect for autonomy$_k$, but this does not rule out the possibility that he puts forth some principle similar to respect for autonomy$_b$, under some other name. In fact, an obvious candidate presents itself. Although the autonomy formulation of the Categorical Imperative does not specify autonomy as an object of special moral consideration (instead saying that autonomous legislation is the *source* of moral principles), the humanity formulation does specify some sort of rational nature as an object of special moral concern. And many authors have in fact seen the humanity formulation as providing a historical basis for the bioethical principle of respect for autonomy.[29] So it is worth considering the possibility that the Kantian moral principle of treating humanity as an end in itself is closely related to the principle of respect for autonomy.

In fact, if Christine Korsgaard or Allen Wood is right in their minimal readings of the humanity formulation, then the humanity formulation does resemble respect for autonomy$_b$ in at least one basic way.[30] Korsgaard takes it that the 'humanity' that must be treated as an end in itself is equivalent to *Willkür*, or the power of choice. Wood thinks the end in itself is this power to make choices or set ends, plus the power to combine those ends into a coherent whole and find effective means to pursue the ends. Either Korsgaard's or Wood's reading of the humanity formulation does make the 'humanity' that is an end in itself into something much like the bioethical conceptions of autonomy. *Willkür*, the power to set ends or make choices, is close to one bioethical conception of autonomy, as the power to choose intentionally. Wood's reading of 'humanity' as the power to set ends and organize those ends into a coherent whole is close to the other bioethical conception of autonomy as the power to make choices in accord with overall values, ends, and plans. So if either Korsgaard's or Wood's minimal reading is correct, then the humanity formulation is similar to the bioethical principle of respect for autonomy at least in so far as both specify similar features of rational agents as the object of special moral requirements.

[29] Some examples are Gauthier, 'Philosophical Foundations', 23–4; Munson, *Intevention and Reflection*, 40; Mappes and DeGrazia, *Biomedical Ethics*, 43.

[30] See Chapter 2 of this book.

But I have argued that Korsgaard's and Wood's minimal readings are mistaken. And Kant's position on autonomy gives a new perspective from which to see how peculiar it would be for him to make the mere power of choice, or choice plus related abilities, an end in itself. Kant expresses an almost disdainful attitude toward conceiving of freedom as merely the power of choice. And freedom as choosing in accord with a coherent package of one's ends and plans would stand no higher in Kant's regard. When he mocks the 'freedom of a turnspit', Kant is, strictly speaking, dismissing these weak conceptions of freedom only in so far as they are unsuitable to play the role of autonomy in the arguments of Second *Critique*. But in spirit, he is also deeming the mere power of choice an inappropriately weak property to mark rational beings off from the rest of nature. It would be exceedingly odd, then, if Kant made mere choice, or choice in accord with goals and plans, into the key feature that has unconditional and incomparable worth, and must be treated always as an end in itself. The humanity formulation does not share its central object of moral concern with the bioethical principle of respect for autonomy. The end in itself is something other than autonomy$_b$.

There is an additional, structural, difference between the humanity formulation and the principle of respect for autonomy$_b$. Kant takes the humanity formulation to be one way of stating the Categorical Imperative, or the single fundamental principle of morality. Kant means this fundamental principle of morality to be the basis of all subsidiary moral rules and requirements. A 'metaphysics of morals' is a system of moral duties, derived from the basic Categorical Imperative and applied to human conditions, and in the book of that name Kant takes himself to be engaging in exactly the task of explicating such a system. Usually, in *Metaphysics of Morals*, Kant relies on the humanity formulation, rather than the universalizability or kingdom of ends formulations. It not clear that the different formulations of the Categorical Imperative are 'basically only so many formulations of precisely the same law', despite Kant's claims that they are (G 436). They certainly look different from one another, and the attempt to draw connections between them has generated a good deal of scholarly debate. But despite the difficulty in supporting Kant's claim that the different formulations are at bottom identical, it is clear at least that they must be consistent. Kant thinks a complete and consistent system of ethical duties can be derived from the Categorical Imperative. This basic Kantian claim could survive even if the different ways of stating the Categorical Imperative cannot be proven identical, but it would suffer a fatal blow if the different formulations actually gave inconsistent prescriptions. No single system of duties could follow from the Categorical Imperative(s) if different formulations of the Categorical Imperative place agents under conflicting obligations. Kant means all ethical questions to be, in theory at least, resolvable in a consistent way, by ultimate appeal to one principle.[31]

In this way, the humanity formulation of the Categorical Imperative has a fundamentally different status from the principle of respect for autonomy$_b$. Respect for autonomy is one principle of bioethics, but there are other, potentially competing principles against which it must be balanced. The principle of beneficence is widely acknowledged to be one. The basic dialectic about the role of physicians is often framed in terms of competing obligations of beneficence (doing what is best for the patient in the physician's judgement) and respect for the patient's autonomy. Beauchamp and Childress, influential on this topic as on many others, list four basic principles of biomedical ethics, adding principles of non-maleficence and justice to the principles of autonomy and beneficence. While not all bioethicists accept exactly this categorization of principles, the standard view is that there are multiple basic principles, and that they can conflict. This means respect for autonomy$_b$ has a significantly different status from Kant's humanity formulation.

In light of the difference between autonomy$_b$ and Kantian 'humanity', and in light of the different status of the humanity formulation and the principle of respect for autonomy, there seems to be relatively little similarity between the two principles.

4. Is a Kantian Approach to Bioethics Viable?

So far, the point of this chapter has mainly been to emphasize how Kant's ethical theory differs from the principle of respect for autonomy$_b$. But this raises the questions of what a genuinely Kantian approach to bioethics would actually say and whether such an approach would be plausible. To develop a complete Kantian system of bioethics based on the humanity formulation is a more daunting task than I am willing to undertake here.[32] Instead, I will focus on three, more limited, goals in this section. First, I will briefly describe what Kant actually says about some of the types of duties that bioethicists base on the principle of respect for autonomy$_b$. Second, I will argue that Kant's ethical theory is not vulnerable to some standard criticisms raised by bioethicists. Finally, I will argue that there is some reason to favour the

[31] For one example of Kant's unambiguous denial of the possibility of genuine conflicts of duty, see MM 224.

[32] Taking steps toward such a project is the goal of Onora O'Neill's *Autonomy and Trust in Bioethics* (Cambridge: Cambridge University Press, 2002). She emphasizes the universalizability formulation as the basis of a Kantian approach.

humanity formulation as a basic ethical principle over the principle of respect for autonomy$_b$.

Kant does not propose a principle of respect for autonomy, but this does not mean that he denies the particular duties that bioethicists usually associate with respect for autonomy. Letting others make choices about their fates, refraining from dissemination of damaging confidential information about them, and providing accurate information rather than manipulative misinformation are all duties that are either explicitly proposed by Kant or plausibly inferred from his theory. The main difference between the bioethics account of these duties and Kant's is that Kant does not group such duties all together, as flowing from one mid-level normative principle. Kant does recognize the need for such mid-level principles, but respect for autonomy is not one of them. Beyond the feature which all moral obligations share, of following in some sense from the Categorical Imperative, the duties that bioethics categorizes as duties of respect for autonomy do not form a particularly homogeneous class for Kant. One must look at several disparate categories of Kantian duties in order to find them.

Kant does recognize a class of duties that he calls 'duties of respect' for persons, but this class does not include most duties of respect for autonomy$_b$ (MM 462–8). I have argued in Chapter 7 that the moral feeling of *Achtung* (respect) plays a role in plausible derivations of most Kantian duties, but only a few duties are related to this moral feeling closely enough to be grouped together by Kant under the heading of 'duties of respect'. In discussing this category of duty, Kant quickly explains that the basic duty is to show a kind of modesty, and absence of contempt, in one's practical dealings with others. This duty follows from recognition of the dignity of every person 'as a moral being'.[33] Kant then lists some vices that violate the duty of respect: arrogance; defamation; and ridicule. Kant says that defamation, meaning the spreading of damaging information, 'diminishes our respect for humanity as such', and one might extend Kant's position to say that treating any confidential information as a source of amusement or profit is incompatible with a proper respect for others. This duty of confidentiality, along with perhaps a duty of courtesy to patients by medical professionals, are the only bioethics duties that seem to fall into Kant's category of 'respect for others'.

For the most basic requirement associated with the bioethics principle of respect for autonomy, the requirement of letting others make decisions about their own lives without interference, one must look elsewhere in Kant's ethics. Some of the passages which best illuminate Kant's position are his discussions

[33] MM 462–4, with the quotation coming from MM 464.

of the duty of beneficence.[34] This may be surprising to those approaching Kant from a bioethics background, since the bioethics principles of beneficence and respect for autonomy are generally taken to be in fundamental tension. But Kant's duty of beneficence is a duty to give weight to others' ends and to assist them in pursuing their ends, rather than to give them what you think will be good for them. It requires recognizing the importance of others' chosen ends, so it intrinsically rules out paternalism and does not conflict with an obligation to let others make their own decisions. Nevertheless, Kant's discussions of beneficence only provide a clue to his reasoning about allowing others to make their own choices, rather than correlating exactly with the bioethics duty. The Kantian duty of beneficence is only an imperfect duty, so one is not required to act beneficently in all circumstances, and it is basically a duty to assist others, not a duty to allow them to make their own decisions. To find an inviolable and negative duty always to avoid interfering with others' morally permissible decisions, one must look to the *Rechtslehre*, part I of the *Metaphysics of Morals*. The most basic underlying idea of the *Rechtslehre* is that it is wrong to infringe upon others' morally permissible decisions. Kant says that to interfere with morally permissible decisions is wrong, because 'this hindrance (resistance) can not coexist with freedom in accordance with a universal law' (MM 230–1). Infringing upon others' decision-making (if their decisions are not themselves immoral) is prohibited by the strongest sort of perfect duty, on the grounds that no such interference can be deemed permissible by the Categorical Imperative (in its universalizability formulation).

Kant prohibits lying in several places, but the most intuitively plausible discussion, and the one which most resembles the bioethics duty of truth-telling by physicians, is his account of what is wrong with making a false promise. This is the second of his four examples of duties that follow from the humanity formulation, in *Groundwork* 429. The problem with false promises (and seemingly also with other cases of stating falsehoods in order to affect others' decisions) is that one is attempting to influence others to act in ways that do not reflect their actual ends. This manipulation treats another person 'merely as a means, without the other at the same time containing in himself the end' that I am attempting to bring about. If I perform an action of this sort, I am failing to give sufficient weight to another rational being's will, and to his ends. By frustrating potential strategies for him to pursue his own ends, I am acting as if ends set by me should carry more weight for him as well as for me. I am acting as if my will and my power to set ends is more important than his.

[34] G 430, MM 452–4. See Chapter 8 above for a detailed discussion of this duty.

So Kant would at least roughly agree with bioethicists about duties of confidentiality, courtesy, allowing others to make their own decisions, and truth-telling by physicians. But to find these duties in Kant's ethics, one must look at many different passages, in different books. For Kant, these duties do not all fall in one category, of 'respect for autonomy'. The only sense in which they all fall under one moral principle is the same sense in which every possible moral requirement also falls under one principle, with the principle being the Categorical Imperative.

The way in which different duties are meant to follow from the Categorical Imperative is worth examining in more detail, because attention to the general structure of Kant's ethical system provides the material to rebut some standard objections. Kant thinks that all moral obligations are derived from one fundamental moral principle, the Categorical Imperative. Kant often groups the duties that follow from the Categorical Imperative by type (duties of love toward others, for example) and thinks some general points can be made about each class of duties (though he does not recognize duties of 'respect for autonomy' as one of these classes). And the general points about a certain class of duties can aid in applying these duties to human circumstances. But Kant's classification of duties is different from the multi-principled approach (often called 'principlism') common in bioethics.[35] Kant's classification of duties, or of moral rules subsidiary to the Categorical Imperative, is meant to result in a consistent system of duties, unlike the principles of bioethics, which are meant to be prima facie principles which can be in fundamental conflict. Kant first argues for a basic, fundamental principle of morality, which will apply to any rational beings. He then attempts to take account of human nature in order to derive a consistent set of more specific moral rules, or a metaphysics of morals, from this principle. But this set of moral rules is still abstract, in that the rules apply to human beings in general, without taking into account all variations in the conditions humans may find themselves in, such as differences in wealth, education, power, and health.[36] So even after arriving at a 'metaphysics of morals', Kant says that

> Just as a passage from the metaphysics of nature to physics is needed—a transition having its own special rules—something similar is rightly required of a metaphysics of morals; a transition which, by applying the pure principles of duty to cases of experience, would schematize these principles, as it were, and present them as ready for morally practical use. (MM 468)

[35] 'Principlism' especially is used to describe the approach Beauchamp and Childress propose, using their four principles, but the general strategy is employed by others who do not agree with Beauchamp and Childress in all details.

[36] For a description and defence of this reading of Kant's metaphysics of morals, see Mary Gregor, *Laws of Freedom* (Oxford: Basil Blackwell, 1963), 1–17.

Kant says that these points of application do not technically count as part of the system of moral rules derived from the Categorical Imperative, since the system itself must 'proceed *a priori* from a rational concept', but that nevertheless 'even this application belongs to the complete presentation of the system' (MM 469).

The point is not that Kant's moral system, the 'metaphysics of morals', is entirely unproblematic. Far from it. As ambitious a project as this is bound to run into some problems of clarity and consistency, and Kant, here as elsewhere, sometimes does a worse job than one might hope of resolving such difficulties. But attention to Kant's overall theory, rough though it is, is enough to rob some seemingly potent objections of their force.

Structural considerations in Kant's theory undermine one common objection, that Kant is an 'absolutist' who believes that moral rules must be applied in all circumstances without exception. Much of the fuel for this objection is to be found in one essay, in which he adamantly argues that it is always wrong to lie.[37] In this essay, Kant insists not only that it is wrong to tell a deliberate untruth in any circumstance (even to a murderer seeking your friend as a victim) but also that 'middle principles' of morality, meaning the moral rules that follow from the Categorical Imperative, in general 'can not contain exceptions'.[38] It would hardly be possible to find more damning evidence, if one seeks to cast Kant as an 'absolutist'. And, though I think the essay is a main inspiration for this view of Kant, it appears there are similar lines of thought in some of his other works as well. In *Metaphysics of Morals*, for instance, Kant seems to treat 'perfect duties' as inviolable prohibitions against certain types of actions. The duty not to lie and the duty not to masturbate are conspicuous and implausible examples.[39]

But it is difficult to see how Kant's overall theory supports such claims. The universalizability formulation of the Categorical Imperative is a test for maxims of action, not for particular action-types. So the universalizability formulation unavoidably leaves a conceptual space for saying that although telling a lie for one kind of purpose, such as to gain material wealth, is always wrong, telling a lie for another purpose, such as to save an innocent person's life, is permissible. And the humanity formulation, like the universalizability formulation, is poorly designed for testing general action-types, such as 'lying' or 'killing', and usually seems to include the rationale for an action as a factor in an action's moral status. For instance, the duty of beneficence does not

[37] Immanuel Kant, 'On a Supposed Right to Lie Because of Philanthropic Concerns', trans. James W. Ellington, in *Grounding for the Metaphysics of Morals* (Indianapolis: Hackett Publishing Company, 1993), 63–7.

[38] Ibid. 67.

[39] MM 429–31 and 424–6, respectively.

include a requirement to further others' immoral ends (MM 480–1), because immoral ends lack value. So, to refuse to give weight to a would-be murderer's end of finding a victim would not violate duties of aid to the murderer, if one refused because of recognizing the immorality of his end. It is hard to see how such reasoning would not also apply to lying to the murderer.[40] So Kant's overall system of moral duties is best taken as allowing or prohibiting actions based on certain reasons or maxims, not all actions of a certain general category. The charge of absolutism is also undermined by the structure of *The Metaphysics of Morals*, where he derives general rules that apply to human nature as such, but then sees the need to take account of specific details of different people's circumstances when applying these rules. This is the only explanation for his habit of appending 'Casuistical Questions' to his discussions of even the supposedly most exceptionless duties, such as when he considers whether white lies 'from mere politeness' are really wrong (MM 431). So, although Kant does sometimes say that some kinds of action are wrong in all circumstances, his overall theory seems not to support such a claim.[41]

Of course, there is a sense in which an essential feature of Kant's ethics is that morality is 'categorical' and allows no exceptions. Actually there are two senses in which this is so. The fundamental principle of morality, upon which all particular duties are based, applies in all circumstances and so is a 'Categorical' Imperative, and no morally permissible action can ever violate it. In addition, if morality actually, all things considered, demands a particular action in some circumstance, then the effects of that action on oneself or others can provide no reason to act contrary to the demands of morality. But effects, motives, and other empirical circumstances are relevant to the conceptually prior determination of what the right action is. For example, Kant entertains the possibility that it is morally acceptable to martyr oneself to save others (MM 423), but argues that it is impermissible to kill oneself to avoid personal pain (MM 422–3, G 421–2, 429). The agents' ends and the effects in the world are relevant to determining whether an action is permissible, but if a particular action is, all things considered, impermissible, then the possible effects of the action are not sufficient to show that it ought to be performed. So

[40] What Kant says about this, both in 'On a Supposed Right to Lie' and in his discussion of lying in MM 429–31, seems to beg the question. He regards lying as a harm to morality or to one's own moral standing, even when the lie does not harm another person, but this appears already to assume that lying is always immoral.

[41] The 'juridical duties' of *Rechtslehre* are apparent exceptions to this, since Kant says they can be prohibited and punished by external authorities because they are types of actions that are always wrong. But this serves to underscore the fact that most of the duties Kant discusses are of a different category, so seemingly are not action-types that are always wrong regardless of the reasons that lead an agent to perform them.

in some senses, moral requirements are 'absolute'. But the sense in which moral requirements are absolute and unaffected by considerations of circumstance is not a sense that supports interpreting Kant's ethics as an inflexible set of prohibitions that looks only at action-types.

Another criticism, that Kant's ethics cannot accommodate cases of conflicting obligation, also rests largely on the belief that Kantian duties are exceptionless demands for, or prohibitions of, particular types of actions. If Kant's ethics consists of rules such as 'Never break a promise', 'Never lie', and 'Never take a human life', then these rules can conflict. And this would be a problem for Kant because if these are exceptionless requirements, but they can conflict, then 'Because moral requirements are categorical for Kant, he seems to say that we are obligated to do the impossible and perform both actions'.[42] But since Kant's ethical theory does not actually result in such 'categorical' moral rules (instead, only the basic Categorical Imperative is exceptionless in this sense), this problem of demanding the impossible is not an apposite criticism. On Kant's account, an apparent moral dilemma is not a conflict between an absolute requirement to perform action *x* and an absolute requirement to perform action *y*, which is incompatible with *x*. Instead, it is a conflict between two reasons for action, and only one of them ends up being, all things considered, a decisive and mandatory reason to perform one of the actions.[43] So Kant's theory does not demand (impossibly) that one perform mutually contradictory actions.

So some common objections to Kant's ethics—that Kant believes that all moral duties are exceptionless demands, and cannot account for conflicts of duty—are based on an incomplete picture of his overall system.

A final criticism, that Kant's ethics is somehow excessively 'moralistic' or judgemental, deserves particular attention. The criticism is especially instructive, because although at first glance it appears to provide a reason to favour the bioethical principle of respect for autonomy over a Kantian approach, a more thorough examination reveals strong reasons for preferring the good will reading of the humanity formulation to the bioethical principle.

Kant allows that a kind of moral judgement of others must sometimes be made, but it is a judgement of the permissibility of their ends, not an assessment of their overall character.[44] One must give some weight to others'

[42] Beauchamp and Childress, *Principles of Biomedical Ethics*, 354. For another statement of the objection, see Munson, *Intevention and Reflection*, 16.

[43] This fits, at least broadly, with an approach proposed by Barbara Herman, 'Obligation and Performance', in *The Practice of Moral Judgement* (Cambridge, Mass.: Harvard University Press, 1993), 159–83. See also Thomas E. Hill, Jr., 'Moral Dilemmas, Gaps, and Residues', in *Human Welfare and Moral Worth* (Oxford: Oxford University Press, 2002), 362–402.

[44] See my Chapter 5 for the arguments that Kant does not require us to pass general judgements on others' characters.

ends, according to Kant's requirement of beneficence, but immoral ends are not to receive any weight at all. I have argued in Chapter 3 that the good will reading provides a rationale for this exclusion of immoral ends, while minimal readings of the humanity formulation do not. According to the good will reading of the humanity formulation, a contingent end has value only because it is set by a properly ordered will. A will that is not regulated by moral requirements is not a properly ordered will, so the ends set by such a will do not have value. But a general judgement about the character of the person setting the end is not needed, in order to conclude that an immoral end should be given no weight. To see why this is so, imagine some immoral end, such as the end of inflicting suffering on an innocent person because of her race. If the end is immoral, then the will of the agent setting the end must be defective in one of two ways. Either she must not be committed to moral principles, in which case her setting of ends does not mean that the ends have value. Or else, if she is committed to morality and so possesses a good will, then the immoral actions that she wills are inconsistent with her will's fundamental principle of giving greater weight to morality than to inclinations. In this case, the inconsistency between the particular ends and the more fundamental commitments means that the particular ends lack value, because they are willed in a defective way. In either case, a defect in the willing that is the source of value implies that an immoral end does not have value and should not receive weight.

Is this view, that immoral ends lack value, a moralistic judgement? To deem someone's end immoral is to render at least a moral judgement, but not necessarily an excessively moralistic one. Nothing about Kant's theory imposes a special obligation to go out of one's way to make such judgements. Instead, the point is just that Kant's theory can accommodate a common pre-theoretical idea, that obviously immoral ends lack value. Despite the pervasive influence of moral relativism, it is routine even today to regard some goals as immoral. People may sometimes differ on exactly which aims are immoral, and may be quite reluctant to pass judgement on others' overall moral character, but acknowledging the existence of some immoral ends is hardly a feature unique to Kant's ethics. Furthermore, whichever ends one deems to be immoral, it is a common practice to regard such ends as worthless. That is, in making decisions about what to do, ordinary people do not regard others' clearly immoral ends as generally providing even prima facie reason for acting. To help a serial killer in his aims, or even to assist a domineering boss in cowing his employees, are not the kind of factors that even ought to enter into consideration in deciding what one ought to do. In this way, Kant's idea that immoral ends should carry no practical weight is consistent with ordinary moral beliefs.

And in this way, the good will reading of the humanity formulation is superior to the bioethical principle of respect for autonomy. A look at one issue commonly discussed in bioethics will make this intuitive advantage of the humanity formulation clearer. The issue is the justifiability of exceptions to the duty of medical confidentiality. This was the focus of the Tarasoff case, one of the classic cases discussed in bioethics, and it is also the central issue in currently pressing questions about revealing or withholding information discovered through genetic testing.

The Tarasoff case is widely used as an illustration of legitimate exceptions to the duty of confidentiality. In 1969, Prosenjit Poddar first told his psychologist that he planned to kill Tatiana Tarasoff, then a few weeks later he carried out his plan. The parents of Tatiana Tarasoff brought legal action against the psychologist, on the grounds that he had acted negligently by failing to warn Tatiana of the threat to her life. The California Supreme Court ruled in favour of the parents, saying that doctors have a duty of due care not only to their patients, but also to potential victims of dangerous patients. In effect, the court ruled that requirements of confidentiality are not absolute. Although some exceptions to confidentiality are now well established, the extent of confidentiality requirements is still controversial in some circumstances. The advances in genetics in the last several years suggest the possibility that it will soon become possible to test for genetic predispositions to many diseases. Among the ethical issues raised by this prospect are issues of medical confidentiality. It is easy to imagine cases in which testing reveals that an individual has a genetic predisposition to some disorder, and this individual requests that the results of the testing be kept secret. Such a request can place medical professionals in a difficult position, because siblings, offspring, and other relatives of the patient may benefit from knowing that they may also be genetically predisposed to the disorder, and may suffer greatly from not knowing. Of course, one obvious step that the medical professional should take is to explain to the patient that her decision will have significant effects on her genetic relatives. And no doubt this will persuade most patients to release the information to relatives. But there is no guarantee that every patient will be moved by consideration of harm to her relatives, and in fact, it seems predictable that some small number of them will not. The moral pressure on medical professionals to make an exception to the rule of confidentiality will be extreme, in the case of disorders which can be prevented. To make the hypothetical case more illustrative for my purposes, we can imagine that the patient actually expresses a lack of concern for the health of her relatives who may develop the disorder, or even states a malicious desire to inflict an avoidable disorder upon them. Such a case would share a feature with the

Tarasoff case, namely that the patient confides to a medical care professional an apparently immoral desire to inflict harm upon another person.

The bioethical principle of respect for autonomy seems to deal with such cases less satisfactorily than the humanity formulation (on the good will reading). Either principle can lead to a reasonable overall conclusion. But respect for autonomy$_b$ seems to give an undue weight to the immoral desires of the patient who wishes to inflict harm on others. A comparison of the two principles' treatment of the situation reveals the intuitive preferability of Kant's principle.

On the good will reading of Kant's humanity formulation, a consideration of the circumstances would admit competing moral reasons in favour of different policies, but would not give any intrinsic weight to the patient's immoral ends. As I mentioned earlier in this chapter, and explained in more detail in Chapter 7, many specific moral considerations are supported by the humanity formulation of the Categorical Imperative. A concern with the continued existence of beings with good will, and with their continued ability to pursue their ends, would justify a strong general policy of maintaining medical confidentiality in most cases. This is for reasons familiar in bioethical discussions of confidentiality—because patients will be more willing to seek medical attention, including psychiatric counselling or genetic testing, if there is a strong requirement of confidentiality. But in cases in which the patient's choices pose a great threat to the continued life or welfare of others, including the Tarasoff case and the hypothetical cases of patients demanding that useful information about preventable genetic disorders be withheld, the immediate concern with life and welfare would provide a more decisive reason for action. There appears to be no reason why a Kantian account, relying on duties based on the humanity formulation, would not arrive at a plausible overall conclusion about exceptions to the confidentiality requirement, for some of the reasons that are already familiar in bioethics discussions. But any supposed value of the patient's immoral ends would be absent from the reasons for action that should be considered, because on the good will reading of the humanity formulation, these ends would have no such value.

A conventional bioethics approach, based on the most widely recognized framework for deliberating about questions in medical ethics, could also arrive at plausible overall decisions about when to make exceptions to confidentiality requirements. But because such a framework recognizes the bioethical principle of respect for autonomy, it seems stuck with an intuitively odd approach to the issue. If there is a prima facie requirement to give weight to intentional and well-informed choices, or to choices that reflect an agent's overall aims and values, then there is no rationale for disregarding ends that meet these requirements but seem clearly immoral. To be sure, duties that follow from the principle of respect for autonomy are only prima facie duties and can be outweighed, since the principlism routinely employed in bioethics treats all moral principles as providing only prima facie guidance, which can be outweighed in a given case by competing moral principles. The problem is not that the principle of respect for autonomy forces an implausible conclusion, for instance that someone who plans to kill an innocent victim must be allowed (or assisted) to do so. Someone who accepts the principle of respect for autonomy could quite reasonably claim that in a particular case, such as when a psychiatric patient states an intention to harm someone, principles of beneficence, or non-maleficence, or some other moral requirement simply outweigh the demand to respect autonomy. The intuitive problem lies in the reasoning that would lead to the conclusion. Someone committed to the bioethics principle of respect for autonomy would necessarily give prima facie weight to a patient's desire to carry out the murder of an innocent person, or to the malicious desire not to release potentially life-saving information gained through genetic testing. These immoral desires are to be given weight (albeit ultimately less weight than other moral considerations), according to the principle of respect for autonomy, if they are intentional choices made in accord with the patient's overall goals and values. This is the problem.

Since the humanity formulation, on the good will reading, does not demand that weight be given to immoral ends, it has an intuitive advantage over the principle of respect for autonomy. And this is not just a particular intuitive difference that arises only in a few quirky cases, a matter for only intellectual curiosity. Instead, it captures a fundamental difference between the two principles. Bioethicists have gone out of their way to make sure that respect for autonomy should embody a pluralistic tolerance of all different sorts of ends. Other moral factors may outweigh the importance of some ends, but the principle of respect for autonomy demands at least prima facie weight for a competent being's ends. But it is this very feature that renders the principle's advice counterintuitive in dealing with clearly immoral ends. And the feature of the good will reading of the humanity formulation that may make it seem unpalatable to some, namely that it does not grant the same status to the wills of good people and bad people, is what allows it to do a better job of handling cases of immoral ends. The supposedly moralistic element of the good will reading, when its limits are properly understood, is not a weakness but a strength.

So, in addition to arguing that Kant's ethics does not support the bioethical principle of respect for autonomy, and pointing out that some tempting criticisms of Kant rest on an incomplete view of his ethical system, I have also provided one way in which Kant's humanity formulation is better than the principle of respect for autonomy. Taken together, this is still much less than a complete exegesis of a thoroughly Kantian approach to bioethics. But it suggests that such a project may be worth exploring. Furthermore, the intuitive advantage of the good will reading of the humanity formulation over the bioethics principle of respect for autonomy provides another example of how the seeming moralism of the good will reading is not in fact repugnant, but unobjectionable and even welcome, when understood within its limits.

11

Autonomy as an End in Itself?

A final point deserves consideration. The issues raised in Chapter 10, in connection with respect for autonomy, urge a re-examination of one version of the minimal reading of the humanity formulation. This version takes autonomy to be the end in itself. In section 3 of Chapter 10, I pointed out that Kant rejects the mere power of choice, or *Willkür*, as a trait important enough to be equivalent to his conception of autonomy. But, conversely, this suggests that autonomy itself is a concept fundamental to Kant's ethics, perhaps fundamental enough to mark the boundary between beings who are ends in themselves and those who are not. So is possessing autonomy, the property of freely and spontaneously providing oneself with reasons for action, sufficient for being an end in oneself? Some commentators think so. Thomas E. Hill, Jr., in a possible modification of his earlier positions on the end in itself, has written recently that 'all rational persons must conceive of themselves as ends in themselves because they have autonomy of the will',[1] and Paul Guyer argues at length for the claim that freedom or autonomy is the end in itself, in several of the essays of *Kant on Freedom, Law and Happiness*.[2]

1. The General Case for Autonomy as an End in Itself

There is undeniably some textual support for taking autonomy to be an end in itself. 'Autonomy is thus the basis of the dignity of human nature and of every rational nature', according to Kant (G 436). In Second *Critique* 87, Kant first says that 'a human being alone, and with him every rational creature, is an end in itself', and then immediately adds, apparently as an explanation of

[1] Immanuel Kant, *Groundwork for the Metaphysics of Morals*, ed. Thomas E. Hill, Jr., and Arnulf Zweig (Oxford: Oxford University Press, 2002), 125.

[2] Paul Guyer, *Kant on Freedom, Law and Happiness* (Cambridge: Cambridge University Press, 2000). See esp. 10, 56–9, 129–71, 203–6, 239–40.

this status, 'by virtue of the autonomy of his freedom, he is the subject of the moral law, which is holy'. And in *Groundwork* 452, Kant says, 'Now, a human being really finds in himself a capacity by which he distinguishes himself from all other things, even from himself insofar as he is affected by objects, and that is reason'. For Kant, reason is pure self-activity, which makes rational beings fundamentally active instead of passive. In his theoretical philosophy, reason is the faculty that spontaneously and freely provides rules for organizing the 'intuitions' of sense that we passively receive. In his practical philosophy, reason freely and spontaneously provides the moral principles that present truly self-given reasons for action, independent of the influence of inclinations. In other words, reason is the faculty that makes autonomy possible. In light of these texts, and of the genuinely central role that Kant gives to reason and autonomy overall, it is easy also to read Kant's frequent statements throughout *Groundwork* and Second *Critique* about the importance and dignity of morality as support for the idea of autonomy or moral self-legislation as an end in itself—that is, to take the 'morality' to which Kant assigns a central role to mean 'self-legislation of moral principles' rather than 'commitment to moral principles'. Since all minimally rational beings possess autonomy, this would mean a minimal reading of the humanity formulation is correct, and the good will reading is wrong.

The positive case for this minimal reading is fairly strong, if considered only in its own right. But if the overall framework for the position is examined, the case is nevertheless weaker than the case for the good will reading. The autonomy reading of the humanity formulation faces major obstacles.

One is that if Kant really means to say autonomy must be treated as an end in itself, he should do a lot more to say so explicitly. The passages that strongly suggest this reading are limited to rare statements like the ones above, so the equivalence of 'humanity' and 'autonomy' is absent in many places in which one would expect to find it.[3] The most conspicuous of these lacunae is in *Groundwork* 432, where Kant first introduces the 'autonomy formulation' of the Categorical Imperative. The discussion immediately follows his discussion of the humanity formulation, and if Kant means to say that the 'humanity' that should be treated as an end in itself is autonomy, he should be expected to say so here. But he does not, instead emphasizing that autonomous self-legislation is the source of moral principles, and that previous moral theories have failed

[3] I am excepting cases in which he attributes dignity to 'making universal law', or 'law-making', for reasons discussed in Chapter 4, section 1. In most of these passages, Kant seems to identify the making of universal laws as acting on universalizable maxims, rather than the *Wille*'s activity of legislating moral principles.

to explain the unconditional nature of morality because they did not see that morality must be based on such autonomous self-legislation. Despite a few passages that seem to identify autonomy as an end in itself, there is a notable paucity of such statements, given the central roles that both autonomy and the humanity formulation play in Kant's ethics.

The second major obstacle to the autonomy reading of the humanity formulation is that even the passages cited above, in which Kant most clearly seems to say that autonomy is the end in itself, are quite tenuous support when placed within their textual surroundings. The passage from *Groundwork* 436, in which Kant says autonomy is the ground of the dignity of rational nature, occurs at the end of the paragraph that begins by asking why a 'morally good disposition, or virtue' has a dignity. It would be odd if the answer were 'Because morally good people have autonomy', since all agents, good or bad, possess autonomy according to Kant, since they all legislate moral principles to themselves. In light of this, it seems more reasonable to view the claim that autonomy is the ground of dignity as stating a loose connection—that autonomous legislation of moral principles is what makes a good will possible, since without such legislation humans could only act on their strongest desires, and would be no different from the rest of nature. (A deeper explanation of the claim is also possible, and will be examined below.) The passage in Second *Critique* 87 similarly precedes a detailed case for the position that only morally good people possess dignity. In light of this, the textual location of the statement that rational beings autonomously legislate moral law (immediately following the claim that rational beings are ends in themselves) is not definitive evidence that autonomy is meant as the defining characteristic that makes a rational being an end in herself. It may again just be saying that autonomy is what makes it possible for a being to act on moral principles, and so what makes it possible for her to possess a good will and thereby be an end in herself. The third quotation cited above in support of the autonomy reading of the humanity formulation, from *Groundwork* 452, does not admit of the same kind of narrowly textual ambiguity as the first two, but all three do lose some of their lustre when viewed in light of a larger-scale feature of Kant's presentation of the idea of autonomy.

This is the third and most important obstacle to treating Kant's claims about autonomy in *Groundwork* and Second *Critique* as strong evidence in favour of taking autonomy to be the end in itself. In both books, Kant emphasizes quite strongly that humans and other finite rational beings exist as part of two radically different worlds, the intelligible or noumenal world and the sensible or empirical world, and he generally attributes autonomy to such beings only in so far as they are members of the intelligible world. The picture that

Kant presents with significant consistency in these works is that, viewed as intelligible beings, we are free or autonomous because (viewed in this way) we are not subject to physical needs, desires, or other inclinations, but viewed as physical beings we are subject to all the same deterministic laws of nature as any other physical objects. Given this picture, that we possess autonomy only in so far as we are intelligible beings free of inclinations, there is no distinction between being autonomous and obeying the moral laws that we autonomously legislate to ourselves. Viewed as beings outside the empirical circumstances of space, time, and causality, we are no different from a holy will and there is nothing to lead us away from the actions that morality requires. So, given the picture that Kant often presents in *Groundwork* and Second *Critique*, any suggestions he makes that autonomy is the end in itself are inconclusive in ruling out the good will reading of the humanity formulation, since in these books he does not clearly distinguish the self-legislation of moral rules from the commitment to obeying them that is the distinguishing feature of a good will. This point renders many passages in the two books, including two cited above (G 436 and C2 87), more comprehensible by explaining why Kant seems to mix together the ideas of legislating moral principles to oneself and obeying those principles. It also precludes taking the *Groundwork* 452 claim, that reason is the feature which distinguishes rational beings from the rest of nature, as evidence against the good will reading. Kant is not distinguishing sharply here between the possession of reason, in virtue of which one freely legislates moral principles to oneself, and the freedom from inclination which would entail that one complies with self-legislated moral demands.

Although current commentators provide strong reasons to discount some of what Kant says on the topic, there is no denying that Kant actually says in many places that humans must view themselves as members of two worlds, one intelligible and one physical, and as possessing freedom, autonomy, and dignity as ends in themselves only as members of the intelligible world. In *Groundwork* 453, Kant says,

> if I were solely a member of the world of understanding, all my actions would conform perfectly to the principle of autonomy of the pure will; if I were solely a part of the sensible world, they would have to be taken as conforming completely to the natural law of desires and inclinations, consequently to the heteronomy of nature.

This fits with Kant's talk in Second *Critique*, that 'the law of a pure will, which is free, puts the will in a sphere quite different from the empirical' (C2 34), and that 'freedom, if attributed to us, transfers us into an intelligible order of things' (C2 42). He also says,

> The sensible nature of rational beings in general is their existence under empirically conditioned laws and is thus, for reason, heteronomy. The supersensible nature of the same beings, on the other hand, is their existence in accordance with laws that are independent of any empirical condition and thus belong to the autonomy of pure reason. (C2 43)

Kant's position is that by thinking of himself as a being with the freedom to act on self-legislated laws, a person also 'puts himself into another order of things' (G 457) in which inclinations are no obstacle to morality. This picture of two different worlds is a continuation of an image that was presented in the First *Critique*, of 'an intelligible world, that is ... the moral world, in the concept of which we leave out of account all the hindrances to morality (the desires)' (C1 A809, B837). And, although the image is generally modified in works written after Second *Critique*, it is at least sometimes still present in later works, such as the Third *Critique*, where Kant says, 'Hence an immense gulf is fixed between the concept of nature, the sensible, and the domain of the concept of freedom, the supersensible, so that no transition to the supersensible ... is possible, just as if they were two different worlds' (C3 175–6).

Of course, Kant does not forget that beings who are rational yet subject to inclinations, like us, are in fact forced to view themselves in both ways, as members of both the intelligible and sensible worlds. In his *Groundwork* and Second *Critique* discussions of our imperfect rationality, he generally maintains the picture of two distinct worlds, and portrays us as bipartite beings, members of both worlds. Kant says that one's self 'as intelligence' is one's own 'true self', and that one's sensible, empirical self is 'necessarily subordinated by reason to the character of the thing in itself', in other words to the principles legislated by one's intelligible self (G 461). He also describes the intelligible world as an 'archetypal world' or 'pattern for the determinations of the will' and says we should 'confer on the sensible world the form of a whole of rational beings', or the form of the intelligible world, by working to make the sensible world conform to the laws of morality (C2 43). More relevantly for the issue of what makes a being an end in herself, Kant says that it is only as an intelligible being, autonomous and ruled by moral principles, that one possesses incomparable dignity. He says that what confers dignity upon a person 'can be nothing less than what elevates a human being above himself (as a part of the sensible world), what connects him with an order of things that only the understanding can think', and that this is 'personality, that is freedom and independence from the mechanism of the whole of nature' (C2 86–7). Reiterating the point in Second *Critique* 161, Kant says that one stage of respect for ourselves is 'consciousness of an independence from inclinations and from circumstances and of the possibility of being sufficient to myself' and that acting immorally makes a person 'worthless and contemptible in his own eyes'. Even a 'malicious villain' recognizes 'examples of honesty of purpose, of faithfulness to good maxims' and wishes to emulate such a good character, and 'By such a wish he proves that with a will free from sensuous impulses he transfers himself in thought into an order of things altogether different from that of his desires in the field of sensibility' (G 454). Kant's picture of two worlds, one world in which a person is a physical being, subject to all the same laws of causation as any other object, and one world in which she is an intelligible being, in which she legislates moral principles and is free of all inclinations that might lead her astray from these principles, explains Kant's overall equivocation in many passages of *Groundwork* and Second *Critique*, where he seems to say both that legislating moral laws makes one an end in oneself and that being committed to obeying these laws makes one an end in oneself.[4] A typical passage is *Groundwork* 439–40, in which Kant begins by asking why we attribute a 'certain dignity and sublimity to the person who fulfills all his duties' and explains that it is because 'the dignity of humanity consists just in this capacity to give universal law, though with the condition of being itself subject to this very lawgiving'. Kant basically views membership in an intelligible realm, which is one of two ways in which all finite rational beings must be viewed, as including both a legislation of moral principles to oneself, and a freedom from inclinations which implies compliance with these principles.

The norm in current scholarship is to take a deflationary reading of Kant's views on this topic, a reading which makes his talk of viewing oneself as an intelligible being into simply a matter of viewing oneself as not bound by deterministic laws. To view oneself in this way is to see oneself as free to choose among different options on the basis of whatever reasons one regards as decisive, and so as being, from a pragmatic standpoint, outside the realm of any deterministic laws of nature.[5] For practical purposes of decision-making, one sees oneself as an intelligible or noumenal being, but only in the sense of not being bound by the causal rules that apply in theoretical thinking. This is

[4] This includes the three passages quoted near the beginning of this chapter as possible evidence for taking autonomy as an end in itself.

[5] For some clear statements of this deflationary position, see Thomas E. Hill, Jr., 'The Kantian Conception of Autonomy', and 'Kant's Argument for the Rationality of Moral Conduct', in *Dignity and Practical Reason in Kant's Moral Theory* (Ithaca, NY: Cornell University Press, 1992), 76–96 and 97–122, respectively.

not best taken as a matter of being a member of another, intelligible realm. I join with the majority of commentators on Kant's ethics in thinking that this deflationary approach is best overall, and Kant himself largely desists from presenting a strong 'two worlds' picture of rational agency in later works. The reason to prefer the deflationary reading is not just the spookiness of the alternative, but also that viewing ourselves as, in part, members of a purely intelligible world obscures an important conceptual distinction. One of the points I emphasized above was that if someone is viewed as a member of a separate, intelligible realm, then as a member of that realm there is nothing to lead her to act contrary to moral principles. This sometimes leads Kant himself into a seeming confusion, of thinking that to exactly the extent that one thinks of rational beings as autonomous (because as members of the intelligible realm they legislate moral principles freely to themselves), one also has reason to think that they will perfectly obey the moral law, because as members of the intelligible realm they have no inclinations to lead them astray. Given this picture, it is hard to keep track of the possibility of beings (like us) who legislate moral law to themselves, yet also frequently act contrary to it.

In fact, it is this strong 'two worlds' image of finite rational agents that leads to a famous and instructive, but ultimately avoidable, criticism of Kant's ethics. This criticism is a *reductio ad absurdum* objection, which maintains that Kant is forced to say that no one is ever responsible for her morally wrong actions.[6] This *reductio* begins by noting that, according to Kant's 'two worlds' image, one is only free to the extent that one is a timeless, intelligible being outside the causal order of nature. But to the extent that one is such a being, one will necessarily act on self-legislated moral principles. So when someone acts immorally, she cannot be seen as choosing actions freely, but instead just as part of a deterministic framework of nature. Since a person is only responsible for free actions, one is only responsible for morally permissible actions, and no one is ever responsible for morally wrong actions.

The response to this *reductio* relies on pointing out the deflationary alternative to the strong 'two-worlds' version of freedom. One must take oneself to be free to choose, whenever one engages in deliberation about choices, so if responsibility accompanies free choice, then one must also take oneself to be responsible. It is common here to cite a distinction from Kant's later works, *Metaphysics of Morals* and *Religion within the Limits of Reason Alone*, to help make the point and ground it in Kant's own statements. The distinction

[6] The example below follows one frequently cited form of the objection, from Robert Paul Wolff, *The Autonomy of Reason* (New York: Harper & Row, 1973), 207–8.

is between the two aspects of the will, *Wille* and *Willkür*. *Willkür* is the power to choose, and to engage in any practical deliberation between different alternatives, one must suppose that one has this power of choice. Since one chooses, one is responsible for one's actions. But, to follow out the line of argument further, one can only be genuinely free to choose if one can act on some other basis than one's strongest desires. The only other bases for action are moral principles, which can only provide a reason for action if they are legislated autonomously, by one's own will. So, since we unavoidably must take ourselves to be free, we also must accept that there are moral principles legislated by our own wills, which apply to us and provide us with reasons for action. The aspect of one's own will that legislates moral principles is different from the power of choice, and Kant calls this aspect *Wille*. The autonomous legislation of moral principles, independently of inclinations, is the activity of *Wille*. Every rational being possesses *Wille*, so they all are autonomous. A holy will, not subject to inclinations, would always choose in accord with the principles of *Wille*. But finite rational beings like us can employ their *Willkür*, or power of choice, to choose to comply with moral principles or act contrary to them. In either case, we are still autonomous in virtue of possessing *Wille*, and in either case, we freely employ our power of choice and so we are responsible for our actions. This picture of rational agency is generally taken to be a more complete and satisfactory amendment to the picture Kant sometimes presents in *Groundwork* and Second *Critique*.

I think this is correct. But to reconstruct a more satisfactory version of Kant's account by relying on later works does not mean the earlier version can be ignored for all purposes. In particular, the occasional passages in *Groundwork* and Second *Critique* in which Kant appears to identify autonomy as an end in itself cannot be taken as counting against the good will reading of the humanity formulation if, in those texts, he often fails to distinguish between autonomous legislation of moral principles and the commitment to those principles that is the distinguishing feature of a good will. Later modifications of his account of autonomy and choice cannot be read back into every passage of earlier works, even if overall the amended picture is more satisfactory.

In light of this, although there is a case to be made for taking autonomy, or the self-legislation of moral principles which makes freedom possible, to be the end in itself, the case is far from conclusive. It relies on a small number of passages, in which Kant fails to distinguish autonomous beings from beings who have good wills. The case is therefore weak. I have argued in Part I of this book that there is a much stronger case for taking good will as the end in itself.

2. Guyer on Freedom as an End in Itself

Paul Guyer has argued that autonomy or freedom (he usually treats them as equivalent) is the end in itself, and that the value of freedom is the central idea of Kant's moral theory. He emphasizes this point heavily, as one of the main insights of his book *Kant on Freedom, Law, and Happiness*, so it is worth giving his position separate consideration.

One typical statement of Guyer's position appears in the introduction of *Kant on Freedom, Law and Happiness*: 'the idea of humanity as an end in itself ... is identical to the idea of the incomparable dignity of human autonomy or freedom governed by the law we give ourselves'.[7] But the statement is ambiguous.[8] When identifying humanity with autonomy, Guyer leaves room for different conceptions of autonomy. This ambiguity is not an anomalous feature of this particular passage, I will argue, but rather reflects a deep ambiguity in Guyer's position. And the vagueness is not Guyer's own invention, but rather reflects just the same ambiguity that Kant himself often displays, between taking autonomy as merely the capacity to act freely on self-given principles and taking autonomy as the property of actually acting on these principles.[9] For the most part, Guyer's arguments are compatible with the good will reading of the humanity formulation, because most of the evidence he offers for an autonomy reading actually relies on taking 'autonomy' in the very strong sense, as the freedom of a rational being who regulates her behaviour with self-legislated moral principles. But Guyer often maintains that autonomy in a weaker sense, as simply freedom, has more fundamental value in Kant's moral theory. I will argue that this reading is less justified.

When Guyer describes his position on the end in itself, whose fundamental value is foundational in Kant's ethics, he usually says that it is freedom, or autonomy in the weaker sense, that plays this role. His statements that Kant's moral theory is 'based upon the fundamental recognition of the intrinsic value of freedom itself' are saying this,[10] as are his supporting references to *Lectures on Ethics*, where Kant says that freedom is the inner value of the world.[11] He also portrays the Categorical Imperative as being based on the importance of

[7] Guyer, *Kant on Freedom*, 10.

[8] The statement is actually loose in another important way as well. By equating incomparable value or dignity with being an end in itself, Guyer leaves aside the question of which is conceptually prior, the attribution of value or the practical requirement to treat something as an end in itself. Above, in Chapter 7, section 3, I argue that Guyer does not show that a value claim is prior.

[9] See section 1 of this chapter.

[10] Guyer, *Kant on Freedom*, 56.

[11] Ibid. 56–7, 96, 129.

the end of freedom, as when he says that 'the moral law, which is formulated by reason, is binding only because it is the necessary means to the preservation and promotion of freedom'.[12] In light of these claims, it is most natural to read his claims about the importance of autonomy—as when he speaks of Kant's 'mature conception of the incomparable dignity of autonomy as the foundation of his moral philosophy'—as also referring to autonomy as freedom, rather than to autonomy in the stronger sense of freely choosing to act on moral principles.[13]

But most of the textual references Guyer gives in support of his view actually favour taking the end in itself to be autonomy in this stronger sense. For example, some unpublished notes of Kant's, which Guyer cites frequently as evidence that freedom is the fundamental value in Kant's ethics, seem actually to be saying 'the good use of freedom' by 'the virtuous person' is what has 'a necessary inner value'.[14] This is the consistent claim of the series of various notes cited by Guyer—that 'virtue' (not just any use of freedom) has 'inner value'.[15] These notes, which Guyer cites in section II of 'Freedom as the Inner Value of the World', are revealing in two ways. Besides the fact that Guyer consistently takes the notes to be attributing a 'special value to freedom',[16] when they are actually attributing this value to the moral use of freedom, the notes also exemplify Kant's own tendency to be misled by an extreme 'two worlds' picture into conflating freedom and virtue. This tendency of Kant's, which I discussed at length in the previous section, is revealed in Kant's statements that one can attain true happiness by acting morally, because 'this is the happiness of the intelligible world ... I must seek on my part to attain the example of perfection in a possible good world'.[17] And by acting morally, 'We then find ourselves in an intellectual world bound in accordance with particular laws, which are moral. And we are pleased therein'.[18] Kant, then, is relying on the image of an intelligible world, more real than the sensible world, and claiming that by acting on moral laws (not just freely legislating these laws) we elevate ourselves into this world and gain a form of happiness independent of desires. Further textual citations by Guyer serve to reinforce Kant's general position that obedience to moral principles is what is sublime. Guyer cites Second *Critique* 86, the passage that begins 'Duty! You sublime, tremendous nature ...', but rather oddly takes it to support the 'absolute value

[12] Ibid. 240. Also 56. [13] Ibid. 99–100. See also, for example, 97.

[14] The passage here is *Reflexionen* 6797, cited by Guyer, *Kant on Freedom*, 110.

[15] *Reflexionen* 7202, cited by Guyer, *Kant on Freedom*, 111–12.

[16] Guyer, *Kant on Freedom* 109.

[17] *Reflexionen* 6907, quoted by Guyer, *Kant on Freedom*, 112.

[18] *Reflexionen* 7260, quoted by Guyer, *Kant on Freedom*, 113.

of freedom'.[19] Guyer also quotes a passage from Third *Critique* 431 as evidence that Kant thinks 'The ultimate end of nature can be nothing less than the freedom by means of which mankind alone can step outside of or beyond nature'.[20] But as I have pointed out in Chapter 4, section 1, this is actually part of a longer discussion in Third *Critique*, which culminates with Kant's claim that the only thing that actually makes a human being the final end of nature is 'the value that he can only give himself, and that consists in what he does, how and on what principles he acts, not as a link in nature, but in the freedom of his power of desire; in other words, I mean a good will' (C3 443). Kant's view that freedom is not valuable by itself, but only when employed morally, is nicely summed up in another of Kant's unpublished notes cited by Guyer: 'the free use of the powers and freedom in general is that which is most important and most noble, but if it is lawless and not unifiable with itself, then it must displease every rational being'.[21] If one does not distinguish carefully between mere freedom and the free choice to obey self-given moral law—a failure to which Kant himself is sometimes prone—then these passages about autonomy may appear to support taking freedom as the end in itself. But when suitably disambiguated, they are better support for the good will reading.

Besides Guyer's textual references, some of his own goals and argumentative strategies lead toward the idea that good will is the end in itself. Guyer points out that *Groundwork* opens with the claim that only a good will has unconditional value, and he takes it that 'the initial intuitive idea of the absolute value of the good will is refined into the notion of the incomparable dignity of autonomy' and that the value of the good will is 'refined and defended in the metaphysics of morals'.[22] Thus it appears that the value of good will remains central to Kant's moral theory. Guyer also expresses dissatisfaction with Korsgaard's regress argument for the end in itself, because Korsgaard incorrectly makes mere end-setting the necessary condition of the goodness of all other ends, which 'does not appear to place any particular constraint on the creative value setting of the agent, that is, to explain why any such agent should set values only in a way compatible with other agents' creation of values'.[23] Although Guyer does not explicitly extend this criticism, to reach the conclusion that good will must actually be the end in itself, this is where the line of thought seems naturally to lead.[24] On a larger scale, Guyer's enlightening discussions of the highest good would be rendered puzzling, if

[19] Guyer, *Kant on Freedom*, 154. [20] Ibid. 169.

[21] *Reflexionen* 6871, quoted by Guyer, *Kant on Freedom*, 116.

[22] Guyer, *Kant on Freedom*, 153 and 147, respectively. See also 139.

[23] Ibid. 151. [24] See my Chapter 6.

the fundamental value at the heart of Kant's ethics is simply freedom, rather than a freely chosen commitment to act on freely legislated moral principles. Guyer usefully develops the idea of the highest good as a harmonious unity of the morally permissible contingent ends of rational beings, and in fact this is one of his central themes in *Kant on Freedom, Law, and Happiness*.[25] Guyer offers several insights on this theme. One is that, although actual empirical (or 'pathological') desires and their satisfaction cannot provide a basis for a universal moral principle, the rationally constructed idea of a unified set of moral beings' desires can.[26] Another is that the sense in which a virtuous person deserves happiness is not just a matter of reward, but also depends on the fact that she actually helps to produce an approximation of this highest good, by helping to preserve others' rational nature and by aiding them in achieving their ends.[27] Without going into more detail, it suffices to say that Guyer provides many intriguing insights along these lines. But if we suppose that the end in itself is just freedom, then the connection between moral law and the highest good threatens to become incoherent. The concept of the highest good is not just of a maximally compossible satisfaction of everyone's actual desires, but instead includes the proviso that only morally permissible desires are to be included, and only in proportion to agents' virtue.[28] Obedience to the Categorical Imperative is the conceptually necessary condition of the inclusion of an agent's ends as part of the highest good. And it is only by obeying the Categorical Imperative that an agent helps to bring about the highest good, 'just as the production of bread for oneself and others both entitles one to eat and also naturally tends to produce the desired outcome'.[29] Just exercising free choice may result in immoral behaviour, which makes one neither deserve nor contribute to the highest good. To make mere freedom the basis of Kant's ethics would turn the highest good into something closely resembling straightforward contractarianism, a mutually agreeable satisfaction of empirically given desires, which would undermine both Kant's own ideas and Guyer's insights. So some of Guyer's own arguments, as well as the Kantian texts he cites, suggest that good will should be taken as the end in itself.

It begins to seem as though Guyer may just be speaking loosely in saying that freedom is the end in itself, that he may have in mind that a moral use of freedom is really what is important. In fact, Guyer does consider this reading of Kant, and even admits that it is roughly the view Kant holds in much of *Groundwork* and Second *Critique*. Guyer describes this view as saying, 'what is

[25] See Guyer, *Kant on Freedom*, 113–25, 224–7, 333–50, 366–8, 385–90, 397–402.

[26] Ibid. 100–7. [27] Ibid. 122–3.

[28] C2 108–20, C3 450, C1 A808–15/B836–43,

[29] Guyer, *Kant on Freedom*, 122. See also 340.

sublime above all else is nothing less than autonomy in the strong sense, that is, freedom that is expressed in or even achieved by adherence to a law other than the law of nature, which is therefore (by elimination) identical to the moral law'.[30] I think this is the position that is most justified, even by the evidence Guyer himself offers. But Guyer presents this view only in order to reject it, in favour of the view that freedom is the more fundamental value for Kant.

Guyer gives his most explicit arguments for this in section IV of 'Morality of Law and Morality of Freedom'. He offers two lines of argument.

First, he tries to show that 'adherence to the moral law itself by itself is not seen as valuable; rather the freedom expressed in and achieved by adherence to the moral law is intrinsically valuable'.[31] So freedom is really the fundamental value that underlies any value that moral action may have. To prove this, Guyer imagines a case of someone acting in accordance with duty but not freely choosing to act this way, and says, 'adherence to the moral law without freedom would also lack absolute value'.[32] Guyer offers a passage from Kant that seems to support this view, in which Kant says that if we were just automatically predisposed to act on moral law then we would not be ends in ourselves.[33] But Guyer's argument here is a straw man. The view Guyer must refute is not that mere mechanical and automatic conformity to moral principles is Kant's fundamental moral value. His hypothetical opponent has not claimed this, nor does the good will reading say that. The view that Guyer must refute says that the free choice to adhere to moral principles is of fundamental value. Whatever our intuition about beings who conform to moral requirements automatically without any choice, it tells us nothing about beings who choose freely to give priority to moral principles.

Guyer's second strategy is to present an alternative view of the most basic structure of Kant's ethics. 'On this [alternative] account, freedom itself is the absolute value and adherence to the law is the condition necessary for the maximal realization of this value rather than part of its very concept'.[34] So the purpose of moral principles is just to ensure that each individual's freedom can be preserved. But the textual evidence for this position is thin. Guyer offers three quotations from Kant's lectures on natural law, and two from *Lectures on Ethics*, notes taken by students in Kant's courses.[35] The first two quotations from the natural law lectures are not clear support for Guyer's position. The

[30] Guyer, *Kant on Freedom*, 155. [31] Ibid. [32] Ibid. 156.

[33] *Naturrecht Feyerabend*, 27: 1321–2, cited by Guyer, *Kant on Freedom*, 156–7.

[34] Guyer, *Kant on Freedom*, 156. See 239–40 for similar statements.

[35] Immanuel Kant, *Naturrecht Feyerabend*, 27: 1321–2, 1319, 1322, and Immanuel Kant, *Lectures on Ethics*, ed. Peter Heath and Jerome Schneewind (Cambridge: Cambridge University Press, 1997), 125 (27: 344), 126–7 (27: 346).

first is the passage mentioned in the previous paragraph, in which the real point is to examine moral actions, and to say that unchosen, mechanical conformity to moral requirements is of less value than freely chosen moral actions. The second just says that the will can only be limited by other wills, a claim which is actually ambiguous between saying that all willing must be given weight or that only everyone's rational and morally permissible willing must be given weight. The third is genuine support for Guyer's position, saying that freedom is the sufficient condition for being an end in oneself.[36] Of the two passages from *Lectures on Ethics*, only the second provides real support for Guyer's position. The first says that freedom must not be restricted except by freedom itself. But this appears to be saying only that principles freely given *by* oneself are the only principles legitimately limiting one's own choices, rather than saying (as Guyer would have it) that 'freedom must be restricted only *for* the sake of freedom itself'.[37] That is, autonomously legislated principles are the only justified limit on freedom, but this leaves open why these limiting principles are justified. The second passage Guyer cites does provide support for his view that the rationale for moral principles is to provide for maximum freedom overall. So the evidence Guyer gives in this section for his unconventional reading boils down to one passage from Kant's lectures on natural law, and one passage from Kant's lectures on ethics. In contrast, in favour of the view that the free choice to adhere to moral principles is of greater value than mere freedom, many of the most central passages from works like *Groundwork* and *Critique of Practical Reason* can be cited. If no further textual evidence can be provided for the unconventional reading, then the most reasonable view would be to regard Kant's occasional statements about the foundational importance of freedom as more loose talk, of a kind he is prone to, in which he really has in mind freedom employed to make moral choices.[38]

However, there is additional textual evidence that seems more promising. Guyer discusses the *Rechtslehre*, or 'doctrine of right', which is part I of *The Metaphysics of Morals*, and which deals specifically with 'duties of right' (legally enforceable duties) instead of ethical duties in general.[39] *Rechtslehre* shows promise as support for Guyer's freedom-based reading of Kant's ethics, since in *Rechtslehre* Kant appears to make freedom, conceived of as unconstrained choice, the fundamental value for political and legal institutions. 'Juridical

[36] See Guyer, *Kant on Freedom*, 156–7.

[37] Ibid. 158. The italics are mine.

[38] This seems more plausible than Guyer's suggestion that in his later, published works, Kant may have refrained from stating that the value of freedom was foundational 'to save himself from spelling out to his readers the argument that he spelled out to his students'. Ibid. 159.

[39] The full title of part I is 'Metaphysical First Principles of the Doctrine of Right' (MM 203–372).

laws', the concern of the *Rechtslehre*, are laws concerned with 'freedom in the external use of choice' (MM 214). The impression that freedom is the basic value to which Kant appeals in *Rechtslehre* is strengthened by his position that 'Any action is right if it can coexist with everyone's freedom in accordance with a universal law' and by his position on the justification—the only justification—for legal coercion. Kant says,

> Now whatever is wrong is a hindrance to freedom in accordance with universal laws. But coercion is a hindrance or resistance to freedom. Therefore, if a certain use of freedom is itself a hindrance to freedom in accordance with universal laws (i.e. wrong) coercion that is opposed to this (as a hindering of hindrance to freedom) is consistent with freedom in accordance with universal laws, that is, it is right. (MM 230)

To someone approaching Kant's position on juridical duties from the well-established liberal tradition of the twenty-first century, it may well appear that freedom of choice is the central concept of Kant's legal and political philosophy, and by extension perhaps of his moral philosophy as well. It is tempting to take Kant to be saying that such freedom of choice is to be promoted to the maximum extent possible, with the only legitimate reason for limiting one individual's freedom being a concern with preventing the infringement upon other individuals' freedom. Guyer does take Kant to be saying this, when Guyer sums up Kant's position as being 'right is the condition in which the external use or the expression of any individual's freedom of choice in freedom of action can coexist with a like active expression of freedom on the part of all others'.[40]

But caution is in order. A good place to start, in interpreting the role of freedom in *Rechtslehre*, is to remember the relationship between Kant's legal philosophy and his overall moral theory. Kant makes clear in the introduction to *The Metaphysics of Morals* that both part I (The Doctrine of Right, or *Rechtslehre*) and part II (The Doctrine of Virtue, or *Tugendslehre*) of the book are based on the Categorical Imperative, or the universal law of morality. All duties, juridical or more generally ethical, are moral duties that are required by the Categorical Imperative (MM 214–19). Kant says, 'all duties, just because they are duties, belong to ethics' (MM 219). Juridical duties are a sub-class of general ethical duties, and can be distinguished from other ethical duties because 'juridical lawgiving is that which can also be external' (MM 220). Kant's idea is that among ethical duties, only some of them are legally enforceable by external authorities, rather than just being required by laws of one's own will. 'What essentially distinguishes a duty of virtue from a duty

[40] Guyer, *Kant on Freedom*, 241.

of right [a juridical duty] is that external constraint to the latter kind of duty is morally possible'.[41] What can be legally prohibited (or subject to legitimate coercion) are actions that clearly violate the Categorical Imperative, with the criterion for violations being 'whether the action of one can be united with the freedom of the other in accordance with universal law' (MM 230). Many actions that are morally wrong are not subject to external punishment, because they violate only imperfect duties, or because their wrongness depends on the agent's motives, which cannot be known with any certainty. Only actions that are clearly inconsistent with the moral requirement of universalizability can be subject to legal coercion.

Since juridical duties are a sub-class of moral duties, the most basic, foundational justification for moral duties in general ought to apply to juridical duties as well. Unless Kant is guilty of a major inconsistency, the best interpretation of his legal philosophy ought to make its conceptual underpinnings consistent with the conceptual bases of his moral philosophy. Guyer is aware of this, and offers a consistent account. In his discussions of *Rechtslehre*, Guyer first emphasizes that the basic purpose of the Categorical Imperative is to preserve freedom, which would be consistent with reading *Rechtslehre* as justifying external enforcement of some duties in order to preserve freedom. 'The end or value which is served by adherence to the fundamental principle of morality is human freedom or autonomy',[42] Guyer says, and so it only makes sense to view legal enforcement as also serving this end of freedom. Guyer's account makes the rationale for juridical duties consistent with the rationale for ethical duties overall. This consistency may appear to be a strength of Guyer's position.

But a different sort of consistency is possible, taking the 'end or value' at the heart of Kant's ethics to be not just freedom as such, but freedom exercised to choose adherence to moral principles. And I have argued that there is an overwhelming preponderance of evidence in favour of this unified approach. In the essays dealing with *Rechtslehre*, Guyer (wrongly, I have argued) takes it as proven that the Categorical Imperative is grounded on the importance of preserving freedom, and does not offer new evidence for this. So if Guyer successfully shows that the *Rechtslehre* is based on the importance of preserving freedom, he is actually showing that *Rechtslehre* has a different aim from the rest of Kant's moral philosophy. If preserving freedom *per se* really is the purpose of the enforcement of juridical duties, while Kant's overall moral theory rests on the importance of freedom exercised within the limits of freely legislated moral principles, then the rationale for Kant's legal philosophy is inconsistent

41 MM 383. The bracketed words are my insertion.

42 Guyer, *Kant on Freedom*, 239. More generally, see 237–40.

with the basis of the overall moral theory of which it is supposed to be one part. Of course, Guyer might respond that the need for consistency is a good reason to read the point of *Rechtslehre* back into Kant's ethics as a whole, and so to think that the real point of Kant's ethics must after all be to preserve freedom as such. And this might be at least one good piece of evidence for a freedom-based reading of Kant's overall moral theory, if *Rechtslehre* were clearly based on the value of mere freedom. But it is not.

The best interpretative strategy to follow, in order to make the point of *Rechtslehre* consistent with the point of Kant's overall moral philosophy, is not to take both of them to be based on the importance of freedom. It is to take them both to be based on the importance of the free choice to accept and act on moral principles. The argument for taking the overall moral system to be based on this end has been given earlier in this chapter, and throughout this book. But it is also the basis of *Rechtslehre*. Kant's emphasis on preserving freedom can easily be misinterpreted, when seen through the lens of contemporary political liberalism. But Kant is actually careful to deny that the freedom he is defending in *Rechtslehre* is the freedom to act in whatever way one pleases. In the introduction to *The Metaphysics of Morals*, Kant says 'Freedom of choice cannot be defined—as some have tried to define it—as the ability to make a choice for or against the law', because 'Only freedom in relation to the internal lawgiving of reason is really an ability; the possibility of deviating from it is an inability'.[43] This explains the otherwise clunky proviso that Kant adds virtually every time he says that the point of the external enforcement of some duties is to preserve freedom. When Kant repeatedly says that an action is legally right if it can coexist with the freedom of everyone, he is consistent in saying that what should be treated as important is not mere freedom, but 'freedom in accordance with universal law' ('Freiheit nach einem allgemeinem Gesetze').[44] The universal law in question is the Categorical Imperative, and the phrase is a reminder that the ultimate standard of morality for all actions is the Categorical Imperative, not a maximization of freedom simpliciter. The idea of uniting everyone's freedom 'in accordance with universal law' is a reminder that not every exercise of freedom is meant to be preserved, but only freedom consistent with the Categorical Imperative's requirement of universalizability. This also fits with Kant's claim that 'in the doctrine of duties', including juridical duties, 'a human being can and should be represented in terms of his personality independent of physical attributes (*homo noumenon*), as distinguished from the same subject represented as affected by physical attributes' (MM 239). Then

[43] The quotations are from MM 226 and 227, respectively.

[44] Kant uses the phrase nine times in MM 230–1.

the idea at the core of *Rechtslehre*, like the idea of Kant's practical philosophy in general, is the importance of acting in accordance with moral principles, not just free choice of any kind.

To avoid confusion, it is important to distinguish between the overall rationale for a system of legally enforceable duties and the motive that individuals may have for complying with externally enforced duties. An individual may act rightly only because she fears punishment, and no external force can compel her to act from a moral motive. This is why Kant emphasizes that the doctrine of right is only concerned with 'the external and indeed practical relation of one person with another' and that no account is taken 'of the end each has in mind' (MM 230). It also explains why Kant says in 'Perpetual Peace' that even a nation of devils would have to invent rules for coexisting ('Perpetual Peace' 8: 366). Individuals may comply with society's sanctions merely from self-interested motives, but this does not mean that the real justification of a legal or political system lies in self-interest. We, as investigators into the justification of a system of right, can see Kant's position that the preservation of morally exercised freedom is the only justification. So even if devils obeyed their diabolical laws from self-interest, we could see that their nation serves no good purpose and would better perish. Their nation would be immoral even if its laws gave the devils the maximally compossible amount of freedom to carry out their evil purposes.

Guyer, then, has offered no conclusive proof that simple freedom is the basis of Kant's moral theory. The claim that freedom must be the end in itself is not reckless or wild—there is some textual support for it, and one can go a fair way toward constructing a consistent picture with the idea as a starting point. But the plausibility of the claim stems largely from the ambiguity in Kant's idea of autonomy. When the confusions are cleared away, there is more to say in favour of taking good will as an end in itself.

12

Some Big Pictures

The good will reading of the humanity formulation is justified not only by a consideration of a few particular texts, and not just by appealing to a few insights that it may provide into Kant's arguments, but by the coherent and compelling overall picture it provides of Kant's moral theory. This may be surprising, given the seemingly alarming and moralistic tone of the good will reading. But the good will reading in fact makes possible an approach to Kant's ethics that renders it quite reasonable and consistent. In this chapter, I will try to present that big picture of Kantian ethics, drawing together the ideas of earlier chapters.

But first, I will examine some influential recent positions on Kant's ethics, to see whether they are compatible with the good will reading. I think that Jerome Schneewind's exegesis of the philosophical history that shaped Kant's work is compatible with the good will reading, and in fact an extension of Schneewind's ideas seems to suggest the good will reading. Another influential picture of Kant's ethics, that it is based on the incomparable dignity of the power of choice, is obviously not compatible with the good will reading. But that is no discredit to the good will reading, since the emphasis on the power of choice is misguided.

1. Kant's Anti-Voluntarism

Jerome Schneewind has succeeded in drawing attention to the proper placement of Kant's moral theory into its context in the history of philosophy. One of the main themes of Schneewind's outstanding and informative book *The Invention of Autonomy* is the importance of religious issues in the historical development of moral philosophy, including Kant's ethics.[1] In particular, previous moral philosophers' positions on voluntarism provide a useful focus for

[1] Jerome Schneewind, *The Invention of Autonomy* (Cambridge: Cambridge University Press, 1998).

understanding Kant's ethics. Schneewind's main historical points are compatible with the good will reading. In fact, although Schneewind's own position on the source of the dignity of humanity is pretty clearly opposed to the good will reading, attention to the historical issues that Schneewind raises actually provides better support for the good will reading than for minimal readings.

Schneewind argues convincingly that Kant's opposition to voluntarism is an essential motivation for his 'invention of autonomy'. Voluntarism is basically the doctrine that the difference between what is morally right and morally wrong is simply a matter of God's fiat. God's omnipotence includes the power to declare any moral order he chooses to the universe. Humans' role is simply to accept and obey God's moral commands, not to understand them. The appeal of this view to some Christians was that it emphasized God's power, humans' appropriately humble position in comparison to God, and the inscrutability of God's nature and knowledge. Kant would have been familiar with the doctrine of voluntarism both from philosophical sources and, more immediately, from the theological position of Martin Luther. Schneewind rightly portrays Kant as deeply opposed to voluntarism. But, as Schneewind also points out, this opposition to voluntarism alone was not what made Kant's ethics revolutionary—the dialectic between voluntarism and anti-voluntarism precedes Kant and provides a historical background for Kant's work. A historical motivation for anti-voluntarism was that it seemed to render praise for God's goodness meaningless. If morality is opaque to humans, then to call God infinitely good is just to say that he does that which he wills. Furthermore, on a voluntarist account, human moral goodness is just a matter of uncomprehending obedience, a kind of servitude rather than freedom. Kant would have been aware of these traditional motivations for opposition to voluntarism.

And Kant's emphasis on autonomy as the basis of morality, which was the revolutionary part of Kant's ethics, provided a new alternative to both voluntarism and previous anti-voluntarist positions. If moral principles are legislated by a part of one's own rational nature, as Kant maintained, then to obey moral principles is not to be a slave to some external authority, but rather to be the very source of universally binding, unconditional practical requirements. The proper moral nature of humans, then, is not to be uncomprehending and servile, but to be co-legislators in an ideal community with God. Humans fall short of divinity in their obedience to the moral principles, but not in their access to or understanding of these principles. Since Kant views all minimally competent adult humans as legislating moral principles as the activity of *Wille*, he stands in opposition not only to voluntarism, but also to a previously dominant anti-voluntarist position. Intellectualism, the position traditionally opposed to voluntarism, maintained that since moral principles are not just the result of God's command, they must be independent truths (presumably necessary truths) discoverable by the human power of reason in the same way that they are more perfectly and immediately known by God. Intellectualism was often accompanied by the claim that some humans, those with a more developed intellect, were better able to grasp these truths than the bulk of mankind. Kant would have found this latter version of intellectualism unsatisfactory for the same reason voluntarism was unsatisfactory, namely that in the name of morality it relegated most humans to the status of servants, either servants of God's revealed commands or of the human intellectual elite. More generally, Kant's view was dissimilar to traditional intellectualism because it did not say that reason discovered independently existing moral principles, but rather that an aspect of reason created moral principles. God is perfect in acting on moral principles, so humans are less perfect than him in their moral commitment, but humans do not fall short of divinity in their access to moral principles, since both humans and God legislate the same principles.[2] Finding both voluntarism and intellectualism unsatisfactory, Kant invented the idea of autonomy as an alternative view of morality's source.

So far, the historical influences that Schneewind points out are compatible with the good will reading of the humanity formulation. Nothing about the good will reading denies the importance of autonomy to Kant's moral theory, or the revolutionary nature of this Kantian insight. But Schneewind emphasizes the similarity between humans' finite rational nature and God's perfectly rational nature, namely that both are co-legislators of moral law, and Schneewind concludes that because of this similarity, 'Kant thought that the ordinary person should be honored even if he acted badly'.[3] Schneewind's position is that all rational beings have an inalienable dignity, as legislators of moral law. But this overlooks the dissimilarity between finite rational beings and God. Both finite rational beings and God legislate moral law, but only God has a holy will which leads him inevitably to act on moral law. Humans must choose between moral principles and the inclinations that sometimes lead them astray. And I have pointed out numerous passages in which Kant says that it is only in virtue of a commitment to actually obeying moral laws that humans possess an incomparable value or dignity, a status as ends in themselves.[4] Two passages deserve special attention on this point. Kant does think that even

[2] Schneewind, *The Invention of Autonomy*, 4. See also Schneewind, 'Why Study Kant's Ethics?', in Immanuel Kant, *Groundwork for the Metaphysics of Morals*, ed. Allen Wood (New Haven: Yale University Press, 2002), 83–91.

[3] Schneewind, *The Invention of Autonomy*, 507.

[4] See Chapter 4 and Chapter 11 above.

the 'humble common man' is worthy of the highest admiration, but only on condition of providing an example of 'uprightness of character' (C2 87). Kant does deny the 'intellectualist' view that intellectual superiority grounds a difference in fundamental moral status, since even the common man has access to moral principles, but the commitment to adhere to these principles provides a basis for difference in moral status. And when Kant compares humans to God, he says that what makes us 'analogous to divinity' is working toward bringing about morally necessary ends, not just our legislation of moral principles.[5] The good will reading is contrary to neither Kant's own stated position, nor the historical forces that shaped his views. It is true that Kant's revolutionary insight was that moral principles must be given autonomously by one's own rational nature if they are to demand unconditional compliance. But Kant did not only emphasize the similarity between ourselves and God, that we all legislate moral law. He also thought the difference between ourselves and God, that humans can choose between giving priority to morality or to desire, was of the utmost importance. Only by giving priority to moral demands, and thus making ourselves closer to divinity, can we give ourselves the highest worth.

This position, like Kant's invention of autonomy, has a strong basis in the religious issues that shaped modern moral philosophy. A religious concern that counts strongly in favour of the good will reading is the concern with preserving an essential role in morality for God, despite the opposition to voluntarism. As Schneewind points out, very few thinkers of the modern period wished to discard God entirely in their moral theories (with Hume being the most notable exception). So anti-voluntarists had to explain why God was still essential to morality, even if morality was not determined simply by what he commanded. Intellectualists faced this problem, because if human reason could discover independent moral truth without revelation, then it was not clear what role was left for God. Kant faced a version of this problem too. If human wills legislate the same moral laws as God's will does, then why put God in the picture at all? Kant's answer is that we have an inescapable reason to accept the Idea of an all-powerful and infinitely just being, because only such a being could make possible the existence of the highest good, which is happiness in proportion to virtue.[6] Humans cannot secure such a good, because we lack both the ability to judge human character accurately and the power to provide rewards in proportion to desert. Yet, Kant maintains, we unavoidably

[5] Immanuel Kant, 'On the Common Saying: This May be True in Theory, but it does Not Apply in Practice', in *Kant: Political Writings*, trans. Hans Reiss (Cambridge: Cambridge University Press, 1991), 65.

[6] The Kantian texts which I am summarizing here are C2 110–48, R 3–6, R 73–8, C1 A804–19, B832–47, and C1 A828, B856.

view virtue unrewarded as a less complete and less satisfying good than virtue rewarded. So our unavoidable expectations make it necessary to accept that God exists, to secure this highest good. This, in very rough outline, is Kant's attempt to show that reason must 'postulate the existence of God' (C2 124). Essential to this argument is the claim that some of us are more deserving of happiness than others, and the characteristic that makes some more deserving is exactly their commitment to morality. God deems some beings essentially better than others, and what makes some of us better and some of us worse is our 'character', our commitment to morality versus self-love. God's role as a judge who deems some of us more worthy and some less is the very thing that allows Kant to say that he is still necessary for a complete moral theory.

Then the historical forces that shaped Kant's moral philosophy, which Schneewind effectively highlights, do not provide reason to reject the good will reading, but rather the opposite.

2. The Power of Choice

I believe the good will reading of the humanity formulation is largely compatible with the historical themes that Schneewind emphasizes. Similarly, I have described throughout this book several ways in which the seemingly alarming and radical claim that good will is the end in itself actually coheres well with some important and illuminating points made by commentators on Kant's ethics in recent years and decades. Some examples of such exegetical points, which I have argued are left intact, or even reinforced, by the good will reading, include: the attempt by many Kantians to show that Kant's ethics is not as moralistic and judgemental as previous generations have thought; Allen Wood's point that, far from being oblivious to human nature and human history, Kant actually develops and relies on many surprisingly plausible and appealing claims about human psychology and history; Christine Korsgaard's 'regress' strategy for reconstructing Kant's argument for the humanity formulation; the position of Barbara Herman and Thomas E. Hill, Jr., that the duty of aid to others is not a strong duty to give others' ends the same status as one's own; and Thomas E. Hill, Jr.'s proposal that the kingdom of ends can be employed as a moral constructivist device for moving from the general demands of the Categorical Imperative to more specific applications. In general, I have frequently emphasized that the good will reading is not as radical as it may seem, and does not imply a rejection of the progress that has been made in Kant scholarship in the last half of the twentieth century and the early years of the twenty-first.

But there is one point that I think must be rejected, both as an interpretation of Kant and as a basis for any satisfactory ethical theory. This is the claim that the feature of rational beings that is of the most fundamental moral significance is their power to choose. I have argued extensively that among the different minimal readings of the humanity formulation, the one that is least satisfactory is the one that takes the central feature of humanity to be *Willkür*, or the power to choose. The claim that the power to choose is the characteristic in virtue of which rational beings must be treated as ends in themselves makes the humanity formulation thematically inconsistent with the other formulations of the Categorical Imperative, since the other formulations all emphasize legislating or acting on moral principles.[7] And the *Willkür* reading of the humanity formulation runs counter to Kant's frequent presentation of humanity as an ideal toward which we should strive, and to Kant's most basic attributions of value in *Groundwork*.[8] It also is inconsistent with particular passages in which Kant explicitly denies that the mere power of choice is what confers dignity upon rational beings.[9] In Chapter 10, I pointed out that Kant not only treats the mere power of choice as too anaemic a conception of freedom to serve as meaningful autonomy, but by implication rejects it as a suitable linchpin for his overall ethical theory. Of course, I have argued against all minimal readings of 'humanity', but the *Willkür* reading consistently fares worst of all, and even those who remain unconvinced by the arguments for the good will reading ought to reject the *Willkür* reading. Even in the *Rechtslehre*, where Kant appears to come closest to treating freedom of action as an important object of moral concern, he does not in fact say that political and legal systems should aim at preserving all free choice, but instead they should aim at preserving free choice that is consistent with moral law. If institutions should be designed so as to leave room for choice, it is not because all choice is valuable and must be preserved. Instead, it is because both institutions and individuals are poorly suited to judge motives, and so should only intervene to prevent or punish actions which clearly display their immorality by infringing on others' (morally 'lawful') freedom. Nowhere does Kant propose enshrining mere choice as unconditionally and incomparably valuable.

And it is hard to see why he should. Choice can be misused in all sorts of ways, as Kant is quite aware. The choice to abuse others, to disregard their interests completely, or to use them manipulatively as tools for one's

[7] See Chapter 3, section 5. [8] See Chapter 3, sections 1 and 2.

[9] See Chapter 4, section 1. The Kantian texts I cite there are C2 61, MM 435–6, C3 437, and C3 443.

own ends is not the sort of thing that ought to be respected or included as intrinsically worthy of special treatment. Of course, there are good reasons to treat freedom of choice as important, but these reasons do not rely on the idea that all choice is good or deserves to be given special status. There is good reason to want state institutions to err on the side of allowing free choice, because there are grave costs to allowing such institutions to intrude too deeply into individuals' lives, and because such institutions are ill suited to assess the real motives of individuals. For these reasons, governments ought to leave individuals space for freedom of choice. But this is not to say that all choices are worth preserving and respecting. Instead, it is to say that tolerating some immoral choices is the cost of preserving a space for morally legitimate choices. Similar reasons apply to individuals who may be tempted to intervene to prevent others' choices that they regard as immoral. It is not that all choices should be allowed because they are equally worthy, but rather that individuals have good reason to be charitable in judging others and to err on the side of allowing poor choices, or even seemingly immoral choices, because individuals tend to be poor and biased judges of which actions are immoral. Many immoral choices ought to be allowed, not because the power of choice is sacred in all its uses and misuses, but because we as individuals or organizations are in a poor position to intervene to prevent such choices without also infringing on morally legitimate choices. A competing picture could claim that freedom of choice is in fact of fundamental importance, and so one individual's freedom should be limited only when it conflicts with others' freedom. Although this picture is familiar, it faces the same intuitive problem that the principle of respect for bioethics autonomy faces.[10] It treats even immoral choices which harm others as being prima facie worth preserving, but as merely outweighed by consideration of others' freedom. This picture seems less satisfying than a picture on which such immoral choices do not have a status that gives them even prima facie theoretical weight. Of course, all of this is just to state my intuition on the matter, and would not convince someone with very different intuitions. But I think when presented with these two competing pictures of the moral significance of immoral choices, many people would share my intuition. And, most importantly for exegetical purposes, Kant shares it.

It appears that some prominent readings of the humanity formulation do take the power of choice as the essential feature of humanity and so as the feature in virtue of which rational beings have dignity and must be treated as ends in themselves. Christine Korsgaard repeatedly states that the

[10] See Chapter 10, section 4.

defining feature of humanity, in the technical sense of the humanity formulation, is the 'capacity for choice' or the 'capacity for setting an end'.[11] And Allen Wood maintains that 'The capacity to set ends through reason holds together the set of capacities constituting our humanity'.[12] The subsidiary capacities Wood has in mind are the ability to find the best means to one's ends, to organize one's ends into a systematic whole, and 'an active sense of my identity and an esteem for myself'. Wood emphasizes that the power to set ends is the central feature that unites these others, and he specifically rules out any rational capacities that 'have specific reference to morality'.[13] So Korsgaard frequently espouses the *Willkür* reading of the humanity formulation, and Wood proposes a reading that at least makes *Willkür* the most characteristic feature of humanity. But do they mean it?

There is some reason for doubt in each case. Although in *Kant's Ethical Thought* Wood displays great clarity of purpose in ruling out any moral characteristic as a defining feature of Kantian humanity, he is more ambivalent in other works. In his paper 'Humanity as End in Itself', published five years before *Kant's Ethical Thought*, he includes the capacity for acting on moral law as an aspect of humanity, and in 'What Is Kantian Ethics?' published two years after *Kant's Ethical Thought*, he says that the kind of beings who have dignity and are ends in themselves are 'rational beings who are moral agents'.[14] This emphasis on moral agency is at least suggestive of a reconsideration of his earlier denial that moral features are an essential feature of humanity. Korsgaard hedges her claim that the power to set ends is the defining feature of humanity, by maintaining that since the power to set ends is part of rational nature, and a good will is nothing but a more perfected rational nature, there is no real difference between saying that the power to set ends is the end in itself and that good will is.[15] So her position seems to be that rational nature is the end in itself, and that it is not significant exactly which aspect or what degree of rationality is taken to be the end in itself. I do not think this is an uncharitable interpretation of her statements, since it seems to be what she actually says in more than one

[11] Christine Korsgaard, *Creating the Kingdom of Ends* (Cambridge: Cambridge University Press, 1996), 17 and 110, respectively. For other citations on this, see Chapter 2, section 2.

[12] Allen Wood, *Kant's Ethical Thought* (Cambridge: Cambridge University Press, 1999), 119. The next quotation is from the same page.

[13] Ibid. 118.

[14] See Allen Wood, 'Humanity as End in Itself', *Proceedings of the Eighth International Kant Congress*, 1/1 (1995), and 301–21, 'What Is Kantian Ethics?', in Immanuel Kant, *Groundwork of the Metaphysics of Morals*, trans. Allen Wood (New Haven: Yale University Press, 2002), 161.

[15] See Korsgaard, *Creating the Kingdom of Ends*, 17, 114, 123–4.

crucial passage. Furthermore, other Kantian ethicists have proposed more or less this same position in correspondence or conversation. But it seems unsatisfactory.[16]

Kant himself thinks it is important to distinguish between different features possessed by rational beings, and it is difficult to see how it could be anything but a deeply important issue in interpreting the humanity formulation. Kant not only thinks it is possible to conceive of beings with *Willkür* but not *Wille*, he also appears to regard non-human animals as such beings.[17] He rules out such beings as deserving treatment as ends in themselves. The question of whether beings who possess both *Willkür* and *Wille*, but lack the commitment to regulate *Willkür* with the moral demands of *Wille*, are to be treated as ends in themselves can hardly be treated as an insignificant question either. All minimally rational beings possess *Wille* and *Willkür*, according to Kant, but not all possess a good will. Only those who are committed to acting on *Wille's* demands have a good will. Part I of this book is a sustained argument that Kant thinks that a finite rational being is an end in herself only if she strives to make moral requirements a sufficient reason for action. An opponent of the good will reading may well offer reasons to reject my arguments, but to do so requires defending a different position, that some feature of humanity possessed by all minimally rational beings is sufficient to make all such beings ends in themselves. The claim that the good will reading is no different from minimal readings is not viable. Whatever feature of rational nature is the distinguishing feature of ends in themselves, it must be some specific feature or set of features. They are not all the same.

At any rate, Korsgaard's overall position on rational agency and normativity seems to be based on something much like the *Willkür* reading of the humanity formulation. A persistent theme in her earlier papers is that choice confers value, and the central ideas of *The Sources of Normativity* seem to be the flowering of this theme.[18] In 'Kant's Formula of Humanity', she assigns the power of choice the fundamental role in the humanity formulation, and defends the picture that I reject above. She says that the power of choice is what has central importance as an end in itself, and that a restriction on this power of choice is that it must not infringe on others' choices.[19] In the later 'Personal Identity and the Unity of Agency: A Kantian Response to

[16] Though I discuss this below, see Chapter 2, section 2 for a more thorough consideration of the issue.

[17] See Chapter 10, section 2.

[18] Christine Korsgaard, *The Sources of Normativity* (Cambridge: Cambridge University Press, 1996).

[19] Korsgaard, *Creating the Kingdom of Ends*, 122–3.

Parfit', she begins with the importance of choice but goes on to emphasize the significance of 'the standpoint from which you deliberate and choose'.[20] Your identity is bound up with the 'principle or way of choosing that you regard as expressive of yourself'. This theme is developed further in *The Sources of Normativity*. There she argues that we must, inescapably, conceive of ourselves as reflective beings who must choose which desires we will act on. This 'forces us to have a conception of our own identity', to accept some actions as consistent with our basic self and regard others as inconsistent with it.[21] Raymond Geuss's criticism of Korsgaard's view, that nothing in her account rules out trivial or even immoral basic commitments, highlights the fact that she is only arguing that some sense of identity is necessary for reflective beings, but not that a commitment to morality is necessary.[22] Similarly, her basic argument in *The Sources of Normativity* regarding obligations to others provides no basis for ruling out others' immoral ends as sources of obligation for an agent. Her argument is that language forces us 'to reason practically together', so reasons for action are fundamentally shared, not private.[23] So others' reasons for action obligate me because 'The space of linguistic consciousness—the space in which meanings and reasons exist—is a space that we occupy together'.[24] There is no obvious way here to bar immoral reasons from the space in question. One may eventually find reason not to act on others' immoral ends, but this must be a matter of them being outweighed by other reasons, not being barred from consideration altogether. Korsgaard's emphasis on the power of choice as the central feature of moral theory is not unique to her interpretation of Kant's humanity formulation, but extends to the more mature views she states as her own.

Maybe I am being uncharitable. I have not devoted much space here to exegesis of Korsgaard or Wood (though I devoted a little more in Chapters 2 and 4), so it is possible that somehow they do not overall endorse taking the power of choice as the main grounding of a rational being's moral status. If they do not think so, then I will be content with making a conditional claim: if anyone takes the humanity formulation to be saying that the power of choice is an end in itself, or that rational beings are ends in themselves just because they have the power to choose, then their reading of the humanity formulation is mistaken.

[20] Ibid. 370. [21] Korsgaard, *Sources*, 113.

[22] Raymond Geuss, 'Morality and Identity', ibid. 193–5.

[23] The quotation is from Korsgaard, *Sources*, 142. More generally, the sustained argument is on 131–45.

[24] Ibid. 145.

3. My Big Picture

Humanity is an ideal, and we ought to live up to this ideal.

This claim is incompatible with viewing 'humanity' as referring to membership in the human species, since we are all human in that sense. It is also contrary to all the minimal readings of the humanity formulation, which take humanity to be something that can never be lost. But it is not contrary to all uses of 'humanity' in English, or of 'die Menschheit' in German. Even in English, we can chastise someone as 'inhuman', or demand that someone act a little more human. In Kant's German, and even more routinely in Yiddish, one can demand that someone be a *Mensch*, and a person can either live up to that demand or fail to live up to it. To live up to the ideal of humanity is to be a basically good or decent person. In several texts, Kant calls humanity an ideal.[25] This makes perfect sense, if humanity is taken to be equivalent to a good will. Every minimally rational being has a will, but not all of us are actually committed to taking morality as a sufficient reason for action. Humans who have this moral commitment live up to the ideal of humanity as a good will. The others have a will, but not a good one. Kant's treatment of humanity as an ideal is consistent with the good will reading, but not with any minimal reading.

Given one of Kant's most important and distinctive ideas, that value is defined by the choices of rational beings, his position that humanity is an ideal to pursue above all else implies that humanity must have an incomparably high value. If humanity is an ideal to be pursued above all else, then it never makes sense to give up this pursuit—to trade one's humanity—for any amount of satisfaction of one's preferences or inclinations. So humanity must have what Kant calls a 'dignity' ('Würde'), and nothing else does. Except that he says good will also has a dignity. This is a contradiction, unless good will is equivalent to humanity. But there is no dilemma here, since Kant does think that good will is equivalent to humanity, and so that good will has an incomparably high value. He says so—he says exactly this—in many passages throughout his practical philosophy.[26]

Kant's claim that good will has an incomparable value is no offhand statement, or casual slip. Besides the fact that he says it repeatedly, it also reinforces the opening claim of *Groundwork*, that only a good will is unconditionally good, or valuable in all possible circumstances. Other (conditionally) good things, whether talents, character traits, or even happiness, are not valuable unless

[25] See Chapter 3, section 3, and also Chapter 4, section 1.

[26] See Chapter 3, section 4, and Chapter 4, section 1.

they are accompanied by a good will. In fact, a good will is the necessary condition of the value of all other possible attributes of a rational being. In the opening pages of *Groundwork*, Kant's position is that common moral intuitions tell us that the talents of a morally bad person are not valuable since they only make the bad person more dangerous, and the happiness of a bad person is not valuable, since no neutral observer can approve of a villain's happiness. The ends of a morally bad person are not really valuable, even if they bring pleasure to the possessor, but the ends of a good person are valuable. So a good will is the necessary condition of the value of an agent's happiness. This is not only the opening claim of *Groundwork*, but also a position that Kant emphasizes in Second *Critique* and *Religion*. In these works, he maintains that the highest good is happiness in proportion to virtue. Kant's justification for the practical postulate of the existence of God is exactly that we must suppose there is a supremely powerful and omniscient being, who sees the true nature of things in themselves, because only such a being could ensure the apportionment of happiness to good character.[27] We humans cannot do so, because our knowledge of others' (or even our own) moral character is uncertain, and because even if we could reliably discern moral character, we lack the power to ensure that good will is rewarded. Again, the basic idea is that happiness is only good on the condition of its possessor having a good will.

Furthermore, the most promising strategy for reconstructing Kant's argument for the humanity formulation depends on this same idea, that a good will is the necessary condition for the value of any of an agent's contingent ends.[28] Humanity, as good will, is an end in itself because it is never reasonable to sacrifice one's good will in order to achieve contingent ends. In other words, it is never reasonable to choose to act immorally in order to satisfy inclinations, because even if this satisfaction is pleasant, it is not actually valuable. To choose self-love over morality is to choose ends that are ultimately lacking in value, because one is sacrificing the necessary condition of contingent ends' value. Then the idea that good will must never be sacrificed in order to satisfy inclinations underlies and unifies several of the central claims of Kant's ethics. It fits with Kant's claims that the highest good is happiness in proportion to virtue, and also with the opening claims of *Groundwork*, that good will is the necessary condition of the value of all contingent ends and so is the only thing good unconditionally. It also underlies the claim that good will is an ideal to be pursued above all else, and so it is a key premiss in the argument for the humanity formulation's claim that humanity is an end in itself, which can

[27] See Chapter 3, section 4. [28] See Chapter 6.

never reasonably be traded for the satisfaction of inclinations. This central and unifying role of the good will reading alone speaks strongly in its favour.

Then why has there been such widespread, and often explicit, rejection of the good will reading? One main motivation has been the apparently judgemental and moralistic demands the good will readings imposes. But these implications are only apparent, not actual. Kant's various formulations of the Categorical Imperative have often been taken to be simple formulae for determining the moral permissibility of actions, roughly on a par with an act-utilitarian principle, ready to be applied to particular situations. But commentators sympathetic to Kant have pointed out that this is not Kant's own view, despite the somewhat facile examples he provides in *Groundwork* of applying the Categorical Imperative. His more considered position is that besides the basic moral principles provided by the Categorical Imperative, one also needs a metaphysics of morals, a systematic application of these general principles to human circumstances. Then it is too quick a move to assume that if the humanity formulation of the Categorical Imperative says to treat good will as an end in itself, then this basic moral principle is accompanied by a demand to make judgements of others' moral character and to apportion moral consideration of others to such assessments. When the humanity formulation is applied to human circumstances, human psychology must be taken into account.[29] Humans' limited epistemological position regarding moral character, and the human tendency to self-aggrandizement at the expense of others, tell strongly against any moral requirement to pass judgement on others. And the importance of encouraging others' moral development and avoiding the dulling of one's own moral feelings are strong reasons to avoid acting on negative moral judgements, even if one cannot help but make them. Pointing out such considerations is not a desperate, ad hoc bulwark against the apparent implausibility of the good will reading. Instead, the duties of tolerance and charity arrived at here are duties that Kant himself lists in the *Metaphysics of Morals*, as following from the humanity formulation. And the psychological grounds for these particular duties are among the more plausible psychological claims that Kant makes. Not only Kant scholars, but anyone interested in moral obligations toward morally imperfect people, should take account of human epistemological limits, the human tendency to self-aggrandizement, the effects of different kinds of treatment on moral development, and the possibility of rendering oneself morally callous. Then there is reason to believe that even if a moral principle, like the humanity formulation, grants the most fundamentally important theoretical role to beings who are committed to morality, it will not

[29] See Chapter 5, section 1, and Chapter 9, sections 3 and 4.

be accompanied by a moral demand to make judgements of moral character at the everyday level.

Kant's position that it is no easy or obvious matter developing a systematic application of the Categorical Imperative has, for the most part, been embraced by commentators, as evidence that Kant's ethics is not vulnerable to the traditional accusation that Kant treats morality as just a matter of applying rigid rules, without regard for the subtleties of human life. I have proposed two ways in which the good will reading is accompanied by supplementary ideas that are useful in moving from the humanity formulation of the Categorical Imperative to particular moral rules. Minimal readings of the humanity formulation lack these useful accessory ideas. The first way in which the good will reading provides an aid for deriving particular duties is that if humanity is good will, then consideration of the concept of humanity inspires a feeling of *Achtung*. This feeling fills a gap that is left by other readings of the humanity formulation. It has become common to say that Kant's ethics demands a certain attitude of respect for rational beings, or that Kantian duties are expressive of such an attitude. But what is the feeling or attitude that is being expressed? The good will reading has an answer. It is the feeling of *Achtung*, which is produced by the moral law, or by rational beings committed to morality, in so far as they too are examples of the awesome power of moral law to subdue opposing inclinations.[30] Other readings are stuck saying, more vaguely, that the attitude is some sort of positive esteem or respect for minimally rational beings. The idea that *Achtung* is the moral feeling on which many particular duties are grounded fits with some of Kant's own discussions, and gives at least some substantial guidance on the kinds of duties that express the moral feeling. But the idea of particular duties as expressive of *Achtung* for humanity, although a useful aid to constructing a metaphysics of morals, no doubt leaves questions about some moral rules unanswered.

If so, then a second supplementary idea, also suggested by the good will reading, may be of further aid. This is the idea of using the kingdom of ends formulation as a moral constructivist device for moving from the humanity formulation to more specific duties.[31] The thought experiment of imagining a union of beings, all committed to treating one another as ends in themselves, may help in focusing our attention on the kinds of moral and empirical considerations that should be considered in resolving particular moral issues. But the idea of such a union, or kingdom of ends, presupposes that they in fact are all committed to treating each other as ends in themselves, and committed to obeying any moral rules promulgated by their legislation. That is the only

[30] See Chapter 7. [31] See Chapter 9, section 3.

way to ensure that the resulting rules will be moral rules that embody the more abstract principle of treating humanity as an end in itself. So the constructivist interpretation of the kingdom of ends presupposes that to be an end in herself, and so to be a member in the hypothetical kingdom of ends, a rational being must be committed to morality. Thus the good will reading of the humanity formulation is accompanied by two interpretative devices for moving from the more abstract principle of the humanity formulation to specific moral rules. And these interpretative strategies are apparently not available to defenders of other readings of the humanity formulation. So the good will reading of the humanity formulation renders it more readily applicable as a viable moral principle.

One of the main ways I have attempted to defuse the criticism that the good will reading is unpalatably moralistic is to emphasize the difference between moral theory and everyday moral demands. I have argued that the pre-eminence of good will over all else, and especially the incomparably higher value of beings with good will over all other beings, is primarily a difference at the level of moral theory. Moral principles are first and foremost principles regarding how to treat beings with good will, and so beings with good will play the central role in moral theory. But, I have maintained, this is compatible with saying that at the level of everyday moral practice, there may be specific moral rules that demand special treatment even for beings who lack good wills. Yet it may strike some as oddly convoluted, even perverse, for particular moral rules to demand something other than the most direct possible application of the more fundamental principle upon which they are based. According to this way of thinking, the good will reading really ought to demand that we seek to make the most accurate possible judgements of moral character, and then leave immoral beings out of the realm of moral consideration.[32] But such a criticism would be misguided. In one important sense, the basic moral principle of good will as an end in itself does give a very direct demand regarding how to act with regard to a good will and less perfect wills. It does this by telling each agent to strive for a good will, to try to accept moral reasons as sufficient reasons for acting. So with regard to oneself, the good will reading of the humanity formulation does give very direct guidance. And it is explicable

[32] This line of criticism somewhat resembles a criticism of rule-consequentialism, that it is not the most direct way to satisfy the underlying moral principle of maximizing utility. But it is not an identical criticism, because the underlying demand to maximize utility appears to be in more direct tension with rules that say to fail to maximize utility on some occasions. The criticism also bears some resemblance to John Rawls's requirement that rules of justice must meet a 'publicity' condition, that the basic principles of justice must be known and publicly chosen, rather than being secret principles that only demand compliance with more specific rules. But my view is not a view about the basic principles for institutions of a society, instead being more generally about moral requirements.

and justifiable why the moral assessment and differential moral treatment of others does not follow as straightforwardly from the humanity formulation. It is because of the limits of human knowledge, and the psychological traits of humans, which make it dangerous to try to pass moral judgements and act on these judgements. But this is not to say that all minimally rational beings are actually deserving of equal treatment. We limited humans ought to treat all beings as if they have good wills, but a being with more perfect insight into real moral character, who also lacks the human tendencies to arrogance and callousness, would be justified in treating beings differently depending on whether they have or lack good wills. Of course, Kant thinks God is such a being, and that we must accept the idea of his existence exactly because of his ability to apportion rewards to moral character. For those of us who doubt this role of God, there is still an important interpretative point. To claim, as I have, that there is room to say both that only some individuals have the highest sort of worth, and yet that we humans should treat everyone as if they have this highest sort of worth, is no high-flown philosophical fancy. It is a common idea that ordinary religious believers have been able to grasp for centuries—that even though some beings have better moral character than others, and deserve better treatment because of this, we humans are in no position to judge this moral worth.

Then there is nothing particularly bizarre or unpalatable about the good will reading of the humanity formulation. It does not demand that one seek to discriminate between beings who have good will and those who lack it, or to punish and reward them accordingly. The reasons why it does not demand this are grounded in reasonable claims about human psychology. And the idea that such psychological considerations must enter into the derivation of particular duties, although contrary to a prevalent caricature of Kant's ethics as disconnected from all empirical considerations, is firmly grounded in Kant's own strategy for developing a system of particular moral rules. The good will reading is an aid, not a hindrance, to the project of applying the humanity formulation to circumstances in the real world, since it provides two interpretative strategies for application—the use of the moral feeling of *Achtung*, and the use of the kingdom of ends as a moral constructivist device. The relevance of human psychology to Kantian ethics also explains why a good will, in human form, is different from a perfectly holy will.[33] Humans will tend to be inattentive and self-deceptive, and so will not always focus adequately on the moral dimensions of their choices. And even when they recognize moral requirements, frailty may lead them

[33] See Chapter 5, section 2.

astray. But all these imperfections are compatible with a commitment to morality. Such imperfections are among the reasons why goodness is always a struggle for humans, but these human limits do not make a good will impossible. In fact, Kant's view, which seems right, is that just by striving for a good will, by genuinely trying to do the right thing, one has attained all the moral perfection that is compatible with human nature. No one of us can ever see her moral goodness as a completed project, but earnestly engaging in this never-completed project is itself the distinguishing mark of a good will.

So, humanity is an ideal toward which we must strive. This is the fundamental demand that the humanity formulation imposes on each of us. It is not accompanied by a demand to judge others' progress toward the goal of good moral character. Instead, with regard to others, we are required generally to treat them charitably, as if they possess good wills. If they seem to act wrongly, we must not aid them in their immoral projects, but instead we must usually act in ways that will encourage their moral progress. We must treat them as ends in themselves, even if some humans do not deserve this treatment. This is not because the power of choice, or the power to act on overall plans of life, or the mere unrealized capacity for morality, confers on every human the highest possible worth. Kant could not think this. Others, like oneself, always have a sufficient reason to accept moral principles as inescapable requirements. When they fail to live up to these requirements, they are irrational. When they possess only the unrealized capacity for a good will, they cannot possess the same incomparable value that they would possess if this capacity were realized.[34] Like oneself, others are flawed if they fail to care about morality's demands. Dignity is not inalienable. But we are in no position to judge others' basic character and worth, and the attempt to do so is fraught with the perils of moralism, insensitivity, and profound arrogance. So the humanity formulation demands that we seek our own perfection, but that we seek to treat others with love and respect.

The basic picture at the core of Kant's ethics is not that all minimally rational beings possess the same incomparable and inalienable dignity, no matter how terribly they choose to act. Instead, the most fundamental ideal is the first-person demand that each of us must strive to recognize moral demands and act on them. Self-love is an obstacle to this moral project that will never be fully overcome, but by struggling to overcome it, one has already shown the commitment to morality that renders a being an end in herself.

[34] See Chapter 4, section 2.

Kant does not think we all are luminous beings, swathed in the inextinguishable glow of moral value and dignity no matter the depths of our depravity and egoism. Instead, he thinks we are all made of clay, but that through our own efforts, we can illuminate ourselves. And this seems about right to me.

Bibliography

Allison, H., *Kant's Theory of Freedom* (Cambridge: Cambridge University Press, 1990).

Atkins, K., 'Autonomy and the Subjective Character of Experience', *Journal of Applied Philosophy*, 17/1 (2000), 71–9.

Baker, R., Caplan, A., Emanuel, L., and Latham, S. (eds.), *The American Medical Ethics Revolution* (Baltimore: Johns Hopkins University Press, 1999).

Barilan, Y. M., and Weintraub, M., 'Persuasion as Respect for Persons: An Alternative Model of Autonomy and of the Limits of Discourse', *Journal of Medicine and Philosophy*, 26/1 (2001), 13–33.

Baron, M., *Kantian Ethics Almost without Apology* (Ithaca, NY: Cornell University Press, 1995).

Beauchamp, T., and Childress, J., *Principles of Biomedical Ethics*, 5th edn. (Oxford: Oxford University Press, 2001).

—— and Faden, R., *A History and Theory of Informed Consent* (Oxford: Oxford University Press, 1986).

—— and Walters, L., *Contemporary Issues in Bioethics*, 6th edn. (Belmont, Calif.: Wadsworth-Thomson Learning, 2003).

Beck, L. W., *A Commentary on Kant's Critique of Practical Reason* (Chicago: University of Chicago Press, 1960).

Blackhall, L., Murphy, S., and Frank, G., 'Ethnicity and Attitudes toward Patient Autonomy', *Journal of the American Medical Association*, 274/10 (1995), 820–5.

Broadie, A., and Pybus, E., 'Kant's Treatment of Animals', *Philosophy*, 49 (1974), 375–83.

Brock, D., *Life and Death: Philosophical Essays in Biomedical Ethics* (Cambridge: Cambridge University Press, 1993).

Callahan, D., 'Autonomy: A Moral Good, Not a Moral Obsession', *Hastings Center Report*, 14/5 (1984), 40–2.

—— 'Can the Moral Commons Survive Autonomy?', *Hastings Center Report*, 26/6 (1996), 41–2.

Carrese, J., and Rhodes, L., 'Western Bioethics on the Navajo Reservation: Benefit or Harm?', *Journal of the American Medical Association*, 274 (1995), 826–9.

Carruthers, P., *The Animals Issue: Moral Theory in Practice* (Cambridge: Cambridge University Press, 1992).

Childress, J., 'The Place of Autonomy in Bioethics', *Hastings Center Report*, 20/1 (1990), 12–16.

Christman, J. (ed.), *The Inner Citadel* (Oxford: Oxford University Press, 1989).

Cohen, J., 'Patient Autonomy and Social Fairness', *Cambridge Quarterly of Healthcare Ethics*, 9 (2000), 391–9.

COOPER, N., 'The Formula of the End in Itself', *Philosophy*, 63 (1988), 401–2.

CRANOR, C., 'Kant's Respect-for-Persons Principle', *International Studies in Philosophy*, 12 (1983), 19–40.

CUMMISKEY, D., *Kantian Consequentialism* (New York: Oxford University Press, 1996).

DENIS, L., 'Kant's Conception of Duties Regarding Animals: Reconstruction and Reconsideration', *History of Philosophy Quarterly*, 17 (2000), 405–23.

DONCHIN, A., 'Understanding Autonomy Relationally: Toward a Reconfiguration of Bioethical Principles', *Journal of Medicine and Philosophy*, 26/4 (2001), 365–86.

DWORKIN, G., *The Theory and Practice of Autonomy* (Cambridge: Cambridge University Press, 1988).

ELLS, C., 'Lessons about Autonomy from the Experience of Disability', *Social Theory and Practice*, 27 (2001), 599–615.

EMANUEL, E., and EMANUEL, L., 'Four Models of the Physician–Patient Relationship', *Journal of the American Medical Association*, 267/16 (1992), 2221–6.

ENGSTROM, S., 'The Concept of the Highest Good in Kant's Moral Theory', *Philosophy and Phenomenological Research*, 52/4 (1992), 747–80.

FETTERS, M., 'The Family in Medical Decision-Making: Japanese Perspectives', *Journal of Clinical Ethics*, 9/2 (1998), 132–46.

FRANKFURT, H., 'Freedom of the Will and the Concept of a Person', *Journal of Philosophy*, 68/1 (1971), 5–20.

GAUTHIER, C. C., 'Philosophical Foundations of Respect for Autonomy', *Kennedy Institute of Ethics Journal*, 3/1 (1993), 21–37.

—— 'The Virtue of Moral Responsibility in Healthcare Decisionmaking', *Cambridge Quarterly of Healthcare Ethics*, 11/3 (2002), 273–81.

GAUTHIER, D., *Morals by Agreement* (Oxford: Oxford University Press, 1986).

GAYLIN, W., and JENNINGS, B., *The Perversion of Autonomy* (Washington, DC: Georgetown University Press, 2003).

GREGOR, M., *Laws of Freedom* (Oxford: Basil Blackwell, 1963).

GUYER, P., *Kant on Freedom, Law, and Happiness* (Cambridge: Cambridge University Press, 2000).

HAIDT, J., 'The Positive Emotion of Elevation', *Prevention and Treatment*, 3/3 (posted 7 Mar. 2000—online journal).

HARE, R. M., 'Could Kant Have Been a Utilitarian?', *Utilitas*, 5/1 (1993), 1–16.

HERMAN, B., *The Practice of Moral Judgment* (Cambridge, Mass.: Harvard University Press, 1993).

HERN, H., Jr., KOENIG, B., MOORE, L. J., and MARSHALL, P., 'The Difference that Culture Can Make in End-of-Life Decisionmaking', *Cambridge Quarterly of Healthcare Ethics*, 7/1 (1998), 27–40.

HILL, T., Jr., *Autonomy and Self-Respect* (Cambridge: Cambridge University Press, 1991).

—— *Dignity and Practical Reason in Kant's Moral Theory* (Ithaca, NY: Cornell University Press, 1992).

—— *Respect, Pluralism, and Justice* (Oxford: Oxford University Press, 2000).

HILL, T., Jr., *Human Welfare and Moral Worth* (Oxford: Oxford University Press, 2002).

HÖFFE, O. (ed.), *Grundlegung zur Metaphysik der Sitten: Ein kooperativer Kommentar* (Frankfurt am Main: Vittorio Klostermann, 1989).

KANT, I., *The Educational Theory of Immanuel Kant*, trans. Edward F. Buckner (Philadelphia: J. B. Lippincott, 1904).

____ *Observations on the Feeling of the Beautiful and the Sublime*, trans. John T. Goldthwait (Berkeley and Los Angeles: University of California Press, 1960).

____ *Lectures on Ethics*, trans. Louis Infield (New York: Harper & Row, 1963).

____ *Critique of Pure Reason*, trans. Norman Kemp Smith (New York: St Martin's Press, 1965).

____ *Anthropology from a Practical Point of View*, trans. Mary Gregor (The Hague: Martinus Nijhoff, 1974).

____ *Critique of Judgment*, trans. Werner S. Pluhar (Indianapolis: Hackett Publishing Company, 1987).

____ *Kant: Political Writings*, trans. Hans Reiss (Cambridge: Cambridge University Press, 1991).

____ 'On a Supposed Right to Lie Because of Philanthropic Concerns', trans. James W. Ellington, in *Grounding for the Metaphysics of Morals* (Indianapolis: Hackett Publishing Company, 1993), 63–7.

____ *The Metaphysics of Morals*, trans. Mary Gregor (Cambridge: Cambridge University Press, 1996).

____ *Critique of Practical Reason*, ed. Mary Gregor (Cambridge: Cambridge University Press, 1997).

____ *Lectures on Ethics*, ed. Peter Heath and Jerome Schneewind (Cambridge: Cambridge University Press, 1997).

____ *Religion within the Boundaries of Mere Reason*, ed. Allen Wood and George di Giovanni (Cambridge: Cambridge University Press, 1998).

____ *Groundwork for the Metaphysics of Morals*, trans. Allen Wood (New Haven: Yale University Press, 2002).

____ *Groundwork for the Metaphysics of Morals*, ed. Thomas E. Hill, Jr., and Arnulf Zweig (Oxford: Oxford University Press, 2002).

KERSTEIN, S., *Kant's Search for the Supreme Principle of Morality* (Cambridge: Cambridge University Press, 2002).

KORSGAARD, C., *Creating the Kingdom of Ends* (Cambridge: Cambridge University Press, 1996).

____ *The Sources of Normativity* (Cambridge: Cambridge University Press, 1996).

MACDONALD, C. 'Relational Professional Autonomy', *Cambridge Quarterly of Healthcare Ethics*, 11/3 (2002), 282–9.

MACKENZIE, C., and STOLJAR, N., *Relational Autonomy: Feminist Perspectives on Autonomy, Agency, and the Self* (New York: Oxford University Press, 2000).

MAPPES, T., and DEGRAZIA, D., *Biomedical Ethics*, 5th ed. (New York: McGraw-Hill, 2001).

MATTHEWS, E., 'Autonomy and the Psychiatric Patient', *Journal of Applied Philosophy*, 17/1 (2000), 59–70.

MILLER, B., 'Autonomy', in W. T. Reich (ed.), *Encyclopedia of Bioethics* (New York: Macmillan, 1995).

MOAZAM, F., 'Families, Patients, and Physicians in Medical Decisionmaking: A Pakistani Perspective', *Hastings Center Report*, 30/6 (2000), 28–37.

MUNSON, R., *Intervention and Reflection: Basic Issues in Medical Ethics* (Belmont, Calif.: Wadsworth/Thomson Learning, 2000).

NEWTON, M., 'Precedent Autonomy: Life-Sustaining Intervention and the Demented Patient', *Cambridge Quarterly of Healthcare Ethics*, 8/2 (1999), 189–99.

O'NEILL, O., *Constructions of Reason* (Cambridge: Cambridge University Press, 1989).

—— *Toward Justice and Virtue* (Cambridge: Cambridge University Press, 1996).

—— *Autonomy and Trust in Bioethics* (Cambridge: Cambridge University Press, 2002).

—— 'Autonomy: The Emperor's New Clothes', *Proceedings of the Aristotelian Society*, Supplement 77 (203), 1–21.

Oxford English Dictionary (Oxford: Oxford University Press, 1989).

PARKS, J., 'A Contextualized Approach to Patient Autonomy within the Therapeutic Relationship', *Journal of Medical Humanities*, 19/4 (1998), 299–311.

PATON, H. J., *The Categorical Imperative* (Philadelphia: University of Pennsylvania Press, 1947).

POTTER, N., 'Kant and the Moral Worth of Actions', *Southern Journal of Philosophy*, 34 (1996), 225–41.

RACHELS, J., *Created from Animals: The Moral Implications of Darwinism* (Oxford: Oxford University Press, 1990).

RAWLS, J., *A Theory of Justice* (Cambridge, Mass.: The Belknap Press of Harvard University Press, 1971).

—— 'Kantian Constructivism in Moral Theory', *Journal of Philosophy*, 77/9 (1980), 515–72.

—— *Lectures on the History of Moral Philosophy*, ed. Barbara Herman (Cambridge, Mass.: Harvard University Press, 2000).

REATH, A., 'Kant's Theory of Moral Sensibility: Respect for the Moral Law and the Influence of Inclination', *Kant-Studien*, 80/3 (1989), 284–302.

—— 'Two Conceptions of the Highest Good in Kant', *Journal of the History of Philosophy*, 26/4 (1989), 593–619.

REGAN, T., *The Case for Animal Rights* (Berkeley and Los Angeles: University of California Press, 1983).

RHODES, R., 'Rethinking Research Ethics', *American Journal of Bioethics*, 5/1 (2005), 7–28.

ROSS, W. D., *Kant's Ethical Theory* (London: Oxford University Press, 1954).

RUMSEY, J., 'The Development of Character in Kant's Moral Theory', *Journal of the History of Philosophy*, 27/2 (1989), 247–65.

SALEM, T., 'Physician-Assisted Suicide: Promoting Autonomy or Medicalizing Suicide?', *Hastings Center Report*, 29/3 (1999), 30–6.

SAUDER, R., and PARKER, L., 'Autonomy's Limits: Living Donation and Health-Related Harm', *Cambridge Quarterly of Healthcare Ethics*, 10/4 (2001), 399–407.

SCANLON, T. M., 'Contractualism and Utilitarianism', in *Utilitarianism and Beyond* (Cambridge: Cambridge University Press, 1982).

SCHALLER, W., 'The Relation of Moral Worth to the Good Will in Kant's Ethics', *Journal of Philosophical Research*, 17 (1992), 351–82.

SCHNEEWIND, J., 'Korsgaard and the Unconditional in Morality', *Ethics*, 109/1 (1998), 36–48.

—— *The Invention of Autonomy* (Cambridge: Cambridge University Press, 1998).

SCHNEIDER, C., *The Practice of Autonomy: Patients, Doctors, and Medical Decisions* (New York: Oxford University Press, 1998).

SCOTT, P. A., 'Autonomy, Power and Control in Palliative Care', *Cambridge Quarterly of Healthcare Ethics*, 8/2 (1999), 139–47.

SECKAR, B., 'The Appearance of Kant's Deontology in Contemporary Kantianism: Concepts of Patient Autonomy in Bioethics', *Journal of Medicine and Philosophy*, 24/1 (1999), 43–66.

SHERWIN, S., *No Longer Patient: Feminist Ethics and Health Care* (Philadelphia: Temple University Press, 1992).

—— *The Politics of Women's Health* (Philadelphia: Temple University Press, 1998).

SHOEMAN, F. (ed.), *Responsibility, Character and the Emotions* (Cambridge: Cambridge University Press, 1987).

SINGER, P., *Animal Liberation* (New York: New York Review of Books, 1975).

STRATTON-LAKE, P., *Kant, Duty, and Moral Worth* (London: Routledge, 2000).

SULLIVAN, R., *Immanuel Kant's Moral Theory* (Cambridge: Cambridge University Press, 1989).

—— *An Introduction to Kant's Ethics* (Cambridge: Cambridge University Press, 1994).

TAYLOR, P., 'The Ethics of Respect for Nature', *Environmental Ethics*, 3 (Fall 1981), 197–218.

VEATCH, R., 'Autonomy's Temporary Triumph', *Hastings Center Report*, 14 (1984), 38–40.

—— 'Which Grounds for Overriding Autonomy are Legitimate?', *Hastings Center Report*, 26/6 (1996), 42–3.

VERKERK, M., 'A Care Perspective on Coercion and Autonomy', *Bioethics*, 13/3–4 (1999), 358–68.

WOLFF, R. P., *The Autonomy of Reason* (New York: Harper & Row, 1973).

WOOD, A., 'Kant on Duties Regarding Nonrational Nature', *Proceedings of the Aristotelian Society*, Supplement 72 (1998), 189–210.

—— *Kant's Ethical Thought* (Cambridge: Cambridge University Press, 1999).

—— 'Humanity as End in Itself', *Proceedings of the Eighth International Kant Congress*, 1/1 (1995), 306–7.

Index